Archaeology at Shiloh
Indian Mounds, 1899–1999

D1546402

A Dan Josselyn Memorial Publication

Archaeology at Shiloh Indian Mounds, 1899–1999

Paul D. Welch

THE UNIVERSITY OF ALABAMA PRESS
Tuscaloosa

Library of Congress Cataloging-in-Publication Data

Welch, Paul D., 1955–
    Archaeology at Shiloh Indian mounds, 1899–1999 / Paul D. Welch.
        p. cm.
    Includes bibliographical references and index.
    ISBN 0-8173-1481-4 (cloth : alk. paper) — ISBN 0-8173-5253-8
(pbk. : alk. paper)
        1. Indians of North America—Tennessee—Shiloh Indian Mounds
National Historic Landmark—Antiquities. 2. Mound-builders—
Tennessee—Shiloh Indian Mounds National Historic Landmark.
3. Excavations—Tennessee—Shiloh Indian Mounds National Historic
Landmark—History. 4. Shiloh Indian Mounds National Historic
Landmark (Tenn.)—Antiquities. I. Title.
    E78.T3W45 2006
    976.8′31—dc22

                                                    2005006877

ISBN 978-0-8173-1481-1 (cloth : alk. paper)
ISBN 978-0-8173-5253-0 (pbk. : alk. paper)
ISBN 978-0-8173-8459-3 (electronic)

Front cover illustration: Trench in Mound F, looking north, courtesy
of the National Anthropological Archives, Smithsonian Institution.

Contents

Figures

Tables

Acknowledgments

This book is a modified version of a report submitted to the Southeast Archeological Center (SEAC) of the National Park Service. To ensure that the information about Shiloh Indian Mounds be available to the archaeological public, SEAC agreed to let me submit the report for publication. This book corrects several minor errors in the SEAC report, omits site-management recommendations and the most excruciating details about preparing the site map, includes newly available (but frustratingly ambiguous) information about excavations by the Park Commissioners in the early 1900s, excludes several lengthy tables and data appendixes, and has an expanded consideration of Shiloh's regional setting in the final chapter.

Many individuals over the course of four years contributed to this report, and it is my pleasure to acknowledge their contributions. The research reported here was funded by: the CUNY-PSC Faculty Research Award Program, grant nos. 66444-0000 and 69491-0029; a Queens College Faculty-Mentored Undergraduate Research award; the Department of Anthropology at Queens College, which contributed one course release to give me time to finish the lab work and start writing; a Smithsonian Institution Short-term Visitor Grant; a grant from the National Park Service's Lower Mississippi Valley Regional Initiative; and three contracts with the National Park Service, nos. 1443PX589098056, 1443PX589098057, and 1443PX532099201. The 1998 excavation at Shiloh N.M.P. was carried out under ARPA Permit SHIL 98-001. My work at Shiloh has been consistently supported, and made enjoyable, by Superintendent Woody Harrell and his staff. At the NPS Southeast Archeological Center in Tallahassee, I received encouragement, support, and patience from Bennie Keel, George Smith, and the center's head, John Ehrenhard.

Fieldwork was carried out with the assistance of a number of people who tolerated some exceedingly hot days. I had the good fortune to have Caroline Steele with me during preliminary reconnaissance and field survey of Shiloh Phase sites in 1996. In both 1998 and 1999 I was assisted by Jennifer Flood, a CUNY graduate student. Patrick Livingood, a University of Michigan graduate student, helped enormously in the field in 1998, taking on all the surveying chores among other things. Other members of the field crews in 1998 and 1999 were Lisa Brando, Tony Castillo, Lazo Dubravko, Adam

Harrell, Vanessa Joseph, Herbert LaCuesta, Kerry McMahon, Rob Menke, Marc Meyer, and Kristi Taft.

I am lucky to have had John Cornelison and David Anderson directing the SEAC fieldwork in 1999, reported in Chapter 7. Their professionalism and dauntingly hard work accomplished far more in two weeks than I had considered possible. I am deeply in debt to them and to John's excellently trained field crew. David and John also read the full draft of this report. Their comments along with those by George Smith and Bennie Keel made my contract report a better, and certainly more understandable, document. The recommendations of Lynne Sullivan, Timothy Pauketat, and an anonymous reviewer helped turn that contract report into a more readable and useful book (though I know they do not agree with everything I say in it).

Other individuals who have helped along the way include John Ross and Ken Hansgen in Savannah and Stacy Allen, Tim Smith, and Brian McCutchen at Shiloh National Park. Suzanne Hoyal of the Tennessee Division of Archaeology searched the state site file for Mississippian mounds east of Shiloh. In New York, Regina Caulfield of the Office of Sponsored Research and Programs at Queens College, CUNY, was an invaluable ally in untangling paperwork snafus. The chair of my department at Queens, James Moore, consistently supported my work and did everything he could to minimize the substantial mess created by a forced move of the archaeology lab from one building to another while I was writing this report. Rob Menke, Kimberly Schaeffer, Kerry McMahon, and Vanessa Joseph put in countless hours washing, sorting, counting, weighing, bagging, and labeling the 60,000 items from the 1998 and 1999 excavations.

Archaeology at Shiloh
Indian Mounds, 1899–1999

1 Introduction

The Shiloh Indian Mounds archaeological site is a late prehistoric community within the boundary of the Shiloh National Military Park, where one of the bloodiest battles of the Civil War was fought in April 1862. The Indian Mounds site is, in its own right, a National Historic Landmark. For over a century the site has been described as having seven earthen mounds. However, there are actually at least eight mounds at the site, and the remains of nearly 100 houses. These all lie atop high tableland that forms a precipitous bluff on the west side of the Tennessee River. To the north and south of the site are steep-sided ravines cut by small streams that feed directly into the river (see Figure 1.1). On the west side, the site was protected by a 900-m-long bastioned palisade wall, built of stout timbers and possibly coated with clay. The habitable area demarcated by the palisade, the ravines, and the river bluff amounts to roughly 19 hectares. Shiloh is only one of several contemporary sites along this stretch of the Tennessee River. I suspect that residents at numerous, scattered farmsteads in the river floodplain, and at those outlying sites with one or two mounds apiece, would have regarded Shiloh as their central settlement or town, much the same way as people in rural areas today speak of going "to town." Shiloh was not the only such town in this stretch of the river valley, for there was also a multimound, palisaded town at the location of modern Savannah, Tennessee. We do not know whether the Savannah site was contemporary with or later than Shiloh. In either case, Shiloh was an unusually large town for its time, which was roughly A.D. 1100 to 1300.

For visitors to the site, its most striking feature is certainly the view of the Tennessee River from the summit of Mound A, the largest of the mounds at the site. Seeing the river flowing immediately below the bluff and the floodplain spreading eastward to the opposing bluffs 5 km away, a visitor may well have the feeling that this mound top is a privileged spot, from which the valley appears to be laid out at one's feet. I imagine that the prehistoric inhabitants of the site would have felt much the same way—that this was their river and their valley. For archaeologists, at least, the site has another, equally striking, characteristic. Because Shiloh has never been plowed, one can walk around the site today and see the collapsed remains of 800-year-old houses

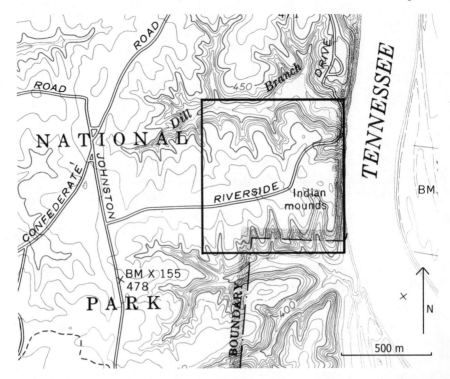

Figure 1.1. Location of Shiloh Indian Mounds (reproduced from 1972 USGS 7 1/2′ Pittsburg Landing Quadrangle)

and the line of the palisade with its bastions. Though there are early historic descriptions of such visible features at many sites in the eastern United States, nearly all such features were obliterated long ago by repeated plowing and its attendant erosion. These ancient houses at Shiloh are visible today only as subtle rises which do not shout of their origins to passersby, yet they are easy to see once attention has been directed to them. Walking over the site, finding these houses and seeing their layout, provides a much more immediate sense of the ancient community that lived here than can be had by studying lines and dots on a paper map. This emotional connection to the ancient inhabitants comes about for precisely the same reason that traveling through the Civil War battlefield at Shiloh involves the emotions in a way deeper and richer than does studying the battle maps. The Shiloh Indian Mounds site is indeed a national treasure.

Far more people know about the Civil War battle at Shiloh than know about the ancient mounds. Rangers at Shiloh National Military Park (Shiloh N.M.P.) report that of the tens of thousands of visitors to the park each year, only a few dozen ask where the mounds are. It is merely an accident that the

battle took place around the mound site, but this accident is directly responsible for the excellent condition of the site today. The Shiloh N.M.P—or
Shiloh Battlefield Park, as it was originally called—was created in 1894. Since
then, the only intentional disturbances to the site have been construction of
a road through the mound area, and excavations by several generations of
archaeologists. At the time of the battle, the area was forested. It was still
forested 32 years later when the park was created and has been mostly wooded
ever since. Trees in the western part of the site are generally younger than
those in the central mound area, indicating that a portion of the site was
cleared except for a few large oaks. Photographs from the 1930s suggest that
this area was allowed to reforest beginning in the 1920s. There is no evidence
from the soil profiles, however, that the cleared area was plowed. Rather, this
area was apparently treated the same as much of the battlefield—the park
burned off low vegetation and thinned the trees to maintain long sight-lines
and permit easy movement across the battlefield by horse-drawn carriages.
Unintentional disturbances of the site include trees blown over and erosion
of the river bluff.

The erosion of the river bluff is the most serious present threat to the site
(see Figure 1.2). To reduce this threat, the base of the bluff is being stabilized
by a gabion wall backed with erosion-control cloth. Unfortunately, this stabilization project will leave the upper portion of the bluff face overly steep,
such that it will continue to slough off until reaching its natural angle of
repose. The bank-stabilization project and the archaeological mitigation that
will be required on the bluff edge are not the subject of this volume. Indirectly, however, the bank situation was partly responsible for the National
Park Service commissioning me in 1998 to prepare a comprehensive report
(Welch 2001) about the archaeology of the Indian Mound site. The present
book differs from that report in being updated in several important details
and in omitting resource management suggestions, lengthy tables, and computer data files that were appended to the technical report. This volume is
intended to make information about the Shiloh site available to the archaeological community at large.

This book attempts to present comprehensive information about the archaeology of this National Historic Landmark. Several far less detailed overviews of the site's archaeology have been produced in previous decades, and
these have appeared only as limited-distribution contract reports. For example,
Brewer (1987) summarized the physical condition of the site and the previous
archaeological investigations. Another review (Beditz 1980b) was produced
when John Ehrenhard and Lindsay Christine Beditz conducted a test excavation on Mound A to delineate the mound's stratigraphy; this was done in
recognition that the mound was threatened by sloughing of the bluff edge.

Figure 1.2. Sloughing of the river bluff below Shiloh Mound A, viewed from east (reproduced from Beditz 1980a:17)

A few years earlier, Gerald Smith (1977) conducted and reported on several new excavations and synthesized what was then known about the site. His excavations confirmed the existence of the palisade and bastions and revealed that parts of the plaza area had a complex construction history. Prior to Smith's work, there had been no recorded archaeological investigation at the site since the extensive excavations in 1933–1934. That project was directed by Frank H. H. Roberts, Jr., of the Smithsonian Institution. It was one of the early archaeological projects to make use of Relief-funded labor, in this case a crew of up to 118 men (Chambers n.d.). Only a brief, nontechnical summary of this project was published, however. Reporting and analyzing the results of the 1933–1934 project is one of the principal contributions of the present volume. I also report, as far as is possible with the very sparse records available, excavations in 1899 and the early 1900s.

To fulfill the goal of synthesizing archaeological knowledge about the site and making sense of decades-old excavation records, I found that additional field exploration was necessary. This work was carried out in 1998 and 1999. In addition to the fieldwork I directed, important additional work was done in 1999 under the direction of John Cornelison and David Anderson of the Southeast Archeological Center, N.P.S. All this fieldwork is reported here, with Anderson and Cornelison coauthoring the chapter on their work. The major part of this book, therefore, consists of reports of the 1933–1934, 1998, and 1999 fieldwork.

Obviously, to report on excavations in various parts of the site, it helps to have a map of the site. Throughout this volume, excavations are keyed to a map of the site (Figure 1.3) that is based on a topographic map made in 1933–1934. That map, made for the excavations directed by Frank Roberts, is reasonably accurate for the central part of the site (though it misplaced one mound by 20 feet), but outside the central area the map's topography is often at odds with reality. Furthermore, the site extends beyond the boundaries of the 1933–1934 map. As funding to prepare a new topographic map was not available, the map used here is essentially the 1933–1934 map, with known errors in the center of the site corrected but the topography near the site edges not corrected. The topographic contours are labeled as having a 60-cm interval, but they are actually traced from the original 2-foot (60.96 cm) contours; this introduces a small distortion, but the raw data required for recontouring are not available. The location and extent of the palisade shown on the map is based on a differential GPS survey in 1999, and the locations of house mounds—far more numerous than on the original 1933–1934 map—were recorded by taped distances and compass bearings. Considerable time in the field and in the lab was spent on trying to match together the grid system of the 1933–1934 map, the grid system used by Smith in 1977, the grid system used by Welch in 1998–1999, and UTM coordinates. To make a long story (Welch 2001:37–46) short, the relationship between most of these grid systems is not known precisely, and depending on which part of the site is considered there may be a mismatch of as little as a few centimeters or as much as a meter or two between reality and what the map indicates.

To set the stage for subsequent parts of the report, Chapter 2 presents a history of archaeological research at the site. Chapter 3 lays out the artifact

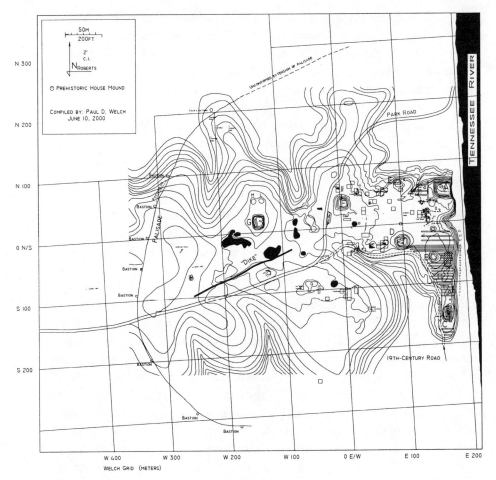

Figure 1.3. Map of excavations at Shiloh Indian Mounds

typology that is used in the remainder of the report, which contains the detailed presentation of the 1933–1934, 1998, and 1999 fieldwork. The 1933–1934 project is reported in Chapter 4. Excavations directed by Welch in 1998 and 1999 are the subjects of Chapters 5 and 6, respectively. Fieldwork directed by Cornelison and Anderson is the subject of Chapter 7. The final chapter, 8, summarizes what we know about Shiloh and neighboring sites and defines the Shiloh Phase.

2   History of Research at Shiloh Indian Mounds

This sketch, brief and imperfect as it is, may afford some data of interest
in regard to the character of the race of men who once thickly peopled
this country, and who have left such surprising monuments of their arts
and industry.

—(Dille 1867:362)

In a survey of Mississippian mound centers, Payne (1994:136) defined seven
size classes ranging from "very small" to very large mound complexes such
as Cahokia. In Payne's terms, the Shiloh Indian Mounds site falls into the
middle-size class, "medium-large," by virtue of having eight mounds. Only
24 Mississippian mound centers (out of 467 in her sample) are known that
have more than 8 mounds. Given Shiloh's size, there should be little surprise
that the site has a lengthy history in the archaeological literature, with a published description as early as 1867. What is more surprising is how little excavation was conducted at the site in the nineteenth and early twentieth centuries, especially in comparison to the extensive excavations at the nearby
Savannah site (Welch 1998a). The site's survival can be traced to its being
more than a few miles from the nearest town and to its inclusion in the
Shiloh Battlefield Park in 1894. The site has thus been frequently visited but
seldom investigated.

DILLE'S 1867 DESCRIPTION OF SHILOH

One early published description of the mounds at Shiloh comes from I. Dille,
who sent to the Smithsonian Institution an account of the mounds he had
observed in Ohio and on travels in the Mississippi valley, including southwestern Tennessee. This description, or recollection, was published in the
Smithsonian's *Annual Report* in 1867. At the end of his report, Dille (1867:362)
cautions the reader that "This hasty sketch of some of the ancient remains
in the Mississippi valley, though the result of the observations of a lifetime,
is principally drawn from memory, and no pretension is made to exactness."

In fact, his memory is inexact in several aspects, but he did remark on several of the key features of the site. His description is reproduced in its entirety below.

> On the battle-field of Shiloh a great many similar right-angled, flat-topped mounds were observed, varying but little in size, form, and height. The mounds of this class are found for miles along the Tennessee river, and are very numerous near the mouth of a small stream, I think called Bear creek, which was in the very midst of one of the battle-fields of our late contest. One of these mounds is on the bank of the river, a little below the mouth of the stream just mentioned, on the side of a high bluff, which affords a fine view of the great bend of the Tennessee river. On its south side it is about seven feet above the level of the land, but situated as it is on the brow of a hill, its north side is raised from twenty-five to thirty feet above the plain below. In the course of a walk of about a mile back from the river, from twelve to fifteen mounds of this class were counted. Their general length is about sixty feet, width forty feet, and height from six to eight feet. Many of them were made the burial places of the slain who fell in the fearful contest.
>
> As in the case of the mound at Fort Pickering [south of Memphis], the surrounding land was marked with small circular mounds, ridges, and crescents, which were so close to each other in some places that I could step from one to the other. No opportunity was afforded to explore any of these mounds, or to form any idea of the purpose for which they were constructed. (Dille 1867:361–362)

Dille's account differs in many of its details from subsequent descriptions. It is important to consider whether the differences are due to Dille's flawed memory or to alterations to the site after he visited it. For a start, the name "Bear creek" is apparently erroneous. His statement that the mounds are "below" the creek's mouth suggests that he is referring to the (unnamed?) creek upriver (south) of the site rather than to Dill Branch. The only importance of this point is that it does indicate that at least some of Dille's details are imprecise.

His mention that Civil War dead were buried in "many" of the mounds also appears to be inaccurate. As far as the records at Shiloh N.M.P. indicate (Stacy Allen, personal communication), only Mound G was used in this way, for the burial of members of the 28th Illinois Infantry. These burials were later relocated to the National Cemetery at Pittsburg Landing.

Dille's statement that there were 12 to 15 right-angled, flat-topped mounds is more interesting, in that it is either an exaggerated recollection or an indication that he was more sensitive to artificial earthworks than most of the subsequent visitors. In 1914, C. B. Moore mapped only seven mounds at the site, though we now realize that he did not include several artificial deposits as mounds. However, to reach a total of 12 to 15 mounds, today one would have to include at least 5 house-sized mounds no more than about 1 m high. It is quite unlikely that erosion or other disturbances before this century removed half a dozen mounds similar to the largest seven at the site. Again, the reasonable conclusion is that Dille's recollection is inaccurate.

The description of the mound atop the high river bluff presumably refers to Mound A. His statement that it was 7 feet high on the south and 25 to 30 feet high on the north either overestimates by a factor of two the height of the apron around the base of Mound A or underestimates by a factor of three the height of the summit above the apron. Given the magnitude of these discrepancies, it is likely that they are due to Dille's faulty memory rather than modification of the site between the time he visited it and the time C. B. Moore mapped the site (1914).

Dille's mention that mounds extend from the riverbank back about a mile is probably also just an imperfect recollection. Of the large, flat-topped, rectangular mounds at the site, Mound G is most distant from the riverbank, at about 300 m (less than one-fifth of a mile). Even if we consider the small house mounds, the one most distant from the bluff is only 500 m (less than one-third of a mile) from the bank. Thus, it appears that all of Dille's numbers are inaccurate.

Despite the inaccuracies, Dille's description is noteworthy for its mention of the "small circular mounds, ridges, and crescents, which were so close to each other in some places that I could step from one to the other" (Dille 1867:361–362). This description likely refers to the dozens of house mounds that lie within the site's defensive palisade. Whether the "ridges" he mentions refer to the palisade embankment, to the feature later called the "Dike," or to much smaller features is not clear. Subsequent visitors also noted the many small, mostly circular, mounds, though no published description of the site counted more than half of the actual number still visible.

It is also noteworthy that Dille does not mention several important features of the site. For example, he does not mention the defensive, bastioned palisade around the site or the ponds or depressions that most subsequent visitors believed to be borrow pits for mound fill.

In short, Dille's description is clearly based on recollection and is not the result of careful observation and recording. To find out how the site may have been altered during the Historic era, we will have to use a later description for our baseline.

PARK COMMISSIONERS DIG INTO MOUND C IN 1899

The next published description of the site appeared in 1902, and it was far more accurate than Dille's. The Shiloh battlefield, including the mound area, had been designated a National Military Park by act of Congress in 1894. For its first few decades, affairs of the park were overseen by a three-member commission, of which the first chairman was Colonel Cornelius Cadle (Smith 2004:32). In 1899 he and the two other commissioners directed an excavation into Mound C. Cadle described the excavation in an article published in 1902, and the park historian (and later commissioner), Major D. W. Reed, published a similar but shortened version 12 years later. Cadle (1902:218) described the site as having "seven prehistoric mounds, within a space of about 25 acres [10 ha]." He also stated that "the excavations for building these mounds are plainly apparent nearby" (Cadle 1902:218). The article gave details about only two of the mounds, Mounds A and C.

Cadle described Mound A as follows: "The largest of these mounds is at the junction of Dill's Branch and the Tennessee river, upon a bluff 125 feet above low water; built immediately upon the edge, and with such a steep descent to the river as to be practically unclimbable. This mound is 80 feet square, about 25 feet high, covered with large white oak trees" (Cadle 1902:218).

This description matches well with the current appearance of the mound, except that erosion of the river bluff has now eaten away a part of the eastern side of the mound. The stated height of 25 ft (7.6 m) is accurate if one measures the mound's apparent height on the north side, though from the west or south the mound projects only about 15 ft (4.6 m) above the surrounding surface (the "surrounding surface" is actually an artificial apron built up around the mound base, but this was not discovered until 30 years later).

There is no mention of the palisade embankment or of the numerous house mounds, probably because Cadle's intent was not to describe the site as a whole but specifically to describe the discovery of the carved stone pipe he found in Mound C. He did specify that, unlike Mound A, "the other mounds are all oval," and he rather unhelpfully says they average about the same size as Mound C (Cadle 1902:218). That is not a very accurate way to describe the larger, rectangular, flat-topped Mounds D, F, and G, though both of the smaller mounds, B and E, may have had an oval, round-topped appearance at the turn of the century. Reed (1914), however, does mention specifically that of the seven prehistoric mounds, four are square and three oval. Reed also mentions the palisade, and provides additional information about the state of preservation of the mounds:

Outside the group of mounds and about a quarter of a mile from the river is a well-defined earth work extending from the river above to Dill Branch below the mounds. Soldiers camping on the battlefield in 1862 made some slight excavations in the tops of two of these mounds and the members of the 28th Illinois regiment buried their dead on top of one of them, but no real effort to open any of them for the purpose of ascertaining what was in them was made until June 1899 when the Shiloh National Military Park Commission undertook a thorough exploration of the oval mound fartherest [sic] up the river. (Reed 1914:21)

Neither Cadle nor Reed provide any particular reason for selecting Mound C for excavation but simply describe how they cut a 4½-foot-wide trench lengthwise from the north edge to the mound center. There is a photograph of the excavation in the archives at Shiloh N.M.P. (Figure 2.1). The mound is described as having an oval base 86 feet long, 56 feet in its short diameter, with the center 10 feet 2 inches above the original ground surface (26 × 17 × 3 m). The trench, roughly 40 ft (12.2 m) long, was excavated "with the utmost care" (Cadle 1902:220), though today's archaeologists will shudder to hear that it took only three days. Only two internal features are described, both of them burials:

In June, 1899, I commenced driving, in one of the smaller mounds, an open cut, 4½ feet wide, its axis the long diameter; commencing at the base. After three days work, and the work was done with the utmost care, the first "find" was a crumbling skeleton, very near the center and 3½ feet from the top. This was evidently an "intrusive" grave, but not recent. The body had been buried in a recumbent position, looking up the Tennessee River, which is in full view, its feet to the north; and at each ear of the skull were two ornaments of shell, concave at the top and lined with very thin copper. The copper had corroded so there was only left upon one, a piece thinner than writing paper, about the size of one's finger nail, but the concavity of each ornament was of the characteristic green copper carbonate color.

Continuing the work we reached the center, driving about 2 feet further. This cut, commencing at the surface, was driven at a slight angle upward for drainage in case of rain, and because I expected to make a "find" on the original surface and at the center. For a space of about 4 by 5 feet in the center, 8 inches above the original surface (the surface of the cut), the ground, upon striking it with the handle of a shovel, sounded hollow. Going back toward the entrance, 1 foot from the resounding area, a hole was dug 2 feet deep and across the cut, and with knife and fingers the earth was slowly taken away, toward

Figure 2.1. Col. Cadle (third from left of the men standing atop mound) and Maj. Reed (rightmost of men standing atop mound) excavating a trench into Mound C in 1899

the supposed "hollow." We were rewarded in an hour or two by finding first that this "hollow" area had been covered with large logs. Carefully removing this wood, which was decayed, we found the remains of three bodies, the crania, the vertebrae, the arm and leg bones; apparently laid upon the surface of the ground before the mound was started, either in a sitting position; or possibly the bones had been brought there for reinterment, and the burial place had been timbered so as to form a cell or room, but the wood in decaying had caused a cave-in, filling up the room. With one of these skeletons was an ear ornament similar to those described above, but more crude in shape and without the copper lining.

About the center of this burial space we struck something that looked like an arm in stone. For two hours we carefully excavated and dug, not daring to use any implement but our knives and fingers, and were rewarded by finding a pipe in human form, bent on one knee, the bowl and place for the mouthpiece in the back. It is about 10 inches high, carved apparently from either "Catlinite," the "red-pipe stone of Minnesota" or a similar stone. It is the most perfect piece of prehistoric carving that I have seen, much superior in artistic work to any thing of the kind described and illustrated in Force, Short, Bancroft, Thruston and others, or that I have seen in various collections. The pipe was broken at the neck, but has been cemented.

Theories regarding the Mound Builders are useless. But the mound in questions seems to show that three persons of importance, with their ceremonial pipe, were placed upon the surface of the ground, covered with logs, and a mound containing about 1,000 cubic yards of earth placed over them.

Pottery was found in the mound, all broken; the pipe was broken. It may be that as their Chiefs had gone to "the shades" they sent, "killing" by breaking, all their paraphernalia, so that the impersonal necessities might become "shades" for their owners' use in the Hereafter. (Cadle 1902:220)

Reed's description provides less detail than Cadle's, omitting any mention of the first, "intrusive" burial:

In excavating, work was commenced at the ground surface on the north side of the mound and a trench made 4½ feet wide which was driven directly toward the center of the mound. Some broken pottery, arrow heads, etc., were found but nothing of importance until at about four feet from the center when it was observed that the ground when struck with pick or shovel gave a hollow sound. Going back a little the excavation was made two feet deeper and then with hands and pocket knives the earth was carefully removed towards the supposed hollow space which proved to be a sort of cellar which had been originally covered with large logs. Carefully removing these decayed logs there was exposed the skeletons of three human bodies, one large, one medium and one of small size. With these skeletons was a perfect Prehistoric Ceremonial Pipe ten inches high made from Minnesota Red Sandstone, or a similar stone with perfect Egyptian features carved in human form, kneeling upon one knee and having in the back the pipe bowl and place for mouth-piece. This pipe was sitting upon a bed of coal and ashes and was surrounded by the bones of the three bodies that had evidently been buried in a sitting posture facing the pipe and the cellar had been covered with logs and this mound of earth over ten feet in height raised over it all.

This pipe, some of the large bones, ear ornaments of shell inlaid with copper, as thin as paper, some shell beads, pieces of coal and of lead that were found with the skeletons are preserved in the office of the Park Commission at Pittsburg Landing, where they may be seen by visitors. (Reed 1914:21–22)

The first burial encountered, as described by Cadle, was clearly Mississippian, as evidenced by the copper-covered shell ear spool. Whether the burial was truly intrusive is uncertain. Excavations in the 1930s uncovered other burials at this depth, but the excavators could discern no actual burial pits and therefore concluded that the burials may have been deposited during construction of the mound.

The central, log-covered burial is, of course, the most interesting feature of Mound C. Log-covered burials are known from the Middle Woodland period and are found widely across the Southeast and Midwest. However, the burial feature at the base of Mound C is not Middle Woodland or even Late Woodland, because the Shiloh pipe (see Figure 2.2) almost certainly dates to the middle of the twelfth century A.D. The pipe is carved from a distinctive red flint clay with white spots. Human figurines of similar size, the same distinctive raw material (Emerson, Wisseman, and Moore 2001; Emerson et al. 2003), and similar style have been found in and around the American Bottom of Illinois. The American Bottom figurines are consistently found in Stirling phase contexts. The raw material for these figurines comes from west-central Missouri, only 40 km or so from the American Bottom (Emerson and Hughes 2000). Given the source of the raw material, the relatively large number and consistent dating of figurines found in the American Bottom, and the clear stylistic similarity between the Shiloh pipe and those from the American Bottom, it is likely that the Shiloh pipe is a mid-1100s import from the American Bottom. This dates the burial chamber beneath Mound C to the Mississippian period.

Cadle and Reed do not mention it, but they did not excavate the entirety of the log-covered tomb. A large part of Mound C was excavated in the 1930s, and the 1899 trench was easily visible (see Figure 2.3 and Chapter 4). Portions of the tomb were intact around the margins of the old trench, particularly on the south side. The 1930s excavators uncovered a number of human bones, which had been deposited as a bundle of defleshed bones rather than in-flesh inhumations. Moreau Chambers described the remaining part of the tomb as follows:

Roofed Burial Pit
The horizontal beam of chestnut or cypress at the south end of the log tomb was about 8 inches in diameter by three feet long; the wooden puncheon that formed the roof of the tomb was approx. one inch thick. Traces of it lay over & in contact with the bunched long bones of several individuals in the south end of the tomb.

Width of grave, 33"; depth of bones from middle of log at top of grave, 12". Wooden covering of grave is traced undisturbed 6½ or 7 ft. north of south end, & traces of the old timbers as far back as 7 ft. further north, but in the digger's trench. (Chambers 1933–1934:48)

Figure 2.2. The Shiloh pipe (SHIL 00386)

Reed's description of the 1899 Mound C excavation mentions that the "pipe, some of the large bones, ear ornaments of shell inlaid with copper, as thin as paper, some shell beads, pieces of coal and of lead [galena?] that were found with the skeletons" were kept for display at the park. Other than the pipe, none of this material is now in the park collections, victims of the tornado that demolished park headquarters in October 1909 (Smith 2004:110).

Figure 2.3. Moreau B. C. Chambers, at right, pointing to outline of the 1899 excavation trench in Mound C (National Anthropological Archives, Smithsonian Institution, negative no. 79-12,606)

CADLE DIGS INTO "MOUND 2" IN 1903

In addition to the excavation into Mound C in 1899, there was at least one other mound excavated by Colonel Cadle. A letter from Cadle to Major Reed in 1903 contains the terse statement "I opened a mound—the one near the road just west of the pipe mound and found *nothing*" (Cadle 1903, emphasis in original). Because none of the large mounds at the site could be described as "just west of the pipe mound"—a ravine is just west of Mound C—the statement must refer to a mound that is near the Browns Ferry Road, which indeed passes just west of Mound C. The other mounds that are near this road include Mounds B, D, and Q. One other possible clue to the identity of this mound comes from a print of a woodcut illustration in the Shiloh park files. The woodcut shows "Shiloh Mound No. 2," with one half cut away and a person kneeling in front of the vertical profile for scale (see Figure 2.4). The illustrated mound is roughly the size of Mound B, too small to be Mound D and too large to be Mound Q. Thus, if "Mound No. 2" is the same as the mound Cadle "opened" in 1903, it is most likely Mound B.

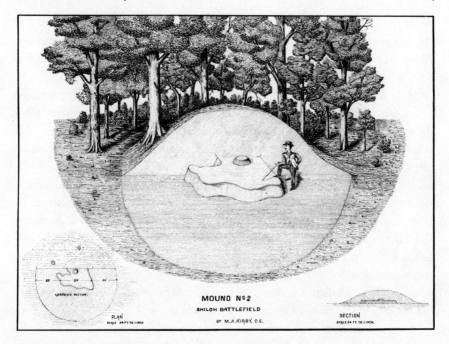

Figure 2.4. Illustration of "Mound No. 2" excavation

The possibility that "Mound No. 2" might be Mound B is given addi-
tional but clearly unreliable support from an interview recorded in 1934 by
Moreau Chambers. Near the end of the 1933–1934 excavation, Mr. L. B.
Philyaw visited the site and Chambers recorded the following information
(I have left the punctuation and line breaks as in the original):

> One of the diggers with Col. Cadle in Mound 2 or B, where pipe was found.
> Mr. L. B. Philyaw, of Shiloh-Selmer (Hwy 57)
> Mound B was being dug on Good Friday, 1899, when men killed in gravel
> pit; pipe found following day.
> Mr. Philyaw stated definitely that the pipe was dug from the base of Mound
> B in a trench from the north, running slightly beyond the middle. Found un-
> accompanied. Doesn't remember finding of bones, wood, etc. Found on base
> of mound. Traces of trench now apparent from east has come since Col.
> Cadle's digging. He thinks Fowler took up the pipe. Mound C hadn't been dug
> into—says Mr. Philyaw—at time of excav. (Chambers 1933–1934:45)

Some parts of Philyaw's story are correct, some clearly incorrect. Philyaw
is correct that the pipe was found in an excavation at the end of a trench that
entered a mound from the north and went to just beyond the mound's mid-

point. But Philyaw is clearly incorrect in attributing the pipe to Mound B; the 1930s excavation of Mound C proves that Cadle and Reed dug into Mound C, just as they describe. Philyaw's memory is clearly flawed in failing to recall the associated bones, artifacts, and wooden covering of the central tomb in Mound C. And Philyaw's association of the finding of the pipe with the deaths of workers in a nearby gravel pit on Good Friday does not match the statements of Cadle and Reed that they excavated Mound C in June. But before dismissing Philyaw's statement that it was Mound B that he helped dig into, we should note that Philyaw also told Chambers that "Simpson Kellar [sic] (bro. of Helen Kellar [sic]) & Mr. Kirby, C.E., took notes while excavations were in progress" (Chambers 1933–1934:46). The woodcut illustration (Figure 2.4) of the excavation of "Mound No. 2" was made by M. A. Kirby, C.E. (Civil Engineer), who was employed by the park, as was Helen Keller's brother, Simpson (Smith 2004). And there was indeed a gravel pit accident in the park on March 31, 1899, that killed three men (Smith 2004:99). Obviously, parts of Philyaw's memory are correct, so it appears that Philyaw had conflated several different events into a single story.

To make matters even more puzzling, an unsigned manuscript copy of a letter (Anonymous 1914) on file at Shiloh N.M.P. describes a set of bones and artifacts found in an oval mound at Shiloh. This letter is part of an exchange between the park superintendent, DeLong Rice, and W. H. Holmes of the Smithsonian Institution. Holmes had seen a copy of C. B. Moore's report on Shiloh—published in 1915, but Holmes must have seen a pre-publication version—which contained an illustration of the effigy pipe. Holmes wrote to the park inquiring whether the Smithsonian might obtain the pipe for display in Washington. Superintendent Rice refused to hand over the pipe but did offer to send some bones and a few other artifacts, an offer Holmes accepted. The letter in question accompanied the bones and artifacts that were sent, whose receipt was acknowledged in a letter on August 29, 1914 (Rathbun 1914). Though the letter probably was sent to the Smithsonian with DeLong Rice's name, the manuscript copy on file in the park is in Major Reed's handwriting, according to Dr. Tim Smith (personal communication), a park ranger and historian of the park's early administration (Smith 2004). The manuscript describes the discovery of the bones and artifacts in an oval mound of roughly the same size as Mound C, but several of the details do not match Cadle's or Reed's published descriptions of Mound C, nor do they match the illustration of "Mound No. 2":

These bones are a few taken from an oval mound 90 × 100 × 12 feet in size on Shiloh Battlefield. Within this mound and distinctly marked is an apparent original mound 30 feet in diameter and 9 feet high, afterward added to to [sic] the extent above stated. At the center of this inner mound and 15 inches above natural surface of ground was found bones, marked No. 1, (one skeleton) lying on its side, with legs drawn up [here a drawing of a fully flexed skeleton lying on left side, hands in front of the face] so, head to the south and facing west.

Bones marked 2 & 3 are a part of many (probably a dozen) skeletons, which were massed closely together and promiscuously placed on the south side of the inner mound and center of the inner mound 2 feet above the natural surface of ground.

The massing shows that they were placed there as bones only. The shell beads enclosed are part of about 50 found among bones of No. 2 group. These being the best specimens. These bones were covered by 10 feet of earth. (Anonymous 1914)

With this manuscript there are drawings of both the plan view and section of the mound, repeating the dimensions stated in the text. The long dimension of the oval is oriented east-west, unlike Mound C. Only Mounds A, C, D, F, and G are large enough to be the mound described in this manuscript. Mounds A, D, F, and G all clearly have flat tops, not the rounded dome shown in the drawing and described in the manuscript. The most likely identification of this mound is C, despite the substantial disparities between the manuscript description and the descriptions of Mound C by both Cadle and Reed. However, given the uncertainties, it is possible that Cadle may have excavated not just in Mound C in 1899, and in "Mound No. 2" in 1903 but possibly in a third mound as well.

The anonymous (1914) manuscript refers to shell beads that were part of the shipment to the Smithsonian, along with the bones. According to Dorothy Lippert (personal communication) of the Repatriation Office of the National Museum of Natural History, the Smithsonian records show that the bones were destroyed and discarded. The beads appear to have gone with them, inasmuch as they are no longer in the Smithsonian collection.

MOORE VISITS AND MAPS THE SITE IN 1914

The Shiloh mounds were visited by C. B. Moore in 1914. He was not able to obtain permission to excavate at the site, so he had to content himself with mapping and describing the mounds and quoting Cadle's description of the trench into Mound C. The letter designations used by Moore on his map (see Table 2.1 and Figure 2.5) are the designations that all subsequent investigators have used. Moore's report (1915) provides several useful details in addition to the map. First, he gives the heights of the seven largest mounds. Mound dimensions provided by Moore are often the earliest accurate measurements

Table 2.1 Heights of mounds at Shiloh given by
C. B. Moore

Mound	Height of summit	
Mound A	14 feet	6 inches
Mound B	8 feet	6 inches
Mound C	10 feet	2 inches
Mound D	9 feet	10 inches
Mound E	5 feet	1 inch
Mound F	9 feet	3 inches
Mound G	11 feet	6 inches

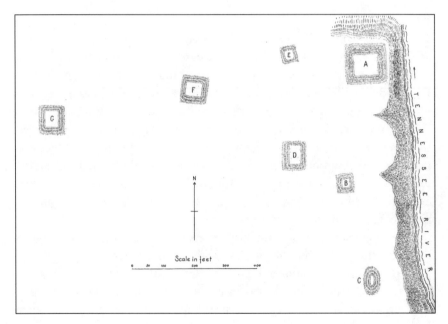

Figure 2.5. Moore's map of Shiloh (Moore 1915:224)

available for mounds that subsequently were later modified or destroyed. Fortunately, there has been little disturbance to the Shiloh Mounds since Moore's
time, though he does comment on disturbances to the mounds before he
arrived.

Moore's second useful comment concerns the mounds and "various low
knolls and humps of aboriginal origin." He states that "most of them have
been investigated, apparently to a very limited extent, with one exception
(Mound C) to be referred to in due course. The humps, however, have been
dug considerably, owing, perhaps, to their convenient size" (Moore 1915:225).

He also mentions the 1862 burial in Mound G of slain members of the 28th Illinois Infantry and their subsequent removal to the National Cemetery.

The third valuable comment of Moore is his mention of the house built atop Mound A, "for the use of the superintendent of the park." Denudation of the surface by the foot traffic during use of this house apparently led to considerable erosion of part of the mound, as revealed by the Ehrenhard/ Beditz excavation in 1979.

So by 1914 or 1915, most of the mounds had received at least superficial disturbance, Mound C had been center-trenched, and Mound G had been trenched to receive, then to remove, Civil War burials. An unknown but not small number of the house mounds or other low mounds had also been dug into, and the park superintendent was using a house built atop Mound A. None of the published descriptions of the site yet provided any details about the palisade around the site, though its existence is mentioned in Reed's (1914) article.

ROBERTS DIRECTS LARGE-SCALE EXCAVATIONS IN 1933–1934

The single greatest human disturbance to the site came in the winter of 1933–1934, when Frank H. H. Roberts, Jr., directed a massive excavation project using a large crew of local laborers paid by the Civil Works Administration (CWA). Roberts, an archaeologist at the Smithsonian Institution, and a single field assistant, Moreau B. C. Chambers, oversaw a crew as large as 118 men for 3 months. This was one of the early Relief-funded excavation projects, and effective management and recording techniques for these large projects were not yet well developed. This may explain why the records of this excavation leave much to be desired even by Relief-era standards. The records, or at least some records, are curated in the National Anthropological Archives at the National Museum of Natural History (part of the Smithsonian Institution). Roberts did not prepare a final report of his excavations, but two separate short overviews appeared in Smithsonian publications (Roberts 1935; Stirling 1935; though published under Stirling's name, the latter was likely written by Roberts). A detailed account of the 1933–1934 excavation appears elsewhere in this report (Chapter 5), so the work is merely summarized here.

The CWA was one of the early Relief agencies; it was created by executive order in November 1933 to help jobless people facing the oncoming winter. Approval to use CWA funds on archaeology projects was granted on December 7 (Lyon 1996:30), with almost immediate results. Roberts, and presumably Chambers, arrived at Shiloh in the evening of December 19, 1933. The next day he and Chambers went to the site and met with the surveyor, named

Williamson, who would map and grid the site, and with CWA officials to arrange for the laborers. The following morning, December 21, excavation commenced. Surveying and gridding of the site also began that morning, so that the early excavations were not dug on a grid system. The surveyor eventually produced a plane-table map of the site with 2-ft contour intervals; the site was eventually staked at 20-ft intervals, and the later excavations were given coordinates in the grid system. The workers for the most part used picks and shovels, rarely trowels—the field notes contain accountings of who was issued trowels—and none of the excavated material was screened. The following passage gives a general impression of the extent of the excavations:

> Investigations included the digging of trenches at regular intervals in the area surrounding and lying between the main mounds; sectioning of the burial mound; trenching two of the platform mounds; examination of a number of house sites; and excavations at several places along the palisade ridge. The trenches through the flats revealed the traces of 30 houses, a temple, and a number of refuse deposits. . . . In two instances remains of white man's dwellings were discovered. (Roberts 1935:65)

The Shiloh project ran through March 30, and the CWA itself was terminated on March 31, 1934, according to Lyon (1996:37). The last date in the field records, however, is March 26. After the fieldwork ceased, the artifact collection was taken back to what was then the U.S. National Museum (now the National Museum of Natural History). Roberts apparently kept the collection in his office or lab for several years, because the collection and supporting documents were not formally accessioned (Accession 152153) into the Smithsonian Institution collections until May 1939. Though Roberts rapidly produced the two brief published reports of his work, there is no evidence that he made any further analysis of the Shiloh materials. It seems likely that his attention soon turned to the Lindenmeier site in Colorado, where he began the first of many excavation seasons half a year after leaving Shiloh (see Wilmsen and Roberts 1978:1–21). Like Roberts, his field assistant, Moreau B. C. Chambers, rapidly became involved in other projects. Chambers (1976:335) reports that after the Shiloh project was closed down, "I tried hard to get it re-established, and was accepted, and then turned it down" to enter full-time employment by the Mississippi Department of Archives and History. By June 1934 he was excavating at the Lyons Bluff site (Galloway 2000).

The excavations of 1933–1934 were very extensive but poorly documented. Describing the excavations in detail, however, is a lengthy and difficult task that will be tackled in Chapter 5.

OTHER EXCAVATION IN 1934

No other excavation is known to have taken place at the site in 1934 after the CWA-funded work closed in March. There is, however, a photograph of a prehistoric pot (Moundville Incised *var. Moundville*) in the park files with the notation "Pot found at Shiloh Indian Mounds on June 14, 1934" penciled on the back. No other information about the provenience of this pot is known, so whether it eroded out a ravine edge or the river bluff, or whether it was excavated, is not known. The pot is no longer in the park collections, nor is there any record that it was ever formally accessioned.

GERALD SMITH'S TEST EXCAVATIONS IN 1976

After the 1930s, no additional archaeological research at Shiloh is recorded until 1976. At that time, Gerald Smith was contracted by the Southeast Archeological Center of the National Park Service to address five principal issues:

1. Examine the collection and records from the 1933–1934 excavation.
2. Emplace three permanent datum markers on a metric grid, for use by future researchers at the site.
3. Examine the feasibility of relocating the 1933–1934 excavations by conducting test excavations in the plaza area.
4. Verify the existence of the palisade and bastions by test excavation.
5. Provide an overview of the place of the Shiloh site in the region's prehistory.

The research conducted by Smith was thoroughly reported, unlike much of the earlier work, so only the relevant conclusions need to be presented here. I address each of the issues listed, in an order that does not correspond to Smith's report but rather one that puts the less successfully-addressed issues before those more successfully addressed.

To assess the largely unpublished work of Roberts in 1933–1934, Smith visited the National Museum of Natural History (NMNH) in Washington, D.C., on September 2, 1975. Unfortunately, one day is inadequate for assessing the collection and records. This is hardly a criticism of Smith, because in my experience the collection's documentation is so fragmentary that it takes many weeks of full-time work to piece together what is recorded and to discover what information is truly missing. Not having a budget for such an expenditure of time, Smith should not be faulted for reaching the conclusion he did: that the records and collection are not of much use and that "the primary contribution from the remaining 1934 data appears to lie in the photographs and contour maps" (Smith 1977:1). The situation is actually better than that, as shown in Chapter 5.

Placing three permanent grid monuments at the site was a goal that Smith had every reason to believe was successfully accomplished. He described these monuments as follows:

> Three benchmarks defining the new metric grid were set adjacent to the asphalt walkway along the north side of the plaza. Each consists of a cast concrete marker approximately 10 inches in diameter and a foot deep, with a central 3/8 inch iron rod marking the point of grid line intersection, and the grid coordinates and elevation incised into the top of the benchmark. The top of each benchmark is slightly below grade. (Smith 1977:3)

Having the locations of these markers, and Smith's grid system as a whole, plotted on a copy of the 1933–1934 topographic map of the site, I expected to relocate them easily in 1998. However, the monuments are not visible on the surface, nor could we find them below surface by probing with chaining pins, trowels, shovels, and a metal detector. After devoting more than 10 person-days to the search, I concluded that the monuments no longer exist, perhaps because frost-heaving raised them to a level at which they were destroyed by the bush-hogs or mowers used in this area by park maintenance crews.

To relocate excavation units from the 1930s, Smith excavated in two locations in the plaza. The first area was immediately northeast of Mound B:

> It was expected that this location next to a mound and near the edge of the plaza would provide a good midden zone, perhaps sealed under mound outwash. Approximate [1933–1934] trench locations were visible on the surface and the area seemed to have been spared the extensive excavation activity suggested by the 1934 field notes for the north, east, and southwest margins of the plaza.
>
> The surface humus was bladed off, exposing faint trench outlines in a hard tan and white mottled clay with extensive iron or manganese concretions. Excavation of and through the approximate old trench locations to a depth of 50 cm produced no artifactual remains and no indication of strata other than subsoil zonation. (Smith 1977:7)

Smith's field notes reveal that he believed the faint trench outline he saw was Roberts's Trench 21, though Smith's excavation is almost certainly too far north for this. Rather, Smith may have observed Trench 22 or 23.

After having little success relocating old excavations northeast of Mound

B, Smith tried excavating in the area south of Mound F. The current ground surface in this part of the plaza has numerous quasi-linear ridges and swales that could be backfilled trenches or the remains of back dirt piles. Smith's crew began with a 50-X-160-cm slot trench, then opened two adjacent 3-X-3-m units separated by a balk 20–30 cm wide. These excavations revealed several pit features, a fire stain, isolated postmolds, and a wall trench 50 cm wide and roughly 1 m deep that ran NW–SE across the excavation. There were 55 cm of cultural deposits, formed of several strata, in this part of the plaza. This is consistent with Roberts's observation that parts of the plaza were built up above the natural surface.

Verifying the existence of the palisade and bastions was the most successful of Smith's undertakings. He relocated the palisade embankment, excavated two sections along the portion of the embankment mapped in the 1930s, and found what he believed was an extension of the palisade north of Mound H. A 1-m-wide test excavation across the possible palisade line north of Mound H did not reveal any postmolds or a wall trench, though a ditch 1 m wide by 30 cm deep may be consistent with the palisade having extended through this location. Visual inspection of this area in 1999 by David Anderson, John Cornelison, and myself did not convince us that this was the palisade, it being somewhat off the line of the palisade as projected from the last definitely known section.

The two excavations across the western portion of the palisade demonstrated that the palisade was built of closely spaced posts set in individual holes with gaps of 5–20 cm between the postmold edges. The postmolds were 12 to 20 cm in diameter, showing that the posts were not as stout as those found at some other palisaded Mississippian sites (e.g., Moundville [Allan 1984; Scarry 1995] and Angel [Black 1967]; for a thorough survey see Milner [1999:118–120]). The postmolds were found in an embankment 35 cm high and 2.5 m wide at its base. The excavation profiles show that the posts had been set into the embankment rather than the embankment having been piled up around the posts. Curiously, one of Smith's excavations lies in the portion of the palisade that the 1933–1934 site map suggests was excavated by Roberts. Smith's excavation encountered no indication that the palisade here had previously been excavated, so perhaps this detail of the 1933–1834 map is merely schematic.

To test whether the rectangular projections protruding from the palisade line are indeed bastions, Smith excavated one (see Figure 2.6). He found that this one was a rectangular bastion 3.2 m wide, projecting 3 m outward from the curtain wall. The bastion, like the rest of the palisade, is built of closely spaced, individually set, small-to-medium-sized posts. Inside the bastion, there were additional postmolds:

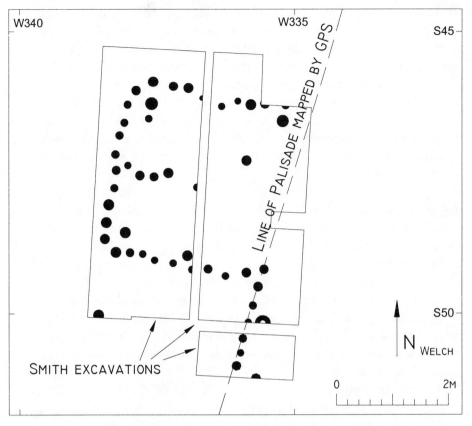

Figure 2.6. Detail of site map showing bastion excavated by G. Smith in 1976

The bastion is open on the inside face, but has a row of postmolds perpendicu-lar to its front wall which divide the outward half of the bastion into approxi-mately equal sections. Inside each corner of the bastion and midway inside each flank is a large extra postmold. These extra postmolds seem best inter-preted as support posts for an interior raised floor within the bastion. (Smith 1977:6)

The final objective of Smith's report was setting Shiloh within the context of the region's prehistory. Here, Smith relied on comparisons with excavated materials elsewhere in the region, considering first the materials from upriver and downriver and then looking westward to the Mississippi alluvial valley. Smith's basic conclusions were that Shiloh had two components, one of Late Woodland age and another of Late Mississippian date:

The Shiloh Mounds Area includes two components, both more closely related to cultures centered in the northern portion of the Mississippi alluvial valley than to earlier ones in the Tennessee River Valley. This is not merely a local phenomenon, but is part of the overall context of cultural development in the Tennessee Valley and must be considered in this perspective. The Late Woodland component is most closely related to components downstream near the Kentucky border, but is part of a general expansion of Mississippi Valley Late Woodland cultures which spread up the Tennessee River at least through Pickwick Basin. The contrast between the Shiloh Late Woodland component and those in Pickwick Basin suggests that different, though roughly contemporaneous groups are involved. The burial pattern in Mound C is clearly Woodland and also quite different from that of nearby Copena burial mounds, but data are lacking to determine whether or not it is part of the occupation represented by the Late Woodland midden deposit found in the 1976 excavations south of Mound F.

The Late Mississippian component includes the most extensive mound-and-plaza complex in the Tennessee Valley and possibly the best preserved Mississippian fortification system left in the nation. Sufficient ceramic data are now available to indicate that it is part of a poorly-known phase restricted to Hardin County, Tennessee, and not part of the Kogers Island Phase of Pickwick Basin fame. Only three other known sites appear likely to be involved in this phase, of which one has already been destroyed. (Smith 1977:23–24)

Several of Smith's chronological assessments no longer appear to be accurate. The Late Woodland, grog-tempered pottery at Shiloh is no more obviously related to grog-tempered pottery downstream near the Kentucky border than it is to grog-tempered pottery upstream in northern Alabama, along the upper Tombigbee River in Mississippi, or along the Black Warrior River in central Alabama (e.g., Futato 1975, 1980, 1987; Jenkins and Krause 1986:73–85; Knight 1990; Mistovich 1988; Rafferty 1986; Walthall 1980:137–141; Welch 1990, 1994). This point will be considered further in the section of the report dealing with pottery. The burials in Mound C are culturally Mississippian rather than Woodland, as demonstrated by the shell- and copper-covered shell ear spools and the imported figurine pipe of Stirling phase style found in the basal deposits. Whether these Mississippian burials were made by people who made shell-tempered pottery or grog-tempered pottery is a vexing question that is still unsettled. Regardless of this point, the people doing the burying were interacting with Mississippian neighbors and were living in a community structured in a typically Mississippian pattern.

Smith's chronological assessment of the Mississippian component of Shiloh is also now superseded by more recently available data. These data include a better understanding of Mississippian chronology in northeast Mississippi and northwest Alabama and radiocarbon assessments from materials at Shiloh itself. The radiocarbon results and comparison of the Mississippian pot-

tery with dated assemblages elsewhere in the region puts the Shiloh component clearly in the earlier half of Mississippian rather than the later half.

The five goals of Smith's 1977 study were addressed with a success that—
with the advantage of hindsight—was more mixed than it appeared to be at
the time. His examination of the 1933–1934 collection in the NMNH under-
estimated the potential of that collection. Relocating 1933–1934 excavation
units in the plaza area turned out to be more difficult than was expected. The
"permanent" datum markers he placed could no longer be found in 1998.
And his chronological assessment of the Late Woodland and Mississippian
components at Shiloh has not been borne out by more recent research. On
the other hand, Smith's excavations along the palisade successfully yielded
clear postmold patterns of both the curtain wall and one complete bastion.
And, perhaps most important, Smith called the attention of archaeologists
to this impressive, well-preserved, important, but poorly known Mississippian site.

BRUCE SMITH ASSEMBLES INFORMATION ABOUT PREVIOUS EXCAVATIONS

In the late 1970s, Bruce D. Smith of the NMNH became interested in the
Shiloh mounds site and began assembling documents and collections. He obtained copies of the field notebooks, maps, 8-X-10-inch prints of the black-
and-white photographs that Roberts had made of the excavations in the
1930s, and other records of that excavation, to go with the artifact collection
stored at the NMNH. Smith also obtained the artifacts, reports, and field
notes of Gerald Smith's work in 1976 and records and collections from subsequent excavation at the site in 1979. Despite having assembled this material, other interests and duties at the Smithsonian prevented Smith from com-
pleting a report on Shiloh, and the materials lay dormant in his office for
almost two decades. The relevance of Smith's activities for this report lies in
the fact that when I became interested in Shiloh, Bruce Smith turned over to
me all the material he had assembled and supported my efforts to conduct
research on the artifacts housed at the NMNH. The fact that he had done so
much of the groundwork has made my job vastly easier and has added in
many ways to the thoroughness of this report.

EHRENHARD AND BEDITZ EXCAVATE ON MOUND A IN 1979

In 1979 archaeologists from the Southeast Archeological Center of the National Park Service excavated stratigraphic test units on Mound A. The objective of the project was to assess the stratigraphy of Mound A, which was

beginning to fall off the side of the river bluff as the bluff episodically slumped away. Work was directed by John Ehrenhard, and results were reported not just in the in-house technical report (Beditz 1980b) but also in a presentation at the 1979 Annual Meeting of the Southeastern Archaeological Conference (Beditz and Bellomo 1980). The presentation was memorable to many archaeologists in the audience for the description of a 1-×-1-m test unit excavated 6.8 m deep, so deep that the crew needed to use spelunking helmets with headlamps just to be able to see down inside it. The unit's walls needed extensive shoring, and workers had to be lowered into the unit on ropes.

Three test units were excavated in the 1979 project. One (Unit 3) was located on the south flank of the mound, in order to see whether there was evidence for a ramp at that location; no such evidence was recognized. Atop the mound's summit, one unit was to be excavated from the summit to premound sediments. The first 1-×-1-m unit (Unit 1) opened atop the summit encountered historic fill to a depth of 1 m. This fill appeared to date from the early part of the 1900s and was interpreted as debris dumped into an erosion gully. The origin of the historic artifacts in the debris was likely the house or cabin built atop the mound for the use of the park commissioner (cf. remarks made by C. B. Moore in 1914) or materials left by Boy Scouts camping at the site.

Abandoning Unit 1, the excavators moved several meters eastward and commenced excavating Unit 2, which turned out to be outside the area of historic fill. Prehistoric fill material, containing sparse artifacts and exhibiting only subtle variations in color and texture, was excavated to a depth of 6.8 m below the summit. This greatly puzzled the excavators, because the ground surface immediately around the mound's base appears to be only about 4.2 m below the summit. No stratigraphic break was seen at the elevation where the premound soil was expected, and artifacts continued to be encountered as much as 2.5 m below the elevation of the expected base of the mound. Both Woodland and Mississippian pottery was noted from these deep deposits.

The explanation for the findings in this deep test unit comes from Roberts's unpublished field notes. Roberts had discovered in 1934 that what appears to be the ground surface around Mound A is an artificial apron. At the middle of the western face of the mound, the apron was 2 m thick, but near the northern end of the western face the depth must be closer to 3 m. Because Roberts had not published this finding, and because Gerald Smith had not discovered this detail in his brief examination of the field records in 1975, the excavators in 1979 had no inkling that Mound A was actually 2–3 m taller than they expected. Had their test excavation extended another meter deeper, they probably would have encountered the premound surface.

Not only did the 1979 test excavation on Mound A fail to encounter the premound surface, but the excavation profile did not exhibit any clear evidence for distinct construction episodes, interrupted by periods of use of the mound summit. There had been at least two shifts of fill sources, as evidenced by a set of arbitrary levels that lacked artifacts, sandwiched between upper and lower deposits containing artifacts. However, none of the soil color or texture variations appeared to form a distinct surface continuous across all sides of the excavation unit. Soil chemistry analyses, measuring pH, and concentrations of calcium, potassium, magnesium, and phosphorous did not display any sudden spikes or troughs that would indicate anthropogenic activity at a particular depth or layer. Radiocarbon samples (Beditz 1980b:23–24) taken from the fill yielded mostly Woodland period age estimates: five charcoal samples yielded estimates between A.D. 140 and 1090, uncalibrated (two shell samples yielded estimates of 325 and 405 B.C., uncalibrated, but dates on freshwater shell minerals are notoriously unreliable). These dates indicate merely that the charcoal was part of the Woodland deposit being quarried as fill for the mound. The excavators concluded that "all evidence points to a single stage of mound construction" (Beditz 1980b:25).

Fortunately, planning for the mitigation excavation of that part of Mound A threatened by bank erosion anticipated that the stratigraphy of the mound might be more complex than indicated by the notorious 1-X1-X-6.8 unit. Excavations in 2001–2003 have revealed multiple mound stages, several of which have multiple resurfacings with superimposed building plans (Welch, Anderson, and Cornelison 2003).

Though it is of interest primarily for demonstrating the multiple inconsistencies between different maps of the site, there is a problem with the grid locations recorded for the Mound A excavations. The Mound A test excavations and the detailed topographic map of Mound A produced during the fieldwork were tied into the metric grid system created in 1975 by Gerald Smith. Or at least, the field workers tied their survey to a concrete monument which they believed to be Smith's N300/W600 monument. It is possible, however, that they mistook another concrete monument near the base of Mound A for Smith's grid monument. Whether or not that is the case, there is a discrepancy between the actual in-the-ground locations of the test excavations (one of which is still visible) and the location that the recorded grid coordinates would have on Gerald Smith's site map. In the long run this does not matter, because in 1999 the still-visible Unit 2 was tied into Welch's metric grid of the site, which is in turn tied into UTM coordinates.

EHRENHARD AND BELLOMO
MAGNETOMETRY SURVEY

Randy Bellomo conducted a small magnetometry survey at the mound site in 1981, focusing on Mounds N and O. It was done as one part of a methodological study of digital filtering techniques on magnetometry data (Bellomo 1983). Bellomo believed, based on what was known at that time, that Mound O had been excavated in the 1930s but that Mound N was intact. Unfortunately, though he had no way of knowing it, Mound N *had* been dug into (see Chapter 6). It is therefore not terribly surprising that he found less difference between the magnetometer results from the two mounds than he had expected. Nevertheless, Bellomo detected magnetic anomalies that indicated the possible presence of a hearth or other features in Mound N, and he extracted 11 small-diameter cores to test this interpretation. Three of the cores did indeed contain charcoal, ash, and fired clay (Bellomo 1983:103–120).

BREWER'S 1987 ARCHAEOLOGICAL OVERVIEW AND ASSESSMENT

National Park Service policy requires that every decade there should be an overview and assessment of each park's resources. The *Overview and Assessment* prepared by David Brewer in 1987 reviews the history of research at the site up to that date. His review was of necessity briefer than this chapter—let alone this report as a whole—but one detail needs to be mentioned. It concerns the designations given to mounds at the site.

The letter designations A–G were applied by C. B. Moore in 1915 and have been used by all researchers subsequently. In 1933–1934, Roberts extended the letter designations to smaller mounds, beginning with H and running through W. All but one of the mounds lettered by Roberts (Mound P) have been located on maps prepared by Roberts or his field assistant, Moreau Chambers. The location of Mound P is not explicitly shown on contemporary maps, but its identity can be firmly fixed by references in the field notes. Thus, there does not now exist any ambiguity about the locations of Mounds A–W. In Brewer's report, these lettered mounds, plus nine other mounds that are not identified in any way at all, are given Park Service List of Classified Structure (LCS) numbers. I have not used these numbers, SHIL 1 through SHIL 33, anywhere in this report, because the park has not been able to locate any map or other document that gives locations for the nine LCS-numbered mounds that are not among the mounds to which letters were assigned in the 1930s (Stacy Allen, personal communication).

In addition to Mounds A–W, there are dozens of other small mounds still visible at the site. Most of them are probably house mounds (i.e., collapsed houses), but a few are possibly intentionally built mounds. In 1998 and 1999, the small mounds that we cored were given number designations by the Queens College field crews. These numbers are independent of the lettering system, such that at least five lettered mounds were given Queens College numbers. In this report, mounds that were labeled in 1933–1934 are consistently referred to by their letter designations, and other mounds are referred to by the numbers assigned in 1998–1999.

WELCH'S RESEARCH, 1994–1997

I became interested in the Shiloh site in the early 1990s. As early as 1980 I had been told, by those who had seen the F. H. H. Roberts collection at the NMNH, that the Shiloh pottery collection resembled that from the Bessemer site in Alabama. I had studied the Bessemer collection in 1980 and eventually published the analysis in 1994 (Welch 1994). I visited Shiloh for the first time in 1994. Because no other archaeologist was working on Mississippian materials in that area, and the archaeological record of Shiloh and outlying, contemporary sites was clearly less well known than a site of this size deserved to be, I decided to begin research in this area.

My long-term research goal was, and remains, assessment of the regional political role of the Shiloh polity and the importance (or lack of importance) of display-good movements along the Tennessee River. In 1995 a small planning grant from the City University of New York enabled me to spend several weeks visiting the known Mississippian mound sites between Pickwick Dam and Swallow Bluff Island. A field assistant and I also conducted a 100 percent coverage survey of 2.8 km^2 in one bend of the Tennessee River, to assess whether nonmound Mississippian settlements such as farmsteads were present. Our survey confirmed that there were indeed such farmsteads and that the outlying mound sites were in varying but generally good states of preservation. The Shiloh polity, with its generally well-preserved sites in the only major undammed stretch of the Tennessee River, seemed to be ideal for a long-range research project.

Having decided to begin research on the Shiloh polity, I applied for and received a Smithsonian Short-term Visitor grant to spend three weeks in July 1996 in Washington, D.C., studying the documents and collections from the 1933–1934 excavations. The collection of artifacts is small, and the collection of field documents is smaller. This afforded me time to examine and record the collection of materials from the Savannah (Tennessee) site, a multimound site protected by two lines of bastioned palisades, only 11 km northeast of Shiloh. Though many of the Savannah mounds turned out to be demonstrably of Middle Woodland date, at least three of the mounds contained Mississippian artifacts (Welch 1998a). The two lines of bastioned palisades around the site are also likely of Mississippian date, inasmuch as bastioned palisades are not known from Middle Woodland contexts. Clearly, Savannah had a

Mississippian occupation, perhaps one as large and important as the nearby Shiloh site, and Savannah must figure prominently in a full accounting of the history of the Shiloh polity.

I arranged to meet with Superintendent Woody Harrell at Shiloh in July 1997 to discuss our respective goals, interests, and desires for research at Shiloh. We found considerable commonalities in our goals. He wanted to learn more about the site so that the park could present information to visitors more effectively and so that he could construct a new walking-tour path with way signs through the site. I wanted to obtain limited excavation data from at least two houses located in different parts of the site in order to assess whether there were differential production of crafts in different parts of the site. Because the excavations I proposed would also provide some of the information he sought, he agreed that excavation would be permissible, and I agreed to assist his planning efforts in any way I could.

WELCH AND HARRELL OBTAIN AMS RADIOCARBON DATES IN 1998

One of the archaeological questions that arose from my restudy of the 1933–1934 excavation collection was the date of the Shiloh occupation. Previously, Gerald Smith had seen some of the Shiloh material and, by analogy to the Lower Mississippi Valley pottery sequence, had suggested a Late Mississippian date, later than A.D. 1400. By contrast, I saw parallels between the Shiloh pottery and the Late Woodland through middle Mississippian pottery sequence from northern and central Alabama and northeast Mississippi. Comparisons to the Alabama and northeast Mississippi sequences suggested a date for Shiloh earlier than A.D. 1300. The radiocarbon dates on isolated pieces of charcoal in the fill of Mound A, recovered by the Ehrenhard-Beditz test excavation, were not helpful in resolving this disparity in cross-dating. I proposed to Superintendent Harrell that we seek funding for radiocarbon analysis of charred plant materials in the collections from the 1933–1934 excavation. He suggested we apply to the Lower Mississippi Valley Regional Initiative, a program within N.P.S., for the funds. Our proposal was approved, and the NMNH permitted us to conduct the (destructive) analysis of three small samples, using the AMS dating technique.

Despite frequent mention of charcoal in the excavation field records, there is not much charred plant material in the collection. There is one accession lot consisting of a mass of charred maize kernels from near the surface southwest of Mound C. Another lot contains several pieces of charred cane, from W330.45/S90.38 (or S-2+96/W-10+84, in Roberts's English grid system). The

Table 2.2 Radiocarbon assays of samples from 1933–1934 excavations

Lab no.	NMNH catalog no.	Conventional ^{14}C age	Calibrated* date ranges
Beta-113780	A385556 #1	840 ± 50**	A385556 assays combined:
Beta-113781	A385556 #2	1000 ± 50***	1σ : AD 1030–1160
			2σ : AD 1020–1210
Beta-113782	A385481	780 ± 50****	1σ : AD 1215–1285
			2σ : AD 1150–1300

*   Calibrations were obtained using OxCal v. 3.4 (Bronk Ramsey 2000)
**   Measured ^{14}C age of 640 ± 50 adjusted for –12.7 o/oo $\delta^{13}C$
***   Measured ^{14}C age of 700 ± 50 adjusted for –7.0 o/oo $\delta^{13}C$
****   Measured ^{14}C age of 810 ± 50 adjusted for –26.7 o/oo $\delta^{13}C$

only other organic material in the collection consists of encrusted, charred, organic materials in the bowls of several ceramic smoking pipes, but NMNH was reluctant to have this material removed for destructive analysis. I obtained two maize kernels and one piece of charred cane. The radiocarbon analysis results are reported in Table 2.2.

Dating the charred cane was straightforward, but assessing the age of the charred maize requires explanation. The two maize kernels were selected from a single accession (A385556) for which a provenience "southwest of Mound C" is listed in the NMNH accession record. This corresponds with the statement in Chambers's field journal that a "mass of charred grain was found near the surface SW of Mound C" (Chambers 1933–1934:3). I am not completely certain that this was the provenience of the dated material, however, because Roberts's original, handwritten Field Catalogue of Artifacts does not specifically list any charred grain or maize. Two sacks of "charcoal" were listed, which, based on their place in the list, most likely came from the area south or southwest of Mound C, but a latter annotation says these sacks were discarded. The only other mention of charred maize in the records is "a few grains of charred corn" found near the pelvis of Burial 5 in Mound C (Chambers 1933–1934:31). There is nothing to suggest that the charred maize from the burial was saved or that it may have become mixed with the mass of charred maize southwest of the mound. Assuming that the A385556 charred maize all came from a single mass southwest of mound C, I would expect that it all was harvested either in a single year or no more than a couple of years apart. Consequently, I have treated the radiocarbon assays for the two maize kernels as independent estimates of the age of the "mass of charred grain." In such a circumstance, it is appropriate to combine the two assays prior to calibration, a procedure which the OxCal v.3.4 (Bronk Ramsey 2000) calibration program carries out. The conventional radiocarbon ages and cali-

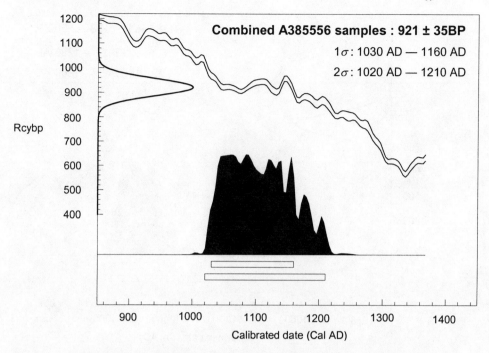

Figure 2.7. Calibration of combined radiocarbon assays on two maize kernels

brated dates are listed in Table 2.2, and the calibrations are illustrated in Figures 2.7 and 2.8.

The calibrated date ranges for the samples center around A.D. 1100 for the maize kernels, and around the mid-1200s for the charred cane. These dates are similar to the radiocarbon determinations from the Owl Creek Mounds, a site 130 km away in northeast Mississippi. At that site there are five radiocarbon determinations with calibrated most-likely dates between A.D. 1133 and 1219 (Rafferty 1995:41–45). Like Shiloh, Owl Creek has mostly plain shell-tempered pottery including jars with noded loop (or loopy strap) handles, with sparse examples of Barton Incised and Moundville Incised motifs. The same pottery diagnostics are found at the Bear Creek mound site in northeast Mississippi, approximately 55 km south of Shiloh (Bohannon 1972:15–24). No chronometric determinations are available for Bear Creek, however. The Shiloh pottery and the AMS determinations also accord well with the pottery and radiocarbon chronology of the Moundville I phase at Moundville, for which dozens of radiocarbon determinations indicate a date range of A.D. 1120 to 1260 (Knight, Konigsberg, and Frankenberg n.d.). The radiocarbon results, as well as the pottery cross-dating, support an A.D. 1100–1300 date for Shiloh, rather than the later date suggested by Gerald Smith.

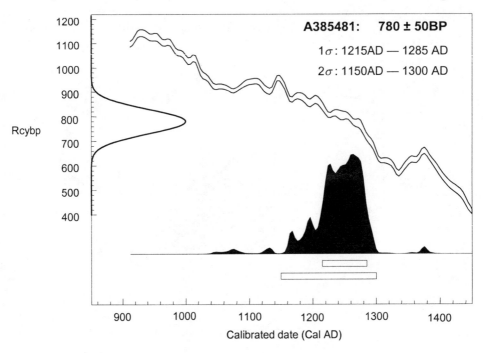

Figure 2.8. Calibration of radiocarbon assay on charred cane

WELCH EXCAVATES TWO HOUSE MOUNDS, 1998–1999

In 1997, Superintendent Harrell and I agreed that excavation of two house mounds would be appropriate. I obtained a CUNY Research Foundation grant to excavate the first one in the summer of 1998, and in the first week of the 1998 field season Superintendent Harrell obtained NPS funding for the second season of work. The 1998 fieldwork, carried out under Archeological Resources Protection Act Permit SHIL 98-001, had three goals:

1. Locate burned houses by looking for burned daub and charcoal in small diameter soil cores from house mounds. Emphasis is on finding burned houses near the palisade.
2. Relocate the monuments for G. Smith's 1975 metric site grid and record cored mound locations and excavation proveniences in the 1975 grid.
3. Excavate a burned house, including some of the area immediately around it, near the periphery of the community.

Results of the 1998 field season were presented in preliminary form shortly after the excavation (Welch 1998b), and the final report comprises Chapter 6 of this book. The season's goals were met with varying degrees of success. The principal failure was the inability to relocate the 1975 grid monuments. As a result, I was forced to create yet another grid system for the site—its third. Markers in this grid system were left in situ at the end of the 1998 field season and were found to be unmoved and still firmly in place at the start of the 1999 season. Consequently, the 1998 grid system was used also for the 1999 Queens College and 1999 SEAC fieldwork and for the more recent NPS mitigation excavations on Mound A.

The most interesting result of the 1998 fieldwork was the discovery that part of the site had experienced considerable erosion during its occupation, leaving the houses pedestalled above the surrounding surface. The evidence for this conclusion is principally the elevation of a house floor some 20 cm above the ground surface surrounding the house mound, with the floor resting atop an undisturbed and obviously ancient weathering profile. By contrast, the surrounding ground surface has a more recent weathering profile developing in a truncated B horizon. Apparently, the house roof protected the house floor from erosion while foot traffic denuded the area around the house, thereby leading to its erosion (Welch 1999). That this is a phenomenon widespread at the site rather than unique to the house we excavated in 1998 is shown by an observation in Roberts's field notes: "House mounds in most cases seem to be at high points of ground. Houses built on rises in each case" (Roberts 1933–1934:30). He apparently found floors above the surrounding ground surface but misunderstood the cause of the phenomenon.

The 1999 excavation, reported in detail in Chapter 7, was planned as an extension of the previous season. Having excavated a house mound near the perimeter of the site in 1998, the principal goal in 1999 was to excavate a burned house near the center of the site. The same technique of coring house mounds was used in 1999, this time with success. In one core from Mound N, the deposits from 46–68 cm below surface consisted of chunks of fired clay; three other cores on the mound failed to penetrate below 37 cm. This was precisely the sort of evidence we were looking for, albeit at a depth considerably greater than the 15–25 cm we had anticipated. One other core, on a low rise southeast of Mound F, yielded considerable charcoal. However, as photographs of the 1933–1934 work showed extensive excavations in this area, I decided it would be safer to excavate on Mound N, for which there was no indication of previous excavation.

As it turned out, Mound N did indeed have previous excavation, though we did not realize this until the middle of the 1999 season. To explore the stratification of the mound before opening up a wider area, we began by excavating an east-west, 1-m-wide trench from the east edge of the mound into the center. For the first 40–50 cm it was clear that we were excavating a fill deposit, as was expected given the thickness of the deposit atop the fired clay of the burned house. Between 40 and 50 cm below the mound summit, the north edge of my excavation trench intersected the north edge of a straight-sided, square-cornered, east-west basin with nearly vertical walls. We quickly ascertained that this basin was about 5 ft wide, that it extended through (and had removed) the fired clay layer seen in the core, and that my excavation trench was almost entirely inside this basin. Apparently somebody, most likely F. H. H. Roberts, excavated a 5-ft-wide trench into the mound precisely where I excavated a 1-m-wide trench.

The 1999 excavation in Mound N encountered four 2-inch-diameter vertical features that had been intentionally filled with sterile, coarse, white and tan sands. These were Randy Bellomo's backfilled sediment cores, and at the time they were a great mystery because park personnel did not have any recollection of anyone coring this mound and I had not yet acquired a copy of Bellomo's (1983) unpublished master's thesis.

Due to the expenditure of time reexcavating the backfilled 1933–1934 trench, only a small portion of the house beneath Mound N was excavated to the floor level. The house had a semisubterranean floor, recessed roughly 10–15 cm below the surrounding surface. From the small portion of the house we excavated, it looks like this recessed basin had been partially filled before the walls burned. However, a rodent burrow had disturbed much of the portion of the house we excavated, and interpretations at this point are necessarily tentative.

SEAC CREW IN 1999 CONDUCTS MAPPING, REMOTE SENSING, AND TEST EXCAVATION

Beginning in the summer of 1998, there were a series of conversations between various NPS staff and myself about the possibility of my preparing a comprehensive report about the archaeology of the Shiloh Mounds site. By spring of 1999 a Scope of Work and a budget figure had been agreed upon, and a purchase order for the report was issued to the Research Foundation of CUNY (on behalf of Queens College). In discussions leading up to the issuance of the Scope of Work, it was agreed that several sets of information that would be of great help in preparing the report but that would require GPS and remote-sensing instruments not available to me could most effectively be obtained by a SEAC field crew using SEAC instruments. Consequently, in

July 1999, a SEAC field crew came to Shiloh under the joint direction of
David Anderson and John Cornelison. Four objectives were specified:

1. Remote sensing survey south of Mound F, north and east of Mound
   D, and west of Mound A to relocate excavations from 1933–1934.
   Ground-penetrating radar (GPR) was expected to be the technology
   of choice, given the problems that historic metal objects and variation in moisture content would present for magnetometry and resistivity techniques.
2. Test excavations to check the "ground-truth" of the remote-sensing
   results and to provide in-the-ground locations for 1933–1934 excavation units which would permit precise matching of the 1933–1934
   grid and the 1998 grid.
3. Test excavation in the "Dike" to assess its construction history. The
   Dike is an artificial, linear, earthen ridge of unknown age or
   significance.
4. A survey of the full extent of the palisade and bastions, using global-
   positioning satellite (GPS) equipment.

These objectives were fulfilled in exemplary fashion. The palisade was
mapped fully, and the GPS receiver also provided decimeter-level UTM coordinates for the 1998 grid datum and all the major mounds at the site. The
GPR survey succeeded beyond my wildest hopes, not only because it rapidly
provided highly accurate indications of the location of the 1933–1934 excavations but because it proceeded so rapidly that there was time to conduct at
least two orthogonal transects across every major mound at the site. The
GPR transects across the mounds detected not only the excavations from
1933–1934 but also mound stratigraphy. In instances where excavations permit
us to check the validity of the GPR indications of stratigraphy, the GPR
results are usually right on target. Reassuringly, much of the stratigraphic
interpretation of the GPR was done "blind," without the interpreter knowing what the excavations had previously revealed. A preliminary report on
the remote sensing results was presented at the 1999 Annual Meeting of the
Southeastern Archaeological Conference (Anderson, Cornelison, Bean, and
Welch 1999).

The test excavations to "ground truth" the GPR indications of 1933–1934
excavation units had mostly positive results. In a minority of cases, there
were no old excavation units found at a location where the GPR had indicated such might exist. But in most instances, the edges of the old excavations were within 20 cm of the location suggested by the radar output. One

of the important results of the GPR survey and test excavations is the dem-
onstration that the 1933–1934 excavations were far more widespread than
either the written or photographic records suggest.

The results of the 1999 SEAC fieldwork are presented in Chapter 8.

WELCH IS CONTRACTED BY NPS/SEAC TO SYNTHESIZE SHILOH ARCHAEOLOGY

After the 1999 fieldwork by Queens College and SEAC crews, the artifacts
from both excavations were brought back to Queens College for cataloging
and analysis. The tasks of washing, sorting, and recording these artifacts (and
those from the 1998 field season) were accomplished by four Queens undergraduate students and were completed in June 2000. All the artifacts and field
records were shipped to the Southeast Archeological Center of the National
Park Service in Tallahassee for curation. Papers (Anderson, Cornelison, Bean,
and Welch 1999; Welch 1996, 1999, 2000) based on this research were presented at annual meetings of the Southeastern Archaeological Conference,
and I submitted the comprehensive report (Welch 2001) in January 2001.

CONCLUSIONS

The earliest recorded archaeological investigations at Shiloh Indian Mounds
are now more than a century old. By today's standards, the published reports
and the unpublished records of excavations in the 1930s and earlier are frustratingly sparse and incomplete. But such complaints about the records of
archaeologists are minor in comparison with a centrally important fact: the
archaeological record at Shiloh—artifacts in context in the ground—is mostly
still there. The site is essentially intact, unplowed and protected from disturbance inside Shiloh National Military Park. The only significant threat to the
site is the erosion of the river bluff. Construction of a bank stabilization
project began in 2001, though unfortunately it has been marred by engineer-
ing failures and delays. From 2001 through 2003, archaeological excavations
removed most of that portion of Mound A that will otherwise slough away.
The work on Mound A is not included in this book, for it will take at least
one other volume on its own. But as a result of that work, I am confident
that the interpretation of Shiloh's prehistoric occupation presented here will
not be the final word on the subject—the inevitable fate of any synthesis of
a discovery-based science.

3   Artifact Typology

The pottery and stone tool types described here are the sort of analytical constructs widely used, and widely understood, by Southeastern archaeologists. They are space-time tools, imprecise tools intended to help us discern the patterns of cultural variation across space and change over time. Though such types have proven to be useful for this purpose, they are imprecise because they do not readily allow us to answer questions such as "what tribe was this?" or "are these the ancestors of the Chickasaw?" The problem is that cultural boundaries and the boundaries of material styles sometimes coincide but not always. We do not yet fully understand why and under what circumstances they do and why sometimes they do not. To use a modern example, would the fact that a person wears blue jeans be a good reason to infer that person is an American? In A.D. 1960 that would have been a reasonable inference but not in A.D. 2000. Reasons for the difference include the hegemonic spread of American movies and television programs, global political interactions, and world economic systems. Now imagine you are an archaeologist looking at a time hundreds of years ago for which there are no written documents and for which you do not even know where all the communities were, let alone the nature of their political and economic ties. In such a setting, what does it signify if two communities make similar pottery or if a style of stone tool spreads across the landscape? Maybe people who used similar styles are culturally related, but maybe not. Perhaps by carefully studying the spatial and temporal distributions of material styles, and combining that with knowledge of the spatial distribution of communities, and knowledge of the networks of political ties and economic exchange, we will be able to reconstruct a cultural geography of prehistory. At present, parts of the outline of that geography are known, but many of the details are still being hashed out in discussions among archaeologists. The next several pages feature just such a discussion, which will be of interest to other archaeologists studying similar materials but which nontechnical readers may find less than riveting (actually, "mind-numbing" was the way one reviewer put it).

For the most part, the type names used in this report are established names already present in the archaeological literature of the region. A type-variety nomenclature for the pottery is used, with several new varieties of extant types introduced. The most interesting typological question that had to be resolved was whether to use type names established in the Mississippi valley or type names established in Alabama. This is not a trivial issue, because it has implications both for what we think about the chronology of occupation at the site and for what we think to have been the cultural ties of the occupants to other communities in the region. In 1977, Gerald Smith argued for use of Mississippi valley type names at Shiloh. This led him to a conclusion that the site was occupied no earlier than A.D. 1300 or 1400. In this chapter I argue that the ties to the west are misplaced and that the connections are instead with communities to the south and east. I am not the first to make this argument; Jenkins (n.d.; see Walthall 1980:137) has been saying the same thing for several decades.

POTTERY

The use of type-variety nomenclature for Mississippian pottery was introduced in Alabama around 1978, when Vincas Steponaitis, Ned Jenkins, and Ben Coblenz agreed on a core set of type names (Steponaitis 1980:50). For the most part, these type names had originally been defined on (or at least in cognizance of) material from Moundville. Thus, the name Moundville Incised was used for unburnished, shell-tempered pottery that has a series of incised arches on the shoulder of globular jars. Pottery with the same motif is called Matthews Incised in the Mississippi valley, but the Alabama archaeologists chose not to extend this term into Alabama. In central Alabama, Moundville Incised pottery, particularly the *Moundville* variety with "eyelashes" above the arches, is restricted to the earlier half of the Mississippian period. In the lower Mississippi valley, Matthews Incised starts later and persists longer (see Morse and Morse 1990:158). While it would certainly be possible to refer to the pottery in Alabama as "Matthews Incised *var. Moundville,*" the decision to employ the term "Moundville Incised *var. Moundville*" in part reflects awareness of the different developmental trajectories and stylistic affinities of pottery in the two regions, and a rejection of the idea that the Moundville community was transplanted from somewhere near Memphis (see Steponaitis 1980:48). What should pottery with this incised-arch motif be called at Shiloh? Shiloh is nearly equidistant from Moundville and the Mississippi valley, so physical geography alone does not suggest an answer. Answering this question is not made any easier by the fact that the Matthews label has been applied to pottery from the lower Ohio valley (Hilgeman 2000:111–115) and central Tennessee (Smith 1992:77–79), with the explicit assumption of a later chronological position in both areas.

Gerald Smith addressed this question directly in his 1977 overview of the Shiloh site. Having examined 535 sherds—he incorrectly believed that was the entire collection—from the 1933–1934 Shiloh excavation, Smith (1977:9–12) decided to employ the Matthews Incised name. His (1977:9–10) reasons for using the Matthews taxon were clearly set out:

> It should be noted here that the terminology for incised types is based on that developed by Stephen Williams for Southeast Missouri and western Kentucky rather than the Moundville-based typology usually used in Alabama. The basic problem here is that the Moundville system does not distinguish among the basic incised motifs present, i.e., the jar shoulder arcades of Matthews v. the jar neck rectilinear guilloche of Beckwith. These two types, as well as at least two varieties of Matthews Incised have quite distinct geographic distributions and therefore should be distinguished in analysis. As used here, "Matthews Incised, *var.* Matthews" refers to the variant with one-to-four-line shoulder arcades, with or without a punctated border. "Matthews Incised, *var.* Moundville" refers to the variant with the arcade defined with a series of straight lines incised upward from the arcade perpendicular to their point of junction with the arcade. Current data indicates that *var.* Matthews is usual in western Kentucky and southeastern Missouri, while *var.* Moundville is usual in Alabama. Contrastive, if not completely complementary, distribution between Matthews Incised and Beckwith Incised is often noted between local areas within their larger zone of distribution.

Several misconceptions and errors in logic are embedded in Smith's rationale for using the Matthews terminology. First, it is not clear why Beckwith Incised (rectilinear guilloche) is even mentioned, since none of the 1,033 sherds in the Shiloh collection bears this motif on jar shoulders. Even odder is the fact that Smith himself mentions only one example of the Beckwith motif, but he noted that it was on the interior of a red-filmed plate rather than the exterior of a jar shoulder. Speculatively, it is conceivable that Smith interpreted some small sherds with parallel straight incised lines on the exterior as fragments of the Beckwith motif on jars rather than portions of the Barton Incised design that, unlike Beckwith, is definitely present in the collection. Given that Smith did not mention the Barton motif, it appears that the sample of sherds he viewed did not happen to contain any of the unambiguous examples of it. In any case, the Beckwith/Moundville issue is irrelevant at Shiloh.

The second misconception in Smith's argument is his statement that incised arches without the "eyelashes" of *var. Moundville* are rare in Alabama and that, because such lashless arches are found at Shiloh, the pottery there is more appropriately classified under the Matthews Incised term. In fact, incised arches without the "eyelashes," or with punctations instead, were illustrated in the publication in which the Moundville Incised type was originally defined (DeJarnette and Wimberly 1941:Fig. 62, bottom left), as well as in the report on the Wheeler Reservoir sites in nearby northern Alabama (Webb 1939:Pl. 89b, Pl. 90b, Pl. 92a, Pl. 106a, Pl. 110a). Though less common than *var. Moundville,* the lashless arch is by no means rare in Alabama.

Moreover, even had Smith been right about the distribution of the "lashless" arches, his rationale for tying Shiloh to the Kentucky-Missouri area is contradicted by his own data. In Smith's classification of a sample of sherds from the 1933–1934 excavation at Shiloh, *var. Moundville* predominated over the "lashless" variety(s) by five to one. In the whole collection of 1,033 sherds from the 1933–1934 excavation (see Table 4.1 in Chapter 4), *var. Moundville* outnumbers the "lashless" varieties by nine to two. Thus, even according to Smith's erroneous notion of the distribution of these varieties, by his own logic he should have concluded that Shiloh was more closely linked to Alabama sites than to sites in Kentucky and Missouri.

Because neither the distributional nor the typological concerns Smith voiced are valid, his linkage of Shiloh to western Kentucky and southeast Missouri rather than to the portion of the Tennessee valley immediately upstream from Shiloh is dubious. In this report, I classify the incised shell-tempered pottery using terminology developed for assemblages in Alabama that are demonstrably far more similar to Shiloh's than are the assemblages of Southeast Missouri. This classification directly affects the ceramic cross-dating of Shiloh.

By drawing parallels with the Mississippi valley, Smith (1977:15–18) was led to infer a Late Mississippian date for Shiloh. But if the Shiloh pottery is compared with assemblages from northern and central Alabama, the result is a distinctly earlier cross-date. This result depends not only on the *var. Moundville* pottery but also on the dates for Barton Incised pottery, vessel shapes, and handle shapes.

The sherds classified as Barton Incised are jar shoulders with panels of oblique, parallel lines incised while the paste was still wet. Though this decorative motif on jar shoulders is not a very useful chronological marker in the Mississippi valley, in north-central Alabama and the upper Tombigbee drainage it appears to be restricted to the earliest part of the Mississippian pottery sequence. In the Moundville area it occurs only in early Moundville I contexts (Jenkins and Meyer 1998:163; Michals 1998; Scarry and Scarry 1995:24–26; Steponaitis 1992; Welch 1994,1998c:166n.1), and similarly early in northeast Mississippi (Rafferty 1995:36). In terms of absolute dates, the Barton motif on jar shoulders is present between A.D. 1050 and 1200. Thus, the presence of Barton Incised jars at Shiloh indicates an early rather than late Mississippian date.

The same cross-dating results from a consideration of vessel shapes. In the northern half of Alabama (see, e.g., Jenkins and Meyer 1998; Scarry and Scarry 1995; Steponaitis 1981; Welch 1994) and the Tombigbee drainage of Mississippi (see, e.g., Jenkins and Krause 1986; Jenkins and Meyer 1998; Mann 1983; Marshall 1977; Rafferty 1995), early Mississippian shell-tempered jars typically have rims that form a distinct angle with the jar shoulder, often nearly a right angle. Jar rims are often folded or thickened, and a distinctive "folded-flattened" rim is diagnostic of early Moundville I and contemporary assemblages. Jar handles (two or four per pot) tend to be loops, loopy straps, or narrow straps with parallel sides (rather than tapering sharply from top to bottom). Other vessel forms known for the A.D. 1050–1300 period are neckless jars, pedestal-based bottles of either slender ovoid or subglobular shape, shallow flaring-rim bowls or plates, simple hemispherical bowls (without beaded rims), and restricted bowls. Shapes such as hemispherical bowls with beaded rims, narrow-neck bottles, deep flaring-rim bowls, short-neck bowls (painted or burnished), and jars with eight or more handles are not present until later. In most respects, Shiloh matches these earlier assemblages and lacks the later vessel modes.

The vessel shapes present among the shell-tempered sherds from Shiloh include nearly everything that would be expected of an assemblage dating between A.D. 1050–1300 in northern and central Alabama. There are neckless jars as well as jars with distinctly angled rims and with folded rims, though none with the folded-flattened rims seen in early Moundville I assemblages. Jar handles are loops, loopy straps, and narrow, parallel-sided straps. There is no evidence for any jar having more than four handles, though in most cases it impossible to tell how many handles were present. There is at least one pedestal-based, slender ovoid bottle, along with subglobular bottles (though the shape of the base is unknown). There are shallow flaring-rim bowls, restricted bowls, and hemispherical bowls. The hemispherical bowls do not have beaded rims. Deep flaring-rim bowls are not present. On the other hand, the vessel assemblage at Shiloh does not precisely duplicate the "expected" assemblage, for there is one narrow-neck bottle and four rims from two different unburnished pots with running-scroll motifs incised on the shoulder of what could be described as either short-neck bowls or neckless jars. Given that these latter are unburnished rather than burnished, they are perhaps best not called short-neck bowls, but the presence of the running scroll motif is itself not expected for an assemblage dating before A.D. 1300.

Another chronological indicator in the shell-tempered pottery is the shape of handles on unburnished jars, an analysis pioneered by Smith himself (1969; see also Steponaitis 1981). At Moundville, Steponaitis found a clear pattern of changing handle shape through time. To illustrate this change, he

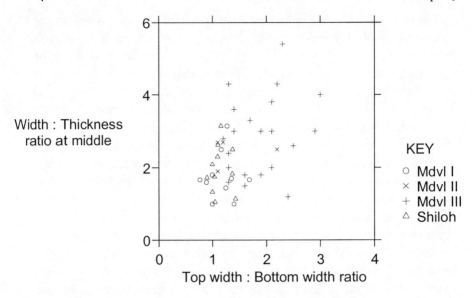

Figure 3.1. Handle shape ratios of unburnished jars from Moundville and Shiloh

constructed a crossplot (Steponaitis 1981:122) of two ratios: the ratio of the width of the handle at its top and at its base (top width:bottom width), and the ratio of the width to the thickness of the handle at its middle (middle width:middle thickness). Steponaitis's plot is reproduced in Figure 3.1, with measurements of the handles from Shiloh (see Table 3.1) added. Steponaitis (1981:119–123) explained the pattern in the graph as follows:

> In fact, by plotting the middle-width : thickness ratio against the top-width : bottom-width ratio for all our specimens combined, we can clearly see not only the trends in handle shape through time, but also the distinctions among the handles from different phases. Early handles, more loop-like and parallel sided, tend to fall in the lower left portion of the scatter, and late handles, more strap-like and tapered, tend to fall in the upper right. Differences attributable to time can be highlighted by dividing the scatter into three parts. The zone to the left of line A contains only jars dating to Moundville I; between lines A and B are most of the jars from Moundville II, mixed with some from Moundville I and III; finally, the zone to the right of line B contains only Moundville III jars, along with a single specimen from late Moundville II.

In Figure 3.1, the Shiloh jar handles (triangles) appear almost identical to the Moundville I jar handles (circles). To the extent that the same chronologi-

Table 3.1 Shape measurements for jar handles from Shiloh

Description	Top width (mm)	Middle width (mm)	Bottom width (mm)	Middle thickness (mm)	Top width/ bottom width ratio	Middle width/ thickness ratio
Mississippi Plain *var. Shiloh*	.	11	.	7	.	1.57
Moundville Incised *var. Carrollton*	.	12	.	12	.	1.00
Moundville Incised *var. Moundville*	.	9	.	5	.	1.80
Mississippi Plain *var. Shiloh*	28	28	27	16	1.03	1.75
Mississippi Plain *var. Shiloh*	.	11	.	9	.	1.22
Mississippi Plain *var. Shiloh*	20	16	14	14	1.42	1.14
Mississippi Plain *var. Shiloh*	24	24	24	18	1.00	1.33
Mississippi Plain *var. Shiloh*	.	.	.	19	.	.
Moundville Incised *var. Moundville*	21	20	20	19	1.05	1.05
Mississippi Plain *var. Shiloh*	22	22	19	7	1.15	3.14
Mississippi Plain *var. Shiloh*	21	21	19	8	1.10	2.625
Mississippi Plain *var. Shiloh*	34	30	31	13	1.09	2.30
Mississippi Plain *var. Shiloh*	33	25	24	10	1.37	2.50
Mississippi Plain *var. Shiloh*	26	22	19	12	1.36	1.83
Mississippi Plain *var. Shiloh*	23	23	23	11	1.00	2.09
Mississippi Plain *var. Shiloh*	18	19	20	11	0.90	1.72

cal pattern of changing handle shape occurred in the Shiloh area as occurred farther south, this suggests that the Shiloh shell-tempered pottery is contemporary with Moundville I, which is now dated between A.D. 1120 and 1260 (Knight, Konigsberg, and Frankenberg n.d.).

The evidence of the incised, shell-tempered pottery, the vessel forms, and the handle forms all suggests that the shell-tempered pottery at Shiloh is early rather than late Mississippian. Shiloh's shell-tempered pottery is distinctly similar to that from the Moundville I (Steponaitis 1981:99–106), Summerville I (Jenkins and Krause 1986:93–94), Bessemer (Walthall 1980:207–211; Welch 1994), and Langston (Walthall 1980:200–205; Futato 1998:226) phases. These parallels imply a date range of A.D. 1050 to 1250 or 1300 for the shell-tempered pottery from Shiloh. This cross-dating agrees with the radiocarbon assays of samples from the 1933–1934 excavation (discussed in Chapter 2) and from the 1998 Queens College excavation (discussed in Chapter 5) and with the date of nonlocal pottery found at Shiloh. However, radiocarbon assays from the 1999 excavation, and from recent excavation on Mound A, yield calibrated dates in the early 1400s. Such a date would be consistent with the sherds that have the running-scroll motif, and consequently the date of the Shiloh occupation is thought to be A.D. 1050–1400 or perhaps even a bit later.

0   cm   5

Figure 3.2. Ramey Incised (A385507)

Among the sample of sherds found at Shiloh in 1933–1934 are several that may be from vessels that were imported to the site. Two rims (see Figure 3.2) have been classified as Ramey Incised, a style centered at the Cahokia site in the American Bottom of Illinois, well dated to A.D. 1050–1250. Based on their similarity of paste and surface characteristics, I have classified four other sherds as Powell Plain, a burnished, shell-tempered type also defined in the American Bottom. The "Ramey Incised" assessment of the sherds at Shiloh was first made by James B. Griffin (1993:4), who had originally defined the type. This assessment was later echoed by George Milner (personal communication), who also offered advice on the likely date of the pottery based on inspection of color photographs of the sherds:

> I would call it Ramey Incised. . . . As far as surface characteristics are concerned, the black Ramey Incised specimen [Fig. 3.2, *left*] has "made in the American Bottom" stamped right on it. Note the definite trailed lines (no hesitation or errors are evident), the horizontal burnishing marks, and the orangish (oxidized) area on the superior rim. It is an example of fine Ramey Incised pottery. The other one [Fig. 3.2, *right*] could easily fit in American Bottom collections, sort of your generic Ramey Incised pottery. Both of the rim forms (judging from your profiles) are classic American Bottom forms, particularly those dating to the Stirling phase. However, I've seen stuff as good elsewhere (as local imitations of the real thing?). . . . About dating, Ramey Incised is clearly and unambiguously associated with the Stirling and Moorehead phases. They are conventionally dated to A.D. 1050–1250 (100 years apiece). If you look at all good context radiocarbon samples, you will see that these dates are a bit

too old . . . my guess is that you might want to move these guess-dates up a couple decades more recently in time, particularly the bottom estimate.

John Kelly and Timothy Pauketat both agree with Milner's assessment of these sherds as good Cahokia or at least American Bottom material. Kelly (personal communication) examined them at the Smithsonian and reported that "the rim morphology in my estimation would place them in early Stirling phase, ca. A.D. 1100–1150." Pauketat, like Milner, had to base his assessment on inspection of color photographs and my hand-drawn rim profiles. Based on the rim protrusion ratio (Holley 1989:21) of ca. 0.71 for both sherds, Pauketat (personal communication) also suggests an early Stirling–phase date for the sherds. He warns, however, that a sample size of only two vessels is slender evidence for making chronological assessments on the basis of the rim protrusion ratio. An early Stirling–phase date is well in line with the other chronological evidence for the Mississippian occupation at Shiloh.

With the Mississippian (i.e., shell-tempered) pottery well dated, we can turn to the more difficult task of assessing the date of the Late Woodland (i.e., grog-tempered) pottery. In calling grog-tempered pottery Late Woodland and shell-tempered pottery Mississippian, we must be careful not to assume that this means that every grog-tempered sherd antedates every shell-tempered sherd. Such instantaneous replacement is likely to have occurred only if the Late Woodland populace was physically replaced by immigrating Mississippians bearing their own new styles of material culture. It seems highly unlikely, after all, that people in the Tennessee valley awoke one morning, cast out all their grog-tempered pottery, and began using only shell-tempered pottery. Thus, if we simply label the grog-tempered pottery "Late Woodland" and consider it to antedate the shell-tempered "Mississippian" pottery, we implicitly assume an answer to a question of some importance: What are the cultural and chronological relationships between people who made grog-tempered pottery and those who tempered their pottery with crushed shell? In the context of this report, the question can be more specifically phrased as "is the grog-tempered pottery at Shiloh a separate component from the shell-tempered pottery, or were at least some of the mounds at the site built by people who used grog-tempered pottery?" For the Pickwick Reservoir area and the nearby Tombigbee and Black Warrior drainages, the archaeological literature on this issue is inconclusive (e.g., Allsbrook 1995; Futato 1987:228–232; Jenkins and Krause 1986:84–85; Mistovich 1988; Walthall 1980:204–205; Webb and DeJarnette 1942:19–20; Welch 1990, 1994).

In the Pickwick Reservoir immediately upstream from Shiloh, Walthall (1980:137–141; see also Futato 1998:219–225) distinguished between McKelvey I and McKelvey II phases. The former is estimated to begin around A.D. 500

and run to around A.D. 700 and the latter from around A.D. 700 to 1000 or 1050. Walthall (1980:137) characterized these two phases as follows:

> McKelvey I is characterized by large percentages of plain and check-stamped ware and by a minority of cord-marked pottery. During McKelvey II times, probably after A.D. 700, cord marking replaced check stamping as a major finish treatment. Toward the end of this latter period, the proportion of plain ware appears to have increased substantially. Check stamping is placed into an early temporal position in this sequence for two major reasons: (1) the Pickwick Basin appears to have been a center for check stamping during late Woodland times, and (2) plain and check-stamped wares represent the dominant pottery types of the local ancestral Copena ceramic complex.

While it is plausible to assume that the predominant surface treatments of Copena would continue into the Late Woodland period, Walthall (1980:137) warns us that there is a "lack of well-stratified sites in the Pickwick Basin region, the McKelvey core area," a problem that remains unsolved today. Futato (1975, 1983) has reported excavations at two single-component McKelvey II sites in the Cedar Creek/Little Bear Creek drainage. At both, Mulberry Creek Cordmarked accounted for roughly 60 percent of the sherds, with McKelvey Plain (in this report called Baytown Plain *var. McKelvey*) accounting for nearly all the rest. A radiocarbon assessment from the Champion site (Futato 1975:54) yielded an uncalibrated age of A.D. 1010 ± 200. The standard deviation on this assessment is regrettably large, but the assay is consistent with the pottery sequence Walthall outlined. To the southwest, in the Tombigbee drainage, cordmarking also gradually increases through the Late Woodland sequence (Jenkins and Krause 1986:83–84).

These comparative sequences suggest that the grog-tempered pottery at Shiloh dates to the later part of the Late Woodland, probably after A.D. 700 or 800. The more difficult question to answer is whether the grog-tempered pottery chronologically overlaps the shell-tempered pottery. Upriver from Shiloh, in the Pickwick Reservoir, there appears to have been a hiatus of a couple centuries between the last occupation by people using grog-tempered pottery and the first settlements with shell-tempered pottery (Walthall 1980: 204–205; Futato 1998:226). Downriver from Shiloh, near the Kentucky state line, the archaeological picture for the interface between Late Woodland and Mississippian has been characterized (Autry and Hinshaw 1981:67) as one of "little completed analysis and almost no published data." One exception to this rather barren picture is the Obion site (Garland 1992), not actually in the Tennessee drainage but only 16 miles (26 km) west of the river. At Obion there are such characteristically Mississippian structures as rectangular platform mounds, wall-trench buildings, and a palisade, but most of the pottery (85 percent) is grog-tempered. The grog-tempered pottery was definitely manufactured and used by the makers of the mounds, buildings, and palisade. Based on a sample of 335 plain rims, the grog-tempered vessels are mostly globular jars with loop handles, hooded bottles, and hemispherical bowls (Garland 1992:64). Jar handles are described as loops, with round or oval cross-sections. Radiocarbon assessments suggest initial occupation of the site beginning around A.D. 1000 (Garland 1992:117–118). Certainly, if the grog-tempered pottery at Shiloh duplicated that at Obion, this would be ample reason to conclude a substantial chronological overlap between grog- and shell-tempering.

The grog-tempered pottery at Shiloh is not much like the Obion grog-tempered pottery. First, unlike the pottery at Shiloh, the "grog" at Obion is mostly not crushed sherds but is instead described as nodules of white or buff fired clay (Garland 1992:63). Second, the vast majority of Obion pottery is plain, and cordmarking is rare (a total of 13 sherds recovered). In the 1933–1934 collection from Shiloh, the cordmarked grog-tempered sherds outnumber the plain grog-tempered sherds 396 to 78. Third, the suite of grog-tempered vessel shapes at Shiloh differs from that at Obion. At Shiloh there are grog-tempered jars with vertical or gently flared rims not unlike some of those at Obion, but there are no known grog-tempered jar handles, nor do any of the grog-tempered jar rims have lugs. Shiloh does have hemispherical bowls, like Obion, but none of the Shiloh bowls are known to have rim lugs. At Shiloh there are no grog-tempered hooded bottles, the second most common vessel shape at Obion. The similarities in vessel shapes are similarities that could be duplicated by virtually any Late Woodland assemblage, whereas the differences involve vessel shapes that at Obion are duplicated on shell-tempered ware. This does not necessarily mean that Shiloh's grog-tempered pottery is earlier than Obion's, just that it is different.

At Shiloh, like at Obion, there is morphological overlap of the grog-tempered pottery and the shell-tempered pottery. The vessel shape that is most clearly duplicated in the two different wares is a globular jar with a vertical or only slightly everted rim. Numerous examples of this vessel shape can be found among the cord-marked, grog-tempered rims, and nearly identical profiles can be found among the unburnished, shell-tempered plain (Mississippi Plain) and Barton Incised rims. This shape is a minority among the shell-tempered jars, with most rims more sharply flared, angled, or thickened. The morphological similarity of some of the grog-tempered and shell-tempered jars may indicate that there was some period during which both kinds of jars were being made, but this is not certain. It is striking that jars of the two wares which are of similar shape have different surface treatments:

the grog-tempered jars are cord-marked, but the shell-tempered jars are plain or incised. This, I believe, leaves us with no clear answer to the question of whether the two wares derive from distinct components separated by a hiatus.

Two conclusions emerge from this discussion of pottery shapes and styles. First, the shell-tempered pottery can be dated fairly confidently to the period from A.D. 1050 to 1400 or perhaps several decades later. Second, the date of the grog-tempered pottery cannot be established on stylistic criteria alone. Other kinds of evidence will be needed to resolve the dating of the grog-tempered pottery.

Having dealt with the chronology and stylistic affinities of Shiloh's pottery, we can now proceed to descriptions of the type and variety names employed in this report (see Table 3.2). The following type descriptions are organized by tempering agent (shell, followed by grog, sand, bone, and limestone), and alphabetically within these ware categories.

Shell-tempered Pottery

Barton Incised

This type encompasses shell-tempered, unburnished vessels with simple, rectilinear, incised motifs such as line-filled triangles and bands of parallel lines. Typically the incisions were made on paste that was still wet, resulting in burrs along the incision margins. Defined originally in the Mississippi valley, pottery that fits this description has also been found eastward in Tennessee, Mississippi, and Alabama. In the Mississippi valley the type is found through the entire Mississippian period, but to the east it is restricted to the early part of the Mississippian period.

variety unspecified (Figures 3.3, 3.4)

Description. Rims from three jars bear panels or blocks of parallel lines incised none too carefully in wet paste. All three jars have sharply angled everted rims; none of the three is known to have had handles or lugs. All three would easily fit within the *Oliver* variety defined at Moundville (Michals 1998:Fig. 8.1, a–e; Welch 1998c:166), but the Shiloh sample provides an awfully slender thread on which to hang such an attribution.

Chronological position. At Moundville (Scarry and Scarry 1995:24–26) and Bessemer (Welch 1994), this type is known only from the early part of the Moundville I phase, A.D. 1120–1200. The type is also present at the Bear Creek site in northeast Mississippi (Bohannon 1972:Fig. 9), for which there are no radiocarbon dates but for which the rest of the pottery suggests a similarly early Mississippian occupation.

Table 3.2 Prehistoric pottery from
the 1933–1934, 1998, and 1999 excavations

Description	Count
Sand-tempered (n=31)	
Baldwin Plain *var. Chalk Bluff* (medium sand)	10
var. Miller Slough (fine sand)	5
Furrs Cordmarked *var. unspecified*	1
Unclassified sand-tempered	15
Bone-tempered (n=2)	
Turkey Paw Cordmarked *var. Moon Lake*	1
Turkey Paw Plain *var. Turkey Paw*	1
Limestone-tempered (n=24)	
Long Branch Fabric-marked *var. unspecified*	10
Mulberry Creek Plain *var. unspecified*	6
Unclassified limestone-tempered red-filmed incised	1
Unclassified limestone-tempered	7
Grit-tempered (n=5)	
Unclassified cordmarked	1
Unclassified grit-tempered, eroded	4
Grog-tempered (n=1,656)	
Baytown Plain *var. McKelvey* (incl. 1 ground triangle)	200
var. The Fork	11
var. unspecified	3
Mulberry Creek Cordmarked *var. Mulberry Creek*	611
var. Coffee Landing	16
Wheeler Check-stamped *var. Edmonds Branch*	1
Unclassified grog-tempered, incised or stamped	1
Unclassified grog-tempered, eroded	803
Unclassified grog-and-sand-tempered, eroded	10
Shell-tempered (n=2,954)	
Barton Incised *var. unspecified* (shell-tempering only)	5
var. unspecified (shell-and-sand-tempering)	1
Bell Plain *var. unspecified*	107
Kimmswick Fabric-impressed *var. Langston*	16
Mississippi Plain *var. Shiloh*	472
var. Shiloh discoidal	1
var. unspecified	7
Mound Place Incised *var. unspecified*	2
Moundville Engraved *var. unspecified*	1

Continued on the next page

Table 3.2 *Continued*

Description	Count
Moundville Incised *var. Carrollton*	1
var. Moundville	12
var. Snows Bend	1
Powell Plain (limestone-tempered variant)	4
Ramey Incised (limestone-tempered variant)	2
Salt Creek Cane-impressed *var. unspecified*	2
Unclassified shell-tempered cordmarked	1
Unclassified shell-tempered incised	3
Unclassified shell-tempered plain	16
Unclassified shell-tempered, eroded (incl. 1 discoidal)	1,708
Unclassified shell-and-grog-tempered, eroded	582
Unclassified shell-and-sand-tempered, eroded	11
Temperless (n=2)	
Unclassified plain	2
Total pottery	4,675

BARTON INCISED

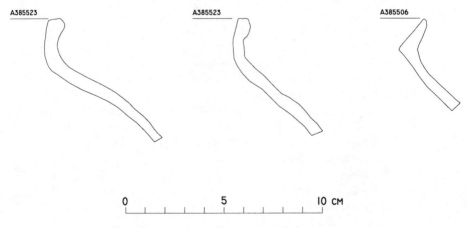

Figure 3.3. Rim profiles of Barton Incised *var. unspecified* jars

Bell Plain

This "supertype" includes all burnished but otherwise undecorated shell-tempered vessels. By including so much, it has little chronological or cultural significance. The shell particles in Bell Plain typically are finely ground, often nearly invisible, but the type is defined on the basis of surface finish rather

Figure 3.4. Barton Incised *var. unspecified* (top, A385523; bottom left, A385523; bottom right, A385506)

than paste characteristics. Paste characteristics have been used in the Mississippi valley and elsewhere for recognizing varieties within the type. Distinguishing such varieties generally requires large samples of well-preserved sherds, and at Shiloh the sample of burnished, shell-tempered pottery is neither large nor well preserved. The majority of sherds in the 1998 and 1999 excavations had eroded surfaces. Of these, some sherds had finely ground shell tempering and may originally have had burnished surfaces, but in the absence of the surface itself no such attribution could be made.

variety unspecified (Figure 4.37)

Description. The known forms of burnished vessels at Shiloh include simple bowls, shallow flaring-rim bowls, narrow-neck bottles (carafes), and a slender ovoid bottle with a pedestal base. Some globular vessel bodies, probably bottles, were gadrooned. The burnished surfaces were usually black or gray, occasionally red, and sometimes a buff color.

Chronological position. Bell Plain is present through the entire Mississippian period in the Alabama-Mississippi-Tennessee area.

Kimmswick Fabric-impressed

Large, thick-walled, shell-tempered pots with fabric impressions on the exterior surface are encountered widely across the southeast during Mississippian times. Usually these pots are shallow, open bowls or trays and are often called "salt pans" in recognition of their abundance at saline springs. Phillips (1970:95) proposed that all fabric-impressed salt pans be classified as Kimmswick, and Jenkins (1981:70) suggested a *Langston* variety in conformity with the Langston Fabric-Impressed type defined by Heimlich (1952:26) for the Guntersville Reservoir in northwest Alabama.

variety Langston (Figure 3.5)

Description. True to form, the fabric-impressed, shell-tempered pots at Shiloh come from vessels with walls usually over 1 cm, sometimes more than 2 cm, thick. Vessel shapes appear to be open, but few rims are known. The fabric impressed on the exterior is a loose, open, twined weave of twisted cords. The tempering is coarse shell.

Chronological position. The type is present throughout the Mississippian period. Along the Tennessee River in north Alabama, the type is common at sites of the early Mississippian Langston phase in northwest Alabama (Walthall 1980:200–205) as well as at sites of the later Kogers Island, Hobbs Island, and Henry Island phases (Walthall 1980:227–245).

Mississippi Plain

Mississippi Plain is the catch-all for unburnished, undecorated, shell-tempered pottery. Numerous varieties have been defined, sometimes on the basis of variations in paste but occasionally merely to have a local name that avoids the implication of cultural ties to distant locales where another variety with identical characteristics was defined. Archaeologists differ as to whether it is appropriate to create a local variety just for the sake of having a local variety,

Figure 3.5. Kimmswick Fabric-impressed *var. Langston* (left, A385513; right, A385523)

and consequently some archaeologists may quibble with the introduction of *variety Shiloh.*

variety Shiloh (Figures 3.6–3.8)

Description. Individual sherds of shell-tempered plain pottery from Shiloh could easily go unnoticed in assemblages of Mississippi Plain pottery from elsewhere in the Southeast. As a group, however, the Shiloh plainware displays a tendency to have small amounts of very fine—nearly silt-sized—sand in the paste. The amount of sand is so small that this admixture is probably not intentional, but instead reflects either the composition of the clay source or the conditions in which the clay is handled and stored before being formed into vessels. Not every sherd displays this minor admixture of sand, however, and usage of the *var. Shiloh* label depends on the characteristics of the assemblage as a whole rather than on the presence or absence of fine sand in individual sherds. In other regards, such as color, hardness, vessel-forming techniques, etc., *var. Shiloh* is like Mississippi Plain elsewhere. Vessel shapes are primarily jars, sometimes with handles that range from loops to parallel-sided straps. The lower ends of handles are usually attached to the bodies by luting, occasionally by riveting through the vessel wall. The upper ends of handles are attached at or on top of the lip, very rarely below it. Nodes, in a variety

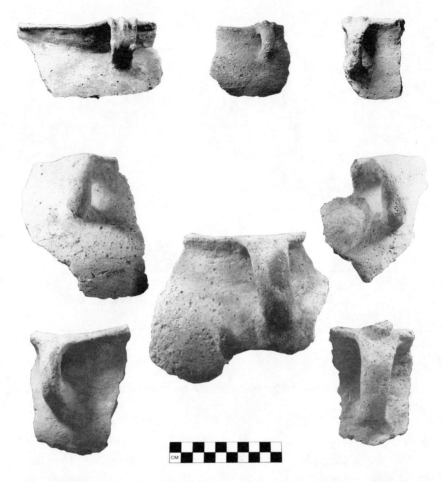

Figure 3.6. Mississippi Plain *var. Shiloh* (top left, A385504; top center, 385531; top right, A385528; lower five, A385533)

of numbers and configurations, are often found on the handles. Lugs are not present in this sample. The necks of jars range from smoothly curved to angular, and there are both simple and thickened rims. Infrequent examples of restricted and vertical-sided bowls are also known.

Chronological position. The handle and rim shapes described above are typical of assemblages dated between A.D. 1050 and 1300, dates that match the radiocarbon assessments from Shiloh. Though the Shiloh site was apparently abandoned ca. A.D. 1300, it is conceivable that *var. Shiloh* pottery continued to be made nearby. For example, the plainware of the Kogers Island phase sites upriver might well be classifiable as *var. Shiloh*.

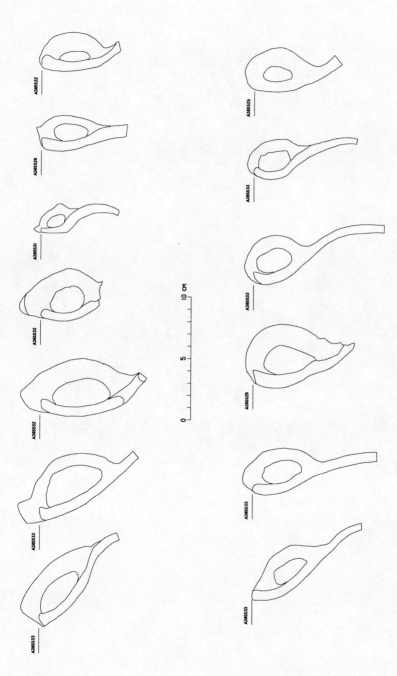

Figure 3.7. Mississippi Plain *var. Shiloh* jar rim and handle profiles

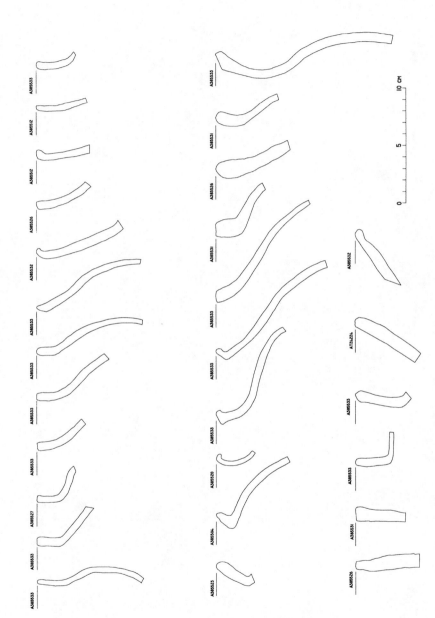

Figure 3.8. Mississippi Plain *var. Shiloh* jar and bowl rim profiles

variety unspecified (shell-and-sand-tempered)

Description. Several sherds had medium-sized quartz sand present in sufficient abundance to suggest it was an intentional addition to the paste. These
may be from nonlocal pots or could represent atypical potters. The sherds are
body rather than rim sherds, so vessel forms are not known.

Chronological distribution. Not known, presumably Mississippian.

Mound Place Incised

Outside of the Moundville area, burnished, shell-tempered bowls with one
or more trailed (broad, U-shaped) lines below and parallel to the lip are called
Mound Place Incised. At Moundville, Steponaitis (1981:53) defined Carthage
Incised *var. Akron* to include such vessels as long as they had two or more
such lines; if only one line was present, he would include the vessel in Bell
Plain *var. Hale.* While this is arguably sensible at Moundville, elsewhere the
merits of separating a bowl with one line from a bowl with two lines are not
evident. Hence, the Mound Place taxon is used in this report.

variety unspecified

Description. Only two sherds of Mound Place Incised have been found at
Shiloh. Aside from noting that they are simple bowls with simple direct rims,
there is little to say about them.

Chronological distribution. Not known, presumably Mississippian.

Moundville Engraved

Steponaitis (1981:54–57) adopted this name for what had previously been
called Moundville Filmed Engraved, deleting along the way any reference to
filming. Technically, the lines on this pottery are not postfiring engraving but
instead dry-paste, fine-line incisions. The shell particles are typically small
and the surface burnished, frequently to a gloss rarely found on burnished
shell-tempered pottery from the lower Mississippi valley. In recognition that
burnished, fine-line incised pottery from the nearby Pickwick Reservoir has
been classified as Moundville Engraved, this type name is used at Shiloh.

variety unspecified

Description. One body sherd of Moundville Engraved was found during
SEAC excavations west of Mound A in 1999. Not enough of the motif is
present to ascertain what it is.

Chronological distribution. At Moundville, engraving (fine-line incision)
appears midway through the Moundville I phase, roughly A.D.1200, and con-
tinues in use to the mid-1500s.

Moundville Incised

The rationale for applying the Moundville Incised label rather than the Matthews Incised label is addressed in detail at the beginning of this chapter. At Shiloh, the variation within the class of unburnished pots with incised arches fits easily into the three varieties defined by Steponaitis (1981:57–58).

variety Carrollton (Figure 3.9, lower right)
   Description. The *Carrollton* variety has incised arches only, with nothing added above or below them. Each arch consists of a single line or sometimes two or three parallel lines. The incisions are usually broad and frequently overhanging. Often the area below each arch is pushed out into a lobe. The only vessel form known at Shiloh is the globular jar.
   Chronological distribution. In the Moundville region, *var. Carrollton* is present in Moundville I and early Moundville II, or from A.D. 1120 to the mid-1300s. It is assumed, but has not been demonstrated, that this span is also valid in north Alabama and northeast Mississippi, at sites such as Bear Creek (Bohannon 1972:Fig. 11, upper left and lower). Unfortunately, Bear Creek has no absolute date determinations, nor do sites in northeast Alabama where *var. Carrollton* is present, such as Hobbs Island (Webb 1939:Pl. 90b, left).

variety Moundville (Figures 3.9, top, 3.10)
   Description. This is the classic incised arch (one to three parallel lines) with straight lines radiating upward. A number of configurations of these radiating lines is known, such as all lines orthogonal to the arch, all lines vertical, and all lines on each side of an arch's apex parallel but slanting opposite to the lines on the other side of the arch. At Shiloh the motif has been found only on jars with angular necks. Some of these jars had handles, but it is not known whether they all did.
   Chronological position. Like the other varieties of Moundville Incised, the presence of this pottery at sites in the region around Shiloh is usually taken to signal an early Mississippian date, by analogy with the Moundville sequence (see, e.g., Rafferty 1995:35–37). Pots of *var. Moundville* are not illustrated in the Pickwick Basin report but were found at sites like Hobbs Island in the Wheeler Basin (Webb 1939:Pl. 106, Pl. 110). The absence (or at least rarity) of Moundville Incised in the Pickwick Basin is one of the reasons for believing the Kogers Island phase to postdate the occupation of Shiloh.

variety Snows Bend (Figure 3.9, lower left)
   Description. This variety is defined by the presence of punctations forming arches on jar shoulders. Frequently the punctations are above an incised line

MOUNDVILLE INCISED *VAR MOUNDVILLE*

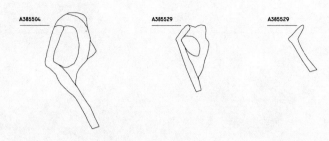

MOUNDVILLE INCISED *VAR SNOWS BEND*   MOUNDVILLE INCISED *VAR CARROLLTON*

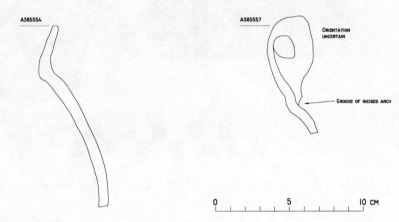

Figure 3.9. Profiles of Moundville Incised jars

(e.g., Webb 1939:Pl. 89b, upper left), which is sometimes overhanging. The incised arch is not strictly required, as it is the arch of punctations that is the defining characteristic. Thus, pots such as the upper and lower left examples in Webb (1939:Pl. 90) would be classified as *var. Snows Bend*. Only one *var. Snows Bend* sherd has been recovered from Shiloh, and it has jab-and-drag punctations above a single overhanging arch. The neck is angular, and the rim is not thickened.

Figure 3.10. Moundville Incised *var. Moundville* (top left, A385513; top right, A385529; lower left, A385504; lower right, A385554)

Chronological position. At sites upriver from Shiloh in north Alabama, this variety is usually found at sites which have *var. Carrollton,* but at some such sites *var. Moundville* is absent. These two varieties may thus persist later than *var. Moundville,* but it is probably already clear that a better knowledge of the chronological position of Moundville Incised in the region around Shiloh would be helpful.

Powell Plain; Ramey Incised

These six sherds have already been described, and the two Ramey Incised sherds illustrated in Figure 3.2. Whether the Powell Plain sherds all came from the two vessels represented by the two Ramey rims is not certain, but all six sherds came from a 20-X-40-ft block west of Mound D.

Salt Creek Cane-impressed

This type includes salt pans that are impressed with matting or basketry made of strips of split cane.

variety unspecified

Description. The type and its established variety were defined in south Alabama by Fuller and Stowe (1982:82–84). Like the pottery described by Fuller, the two sherds at Shiloh bear the impression of plaited basketry made of 0.5-cm-wide strips of what appears to be split cane. The sherds are thick, as is usual for salt pans, but as neither is a rim the vessel form is not known.

Chronological position. Presumably similar to Kimmswick Fabric-impressed, which is to say Mississippian in general.

Unclassified Shell-tempered Cordmarked

One body sherd bearing cordmarking was found in excavations on the apron west of Mound A in 1999. Given its solitary status and unknown vessel shape, it is not clear whether this might be an import from, say, southern Illinois or whether it might be from a Late Mississippian/Protohistoric McKee Island Cordmarked pot.

Unclassified Shell-tempered Incised

There are sherds from at least three vessels that bear incised running scrolls composed of four, five, or more lines (Figures 3.11, 3.12). All are vessels that could be called either short-neck bowls or restricted jars. One, somewhat eroded, appears to have been burnished and has U-shaped lines made on leather-hard paste. In terms of motif and execution, this sherd could be classified as the Mississippi valley type Leland Incised *var. Williams* (Williams and Brain 1983:179), but Leland Incised pots are usually hemispherical bowls. The other sherds, of precisely the same vessel form and decorative motif, are clearly unburnished and have the incisions made on wet paste. These could be called Winterville Incised *var. Rising Sun* (Williams and Brain 1983:209). However, assigning these Mississippi Valley labels may mislead us into thinking the sherds indicate a western connection. Given the similarity of these running-scroll vessels, and the suggestion by Williams and Brain (1983:209) that in the lower Mississippi valley this motif on jar shoulders derives from Cahokia, I suspect these Shiloh sherds may be a local "knockoff" of Ramey Incised rather than material or ideas arriving from western Mississippi.

Other unclassified incised sherds include five that have rectilinear, wet-

Figure 3.11. Unclassified shell-tempered pottery with incised running scroll (top row, A385522; lower left, A385526; lower right, A385506)

paste incision. These could be either Barton Incised or Moundville Incised *var. Moundville.*

Another addition to the unclassified incised category is a restricted bowl with very sloppy, broad chevrons incised in very wet paste (Figure 3.13, right). This could be someone's loose interpretation of Barton Incised, but the sherd is so small that firm attribution seems unwarranted.

And finally we come to the red-filmed, shallow, flaring-rim bowl sherd illustrated in Figure 3.13 (left). This appears to be the sherd that Smith (1977:9–10) had in mind when he talked about the problem of conflating Beckwith Incised with Matthews Incised at Shiloh, inasmuch as no other sherd in the collection is any closer to having a rectilinear guilloche motif than this. On the inside of the rim there are broad, trailed lines crossing more or less at right angles. This sherd could be called O'Byam Incised *var. O'Byam*

SHELL-TEMPERED INCISED, RUNNING SCROLL

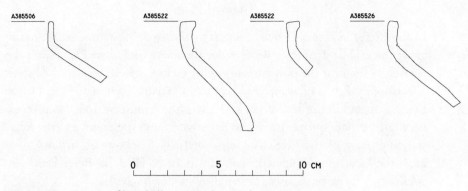

Figure 3.12. Rim profiles, shell-tempered incised pottery

Figure 3.13. Unclassified shell-tempered incised pottery (A385517)

(Phillips 1970:144), Wells Broad Trailed (Kelly 2001; Vogel 1975:104–106), or a weird variant on Carthage Incised *var. Moon Lake* (Steponaitis 1981:54), but given its splendid isolation at Shiloh it seems wisest to leave it unnamed.

Unclassified Shell-tempered Eroded;
Unclassified Shell-and-Grog-tempered Eroded;
Unclassified Shell-and-Sand-tempered Eroded

These residual categories comprise sherds whose surface is no longer present, so that paste characteristics are the only remaining basis on which to sort them. They are mostly body sherds, and they are mostly small.

Grog-Tempered Pottery

Baytown Plain

In the late 1930s, Haag (1939:15, 1942:517–518) gave grog-tempered plainware along the middle Tennessee River valley the name McKelvey Plain, after the McKelvey site near the downstream end of Pickwick Reservoir. In the Lower Mississippi valley, similar material acquired the name Baytown Plain, a usage that has spread out of that valley and across the Southeast. In a compromise between the widespread use of the Baytown Plain type name and the long-standing usage of the McKelvey term for the grog plainware in the Shiloh area, the local grog-tempered plainware is here called Baytown Plain *var. McKelvey,* a usage previously suggested by Futato (1998:19).

In 1996, pottery was collected from the surface of a number of small sites in a bend of the Tennessee River several kilometers downstream of Shiloh. The sites turned out to differ, sometimes strikingly, in whether the temper was grog only, or a mixture of grog and sand. Without larger collections, and pottery from well-dated or stratified contexts, it is not yet clear whether there is any chronological or cultural significance to this variation. But on the chance that the difference might be significant, I have segregated the grog-and-sand material into a separate variety, here labeled *The Fork* in honor of the local name for the area where the 1996 surface collections were made. In the Tombigbee drainage to the south, similar variation was recognized by a distinction between the grog-only *var. Roper* and the grog-plus-sand *var. Tishomingo* (Jenkins 1981:87–91). Unlike *var. Tishomingo,* in which the sand temper is more abundant than the grog, in *var. The Fork* sand is usually less than half as abundant as grog.

Many grog-tempered sherds from Shiloh appear to have smoothed-over cordmarking, and the classificatory boundary between plain and cordmarked is indistinct. If the surface irregularity was clearly caused by cordmarking, I called the sherd Mulberry Creek Cordmarked. If the irregularity of surface could not be definitely attributed to cordmarking but might instead have been due another cause such as protruding temper particles, I called the sherd Baytown Plain. Where this criterion yields contradictory classification for different parts of a single sherd, the presence of recognizable cordmarking was given priority and the sherd was called Mulberry Creek Cordmarked.

variety McKelvey (Figure 3.14)
   Description. The paste characteristics were well described by Haag (1939:15, 1942:517–518), though his description lumps together the material here distinguished as *var. McKelvey* and *var. The Fork.* Vessel forms include simple bowls of hemispherical to restricted shape and jars with vertical to inslanting rims.

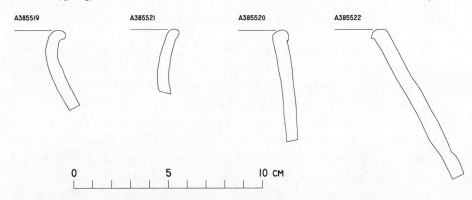

Figure 3.14. Rim profiles of Baytown Plain *var. McKelvey*

The bases of all vessels appear to be round rather than pointed or flat. Surfaces, both interior and exterior, are casually smoothed rather than being carefully finished, and wiping is common.

Chronological position. As discussed early in this chapter, the grog-tempered pottery is generally of Late Woodland date, but we do not know whether or how extensively it overlaps in time with the shell-tempered pottery. Chronological change in the relative frequency of *var. McKelvey* and *var. The Fork* is not yet understood. Walthall (1980:137–138) and Futato (1998:225) suggest that *McKelvey* is more abundant than cordmarked pottery in McKelvey I times (A.D. 500–700) and the reverse in McKelvey II times (A.D. 700 to 1000 or 1100), but there is precious little data to test this suggestion.

variety The Fork

Description. Fine to medium sand added to the paste usually comprises less than half the temper particles. Surfaces of these sherds usually feel sandy, often because wiping of the surfaces exposed the temper particles. The variety is far less common at Shiloh than *var. McKelvey,* and because none of the recovered sherds are rims, the vessel forms are unknown.

Chronological position. See discussion of *var. McKelvey.*

variety unspecified

Two sherds were left without a variety name specified. One looks like standard-issue *var. McKelvey* except that it has a few particles of shell in the paste. The other has only grog tempering but has firmly compacted, smooth surfaces quite unlike the rest of the Baytown Plain material. While this may be some nonlocal variety such as *var. Vicksburg* (Phillips 1970:56–57), the sherd is so small that any definite assignment is unwarranted.

Mulberry Creek Cordmarked

When Phillips (1970:136) adopted Mulberry Creek as the type name for cord-marked, grog-tempered pottery in the Yazoo Basin, he noted that "according to the rule of priority, the northern Alabama material becomes the established variety" of the type. The northern Alabama material was described by Haag (1939:17, 1942:518). As with McKelvey Plain, Haag did not distinguish between sherds with only grog temper and those with small amounts of sand added. To maintain a parallel with the distinction between Baytown Plain *vars. McKelvey* and *The Fork,* a distinction is made here between Mulberry Creek Cordmarked *vars. Mulberry Creek* (grog only) and *Coffee Landing* (grog and sand).

variety Mulberry Creek (Figures 3.15–3.17)

   Description. Paste is the same as Baytown Plain *var. McKelvey.* As Haag (1942:518) noted, cordmarking "covers the vessel from lip to base and apparently was applied in a haphazard manner." Often the cordmarking is partially obliterated by smoothing. Vessel lips are also sometimes cordmarked, with the marks oblique or orthogonal to the lip, but the lips are usually rounded or sometimes slightly rolled to the exterior. Vessel forms are jars with vertical to inslanting necks and bowls of hemispherical to restricted shape. Vessel bases are round, not flat or conical.

   Chronological position. On the whole earlier than shell-tempered pottery, but as discussed earlier in the chapter, there are unanswered questions about the chronological position of the grog-tempered pottery at Shiloh. Walthall (1980:137–138) and Futato (1998:225) suggest that *McKelvey* is more abundant than cordmarked pottery in McKelvey I times (A.D. 500–700) and the reverse in McKelvey II times (A.D. 700 to 1000 or 1100).

variety Coffee Landing

   Description. Paste is the same as Baytown Plain *var. The Fork.* Just as *The Fork* is strongly outnumbered by *McKelvey* at Shiloh, so too *Coffee Landing* is strongly outnumbered by *Mulberry Creek.* None of the recovered *Coffee Landing* sherds are rims, so vessel forms are not attested.

   Chronological position. See comments under *var. Mulberry Creek.*

Wheeler Check-stamped

This is another Pickwick Reservoir type for which variety names are being introduced. Haag (1939:16, 1942:518) described both square- and diamond-shaped checks for Wheeler. Whether that distinction is culturally or chrono-

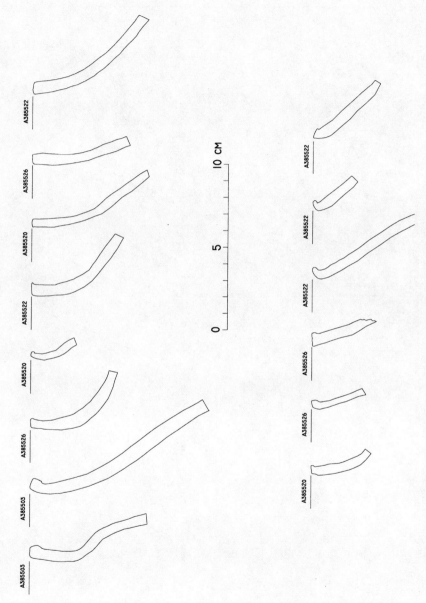

Figure 3.15. Rim profiles of Mulberry Creek Cordmarked *var. Mulberry Creek* jars

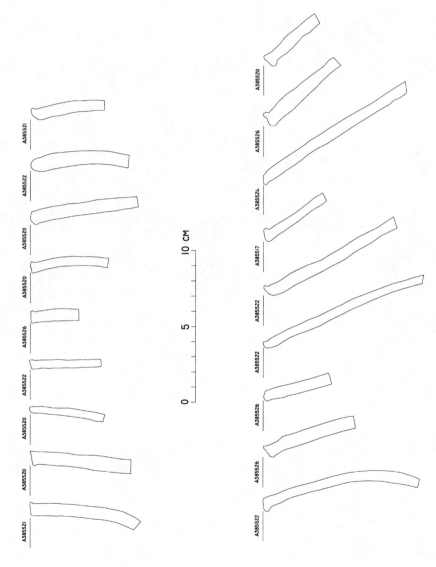

Figure 3.16. Rim profiles of Mulberry Creek Cordmarked *var. Mulberry Creek* bowls

Figure 3.17. Mulberry Creek Cordmarked *var. Mulberry Creek* bowls (top row, A385522) and jars (middle and lower, A385503)

logically significant remains unknown, but on the chance that it is, a distinction is made here between *var. Wheeler* and *var. Edmonds Branch*. The established variety, *Wheeler,* which has diamond or rhomboidal checks, was not found at Shiloh but has been recovered at nearby floodplain sites. At these sites both *Wheeler* and *Edmonds Branch* are usually found with the checks smoothed over, sometimes nearly to the point of obliteration.

Figure 3.18. Unclassified limestone-tempered red filmed incised (left, A385557) and Wheeler Check-stamped *var. Edmonds Branch* (right, A385510)

variety Edmonds Branch (Figure 3.18, right)

Description. Because only one sherd of Wheeler Check-Stamped was found at Shiloh, we will simply rely on Haag's (1939:16, 1942:518) description, except that only square or rectangular checks are included in this variety. Checks are between 2 and 10 mm on a side, usually 3 to 3.5 mm. Vessel shapes are similar to Mulberry Creek Cordmarked.

Chronological position. In assemblages of grog-tempered pottery in the Pickwick Reservoir, the relative abundance of check-stamped pottery patterns the same way as plain pottery (Walthall 1980:137–138; Futato 1998:219, 225). That is, plain and check-stamped pottery predominates in McKelvey I times (A.D. 500–700), but they are outnumbered by cordmarked pottery in McKelvey II times (A.D. 700 to 1000 or 1100).

Unclassified Grog-tempered Incised or Stamped

One grog-tempered sherd had an exterior surface with some sort of marking, but whether that marking was created by incision or by stamping could not be discerned.

Unclassified Grog-tempered Eroded,
Unclassified Grog-and-Sand-tempered Eroded

Given the predominance of cordmarking over other surface finishes among the grog-tempered pottery at Shiloh, the majority of these sherds were probably originally cordmarked. Weathering of the surfaces, however, prevents any definite classification.

Pottery Tempered with Limestone, Bone, Grit, or Sand

The following types significantly antedate the principal occupation(s) at Shiloh. As they are of secondary interest, their descriptions are presented in less detail than the preceding types.

Long Branch Fabric-marked

Ten sherds of this limestone-tempered type were found at Shiloh. Despite the earlier dates associated with such pottery in east Tennessee, north Georgia, and northeast Alabama (e.g., Chapman 1995:56; Futato 1977:241; Lafferty 1981:503–505), in the region around Shiloh this type consistently dates to the early part of the Middle Woodland period, being most abundant in the first couple of centuries B.C. (Butler and Jefferies 1986:531; Futato 1998:217–224; Welch 1998a:84–86). Two of the sherds are rims, both of jars or bowls with inslanting rims and squared, slightly thickened lips.

Mulberry Creek Plain

This limestone-tempered type is known from Middle Woodland sites along the central and lower Tennessee River (Futato 1988, 1998:218–224; Peterson 1980; Welch 1998a). For description of the type, see Haag (1942:516). For review of local Middle Woodland chronology, see Futato (1988, 1998:217–224) and Welch (1998a:84–86). Of the six sherds recovered at Shiloh, three are body sherds, two are rims of indeterminate shape, and one is an outslanting rim with a squared-off lip.

Unclassified Limestone-tempered, Red-filmed, and Incised (Figure 3.18, left)

A well-made red-filmed beaker had fine incised or engraved lines forming line-filled triangles on the exterior. The temper particles, which had leached away, were blocky rather than plate-shaped; hence the sherd is thought to have had limestone rather than shell temper. The author is uncertain what to make of this sherd. In terms of vessel shape and decorative treatment, it is not dissimilar from incised, shell-tempered beakers found at a number of earlier Mississippian sites such as Moundville and Cemochechobee. Conceivably the temper really was shell rather than limestone. On the other hand, both red-filming and incised rectilinear decoration are known on limestone-tempered Middle Woodland pottery farther up the Tennessee River (e.g.,

Prospect Red Filmed [Heimlich 1952:19]). No statement will be made here as to the chronological position of this sherd.

Unclassified Limestone-tempered

This is a residual category for sherds whose surface was eroded or that were too small to classify reliably.

Turkey Paw Cordmarked *variety Moon Lake;*
Turkey Paw Plain *variety Turkey Paw*

Along the Tombigbee River near the Alabama-Mississippi state line, Jenkins (1981:157–158) found pottery tempered with a combination of crushed bone and grog (and/or sand). The Turkey Paw types and varieties listed here are copied from his report. The context for this pottery was consistently late Miller II, A.D. 400–550. Previously, Cotter and Corbett (1951:22) had found a few bone-tempered sherds at the Bynum site, now dated between 250–60 B.C. (Walling et al. 1991). And to confuse the chronological picture further, Jennings (1941:189) reports finding bone fragments in Historic Chickasaw pottery in northeast Mississippi. One plain sherd and one cordmarked sherd found at Shiloh had enough bone fragments to suggest that the addition of bone was intentional, though neither sherd had quite as much bone as Jenkins describes for the types and varieties named above.

Unclassified Grit-tempered Cordmarked;
Unclassified Grit-tempered Eroded

Five sherds tempered with medium to coarse angular grit have been found at Shiloh. One was cordmarked, the rest are eroded.

Baldwin Plain *vars. Chalk Bluff* and *Miller Slough*

Sand-tempered plain pottery is common in northwest Mississippi and west Tennessee during most of the Woodland period. There appears to be variation over time in the coarseness and amount of sand used, but Jenkins (1981:123) reported that such criteria are known sometimes to produce chronological misattributions. Consequently, no position is taken here on the chronological position of the two varieties recognized. Sand-tempered plain pottery in surface collections from sites on the Tennessee floodplain several kilometers north of Shiloh fairly consistently had either abundant medium-to-fine sand or sparse fine-to-very-fine sand. Those sherds with abundant medium-to-fine sand are classified as Baldwin Plain *var. Chalk Bluff* and those with the sparse finer temper as *var. Miller Slough*. As a total of only 15 sherds of the two varieties combined was recovered at Shiloh, the site was not much used during whatever period(s) this pottery represents.

Furrs Cordmarked *variety unspecified*

Furrs is characteristic of the Miller cultural sequence in northwest Mississippi and west Tennessee. With only one sherd recovered at Shiloh, the reader is referred to Jennings (1941) and Jenkins (1981) for further discussion of this type.

Unclassified Sand-tempered Eroded

Eroded sand-tempered sherds could be sorted according to the same paste characteristics used to distinguish the varieties of Baldwin Plain, but without any idea what the original surface finish was, there seemed to be little point in doing so. The eroded sand-tempered sherds have thus been left undifferentiated.

Temperless Pottery

Two small plain sherds had no visible temper. Both had compact, gray paste. Whether they represent a potter's momentary aberration or something more significant is not known, but they are reported separately in case a later researcher is able to make more sense of them.

CHIPPED STONE TOOLS

Counts of the formal chipped stone tools from the 1933–1934, 1998, and 1999 excavations are listed in Table 3.3. Typology for the projectile points, or projectile-point/knives as some researchers would cautiously say, is drawn primarily from Justice (1987), supplemented by Cambron and Hulse (1975). Other categories of tools, lacking formal type names, are morphological groupings. Though the functions for tools in several of these groups are inferred, no microscopic edge-wear analysis has been performed, and thus the inferred functions should be regarded as hypotheses for future testing. Tools of the named types will be described first in the order of their chronology, followed by the morphological groups.

Projectile Points

Decatur Projectile Point (Figure 3.19, top left)

This Early Archaic point may be the oldest artifact from the site, dating between 7500 and 7000 B.C. It was recovered in the vicinity of Mound T in 1933–1934.

Table 3.3 Chipped stone tools from the
1933–1934, 1998, and 1999 excavations

Description	Count
Kirk corner-notched projectile point	2
Kirk stemmed projectile point	1
Decatur projectile point	1
Benton stemmed projectile point	1
Brewerton corner-notched projectile point	1
Pickwick projectile point retouched to make a drill or awl	1
Little Bear Creek projectile point	4
Bradley Spike	1
Wade projectile point	1
Adena projectile point	1
Bakers Creek projectile point	1
Copena pentagonal projectile point	5
Jacks Reef corner-notched projectile point	1
Hamilton projectile point	8
Madison projectile point	15
Unclassified side-notched projectile point	1
Unclassified stemless point	1
Flake tool (utilized flake)	62
Uniface	1
Biface or biface fragment	39
Awl	1
Drill	19
Graver	1
Scraper	4
Hoe or hoe fragment	5
Hoe or axe preform	1

Kirk Corner-notched Projectile Point (Figure 3.19, top row, second from left)

Two of these Early Archaic (7500–6900 B.C.) points have come from Shiloh. One, found in the 1933–1934 excavations, is a dark gray material with solution cavities; it may be Tallahatta quartzite, but that is not a secure identification. The other, found in the 1999 excavation in Mound N, is made of Ft. Payne chert.

Kirk Stemmed Projectile Point

One of the Early Archaic (6900–6000 B.C.) points came from excavations west of Mound D in 1933–1934. The raw material is Ft. Payne chert.

Figure 3.19. Stemmed and notched projectile points, from left to right, top row: Decatur (A385402), Kirk Corner Notched (SHIL 08693), Benton Stemmed (A385387), Little Bear Creek (SHIL 06039); bottom row: Wade (A385387), Bakers Creek (A385404), Copena (A385387), Jacks Reef Corner Notched (A385411)

Benton Stemmed Projectile Point (Figure 3.19, top row, third from left)

The lone Benton point from the site is made of Ft. Payne chert and was found east of Mound F in 1933–1934. The type is of Middle to Late Archaic date, between 3500 and 2000 B.C.

Brewerton Corner-notched Projectile Point

This example, made of Ft. Payne chert, is somewhat far afield from the north-eastern/Great Lakes region where Brewerton is more commonly found. The type dates between 3000 and 1700 B.C.

Pickwick Point Retouched to Make a Drill or an Awl

Found north of Mound B in 1933–1934, this tool looks almost exactly like the Pickwick-based drill illustrated in Justice (1987:152). Pickwick points are of Late Archaic age, about 2500 to 1000 B.C.

Bradley Spike

This point is classified as a Bradley Spike somewhat by default because of lack of any better identification. It is small in comparison to most points of the Late Archaic/Gulf Formational era in which contracting-stemmed points such as Pickwick were made. The raw material is heat-treated Tuscaloosa chert. Given the tentative identification as a Bradley Spike, it is perhaps only fitting that the age range of Bradley Spikes is also not well established. Cambron and Hulse (1975:19) suggest a range of "about 2000 B.C. to sometime A.D."

Little Bear Creek Point (Figure 3.19, top right)

These Late Archaic or Gulf Formational points date between 1500 and 500 B.C. The one found at Shiloh came from the 1998 excavation of House Mound 7. It is made of an unidentified gray-speckled chert.

Wade Point (Figure 3.19, lower left)

This style of point has the same Late Archaic or Gulf Formational age range as Little Bear Creek points. The Wade point from Shiloh was found east of Mound F in the 1930s and is made of a chert tentatively identified as Dover.

Adena Stemmed Point

A few centuries more recent than the Wade point is this Adena point made of heat-treated Tuscaloosa chert, with an age estimated between 800 and 300 B.C. It came from west of Mound D and was excavated in 1933–1934.

Bakers Creek Point (Figure 3.19, lower row, second from left)

The point I have called Bakers Creek is made of Ft. Payne chert and came from south of Mound E in 1933–1934. This specimen has an unusually short stem for Bakers Creek, and the incurvate base is also unusual in this type. The point might alternatively be classified in the slightly later Jacks Reef Corner Notched taxon, although that is not a perfect fit either. Bakers Creek points date to the Copena period, from around A.D. 150 to perhaps 600, and Jacks Reef dates from around A.D. 500 to 1000. Perhaps this specimen comes from somewhere in the middle, around A.D. 500 or so.

Copena Point (Figure 3.19, lower row, third from left)

Two whole points and three fragments were classified as Copena points, A.D. 150 to 500. One whole point was made of Dover chert, and it is 8.3 × 2.4 cm, unusually long for a Copena point. It was found in excavation northeast of Mound D in the 1930s. The other whole point (shown in Figure 3.19) was found east of Mound F in the 1930s. My notes do not contain a record of the raw material. One of the fragmentary examples, made of an unidentified agate-like material, was recovered in the 1930s from mound fill on the southeast side of Mound C. Another fragmentary example was found in the fill of Mound F, at a depth of 10 ft below the summit. It was made of a banded purplish-grayish-tan chert. The other fragmentary example was found in 1999 on the apron west of Mound A.

Jacks Reef Corner Notched Point (Figure 3.19, lower right)

This is a Late Woodland style, antecedent to or contemporary with the small triangular points classified as Hamilton or Madison. The date range for Jacks Reef is A.D. 500 to perhaps as late as A.D. 1000. The sole example from Shiloh is made of Ft. Payne chert and was found at a depth of 12 inches in Mound Q in the 1930s.

Hamilton Point (Figure 3.20, lower right)

Hamilton and Madison points are small isoceles triangles, differing in their blade edges. In the terminology of Justice (1987:224–229), Hamilton is defined as having incurvate blade edges and, classically, incurvate bases, while the Madison taxon includes points with straight or excurvate edges and straight or incurvate bases. Justice imputes an earlier date to Hamilton (Late Woodland) than to Madison (Mississippian), but careful studies in the Tombigbee drainage (Peacock 1986) and Tennessee (Boyd 1982) showed that the two forms appear at the same time in the Late Woodland period. Both forms are present in the Alabama-Mississippi-Tennessee area from A.D. 800 well into the Mississippian period, though the incurvate-sided form may have been discontinued before the end of the Mississippian era. Just in case the form of the blade edges is chronologically, functionally, or socially significant, I have distinguished between Hamiltons and Madisons. As the points in the lower row of Figure 3.20 demonstrate, this distinction is sometimes so narrow as to appear arbitrary.

I classified eight points as Hamiltons. Of these, five were made of heat-

Figure 3.20. Madison points (left to right): top row, SHIL 06432, A385397, SHIL 09129; middle row, SHIL 09855, SHIL 09012, SHIL 09431, SHIL 06476; bottom row, SHIL 07509, A385401, SHIL 10269,) and Hamilton point (lower left, SHIL 08821)

treated Tuscaloosa chert, one of Dover, and one of an unidentified white chert. For the eighth example my notes do not record a material identification, which probably means I did not know what it was. The quality of manufacture varies considerably, from crude to the exquisitely pointed example in the lower right corner of Figure 3.20.

Madison Points (Figure 3.20)

This is the most common style of point found at the site, consistent with the Mississippian occupation. Of the 15 examples found, 7 were made of Tuscaloosa chert, 3 of Dover chert, 2 of unidentified gray cherts, 1 of a gray-speckled chert, and 1 of a white chert with light gray mottles and sparse dark gray-brown spots; the raw material of the remaining one is not recorded. The quality of manufacture ranges from crude to the finely worked examples at the top and center right of Figure 3.20.

Unclassified Side-notched Point

Inside the house beneath Mound N, a broken and incomplete side-notched projectile point was found. There is barely enough of the proximal portion of the tool to discern that it was side-notched, but no typological identification is possible. The raw material is an unidentified gray chert.

Unclassified Stemless Point

One stemless point from 1999 excavations west of Mound A was left unclassified. It is a tiny flake, less than 1 cm long, whose edges appear to have been chipped to form a tiny triangular point. The material is heat-treated Tuscaloosa chert.

Flake Tools (n=62)

Flakes exhibiting a macroscopic pattern of edge modification that was not clearly just the result of trampling were classified as flake tools. Because no microwear analysis was attempted, the purposes to which these tools were put is not known. For that matter, many flakes that did not exhibit macroscopic edge modification may also have been used expediently for cutting or other tasks. The majority of flake tools (56, or 90 percent) came from the fill of Mound N. Because the same recovery techniques were used by the 1999 SEAC crew and by the 1998 excavation of House Mound 7, this disproportionate abundance is not just a result of different sampling biases. Wherever the fill for Mound N came from, flake tools were discarded in unusual abundance there.

Uniface (n=1)

The hallmark of unifaces is intentional retouch on one face of a flake. The edge modification on flake tools was also usually unifacial, but unlike flake tools the single specimen classified as a uniface had edge retouch sufficiently systematic to indicate intentionality. Aside from the edge retouch, the tool was not otherwise modified.

Bifaces (n=39)

This is a catchall category for nondiagnostic fragments of formal tools or entire but nondiagnostic bifacially worked tools. The majority of such specimens (24, or 62 percent) came from the 1933–1934 excavations. That is probably because workers in the 1930s were more likely to collect items that were obviously parts of formal tools than they were to collect nondiagnostic items like unifaces or flake tools.

Awl (n=1)

One tool from Mound N was classified as an awl. It is a prismatic blade of Ft. Payne chert on which the distal end has a diagonal transverse edge finely serrated and terminating in a sharp point. Given its form, the tool may have been used as a perforator, or perhaps as a scratcher.

Drills (n=19; Figure 3.21)

Two distinct kinds of tool are represented by this term. First, there are bifacially worked tools with formal hafts. Some of these may have been projectile points that were modified (but are no longer diagnostic, unlike the Pickwick drill reported above). Two such tools, or fragments thereof, were recovered in the 1930s and one in 1998 at House Mound 7.

The other sort of tools labeled drills are small flakes or blades with steep, bilateral, unifacial retouch producing a shaft with a rectanguloid cross-section and a sharp tip. These have been found only in the fill of Mound N, and a more complete discussion of these tools will be found in Chapter 6. Sixteen are illustrated in Figure 3.21; the other is fragmentary and is not illustrated. The raw material is mostly heat-treated Tuscaloosa chert, but a couple of Ft. Payne examples and one specimen of caramel-colored chert are also present.

Graver (n=1)

The sole graver is a broad flake with one or possibly two graver spurs. The raw material is Dover chert.

Figure 3.21. Drills from Mound N (left to right) top row: SHIL 08688, SHIL 06968, SHIL 09090, SHIL 07914; second row: SHIL 08605, SHIL 08707, SHIL 08530, SHIL 07555; third row: SHIL 06854, SHIL 08939, SHIL 08816, SHIL 08411; bottom row: SHIL 06830, SHIL 07553, SHIL 07316, SHIL 08332)

Scrapers (n=4)

Four scrapers were found in the fill of Mound N in 1999. It is curious that
none has been found elsewhere on the site, despite the use of identical recovery techniques in 1998 and by the SEAC crew in 1999. Aside from having the
steep marginal retouch characteristic of scrapers, these four tools have little
in common. One is made of unidentified gray chert (perhaps low quality Ft.
Payne), one of an unidentified cream/tan chert, one of an unidentified white
chert, and one of Dover chert.

Hoes (n=5)

Hoes are distinctive Mississippian tools, frequently made of either Dover
chert from west-central Tennessee or Mill Creek chert from southern Illinois.
Three whole or nearly whole hoes have been found at Shiloh, all during the
1930s. One is made of an unidentified banded chert and a second of limestone. The third, made of Mill Creek chert, is unusually small but has the
characteristic hoe polish on the bit end. Two hoe fragments were found in
excavations during the 1990s, and they are described in later chapters.

Hoe Preform (n=1)

This item appears to be a blank or preform for a hoe or possibly for an ax. It
is made of an unidentified chert that has bands of dark blue-gray, light gray,
and purple.

Hoe Fragments (n=2) and Hoe Flakes (n=10)

Unlike whole hoes, which probably were not intentionally discarded, fragments of broken hoes and flakes created either during the use or resharpening
of hoes probably do represent intentional discards. Two fragments of hoes,
both of Mill Creek chert, were found in the 1930s. Ten small flakes with the
distinctive hoe polish on their dorsal surface(s) were found in 1998–1999.
Seven of these were Mill Creek chert, two Dover chert, and one an unidentified chert.

GROUND STONE TOOLS

The categories in which ground stone tools are reported (see Table 3.4) are
defined below. For the most part these are morphological types, whose function in some instances is only tenuously inferred. In other cases, like that of

Table 3.4 Ground stone tools from the 1933–1934, 1998, and 1999 excavations

Description	Count
Abrader	2
Adze	1
Celts or celt fragments	16
Celt-shaped cobble	1
Chunkey stones	12
Discoidals	2
"Drill rest" (or ornament?) of red shale	1
Flaked and ground fragment	1
Gorget or gorget fragments	2
Grinding stones or mortars	10
Ground stone	9
Hammerstones	8
Nutting stone	2
Rectangular prism, drilled, red shale	1
Ring or torus of coquina	1
Sharpening stones (grooved abraders)	2
Ground stone pentagon	1
Saw	5

ax heads, the function is well established even if it is not always clear whether a given ax head was used on wood or on enemies. The descriptions below are organized into two groups: the first is tools of a technomic nature, and the second includes ornaments, gaming pieces, or other items of a sociotechnic or idiotechnic nature.

Abraders (n=4)

These are pieces of rock—they all happen to be sandstone—against which something hard such as a tool was sharpened or abraded. The action of the tool against the abrader creates grooving, which distinguishes abraders from grinding stones.

Adze (n=1)

The distinction between the head of an adze and the head of an ax is the off-center placement of the bit on an adze. The one such tool found at Shiloh is made of a medium gray metamorphic rock.

Axes (n=16; Figure 3.22)

Ax heads (also called celts) and fragments of ax heads are the most numerous category of ground stone tool in the collections from Shiloh. All but one are made of metamorphic rock, frequently greenstone. The exception is a chipped and polished ax head made of Tuscaloosa chert (Figure 3.22, upper left).

To my knowledge nobody has presented a typology for Woodland and Mississippian ground stone ax heads in the Southeast. There is, however, some reason to think that formal variation over time has some patterning. The ground stone ax heads found in Copena burial mounds, for example, all have oval cross-sections. In contrast, some of the ax heads found at Shiloh and other Mississippian sites have rectangular or rectanguloid cross-sections. The separation is not perfect, however, for oval-section ax heads have been found at many Mississippian sites. Thus, the rectangular cross-section may be distinctively Mississippian, but oval cross-sections do not appear to be chronologically distinctive. In reporting the results of the 1933–1934 excavations in Chapter 4, the form of the cross-sections of ax heads is mentioned for the sake of completeness, but no spatial patterning is evident.

At other sites, ax heads discarded or lost during the manufacturing process reveal that they were first chipped to rough shape, then pecked, and finally ground (e.g., Wilson 2001). Occasionally, however, ax heads discarded during manufacture have saw marks, such as the one in Figure 3.22 at the lower left. In this instance, it looks like a finished ax broke, and the butt end was being refashioned into a smaller tool.

Grinding Stones (n=10)

Items categorized as grinding stones have surfaces against which something was ground, but those surfaces were flat or basin-shaped rather than grooved. Mineral pigments, nutmeats, maize, or many other materials may have been ground on these surfaces. All the grinding stones are made of sandstone.

Ground Stone (n=10)

This is a residual category for items that have one or more artificially smooth surfaces but that are too fragmentary to identify as any other category of ground stone artifact.

Hammerstones (n=8)

Eight hammerstones were recovered during the 1933–1934 excavations. One is quartzite, four are sandstone, and the rest could be either a well-indurated

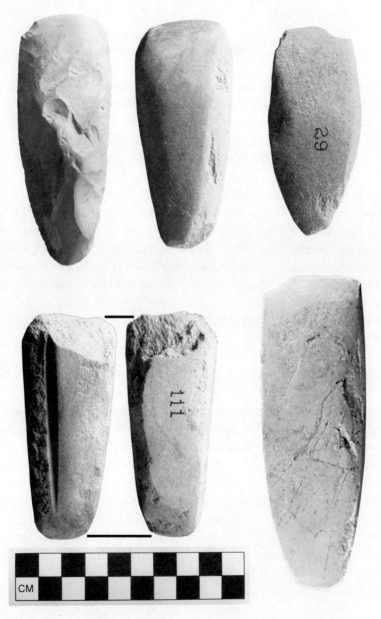

Figure 3.22. Ax heads (left to right) top row first: chert, A385431; greenstone, A385441; gray metamorphic, A385434; greenstone with sawn groove, obverse and reverse, A385449; greenstone, A385440)

sandstone or a fine-grained quartzite. All bear the fine pitting characteristic of hammerstones, and two have been used to such an extent as to become rounded like a discoidal.

Nutting Stones (n=2)

Two pieces of sandstone bear the small, hemispherical depressions that archaeologists generally believe were used for holding nuts that were about to be smashed.

Saws (n=5; Figure 3.23)

More is said about the possible function and the context of these tools in Chapter 6, for the only place on the site where they have been found is in the fill of Mound N. All the examples are thin sheets of ferruginous sandstone, such as can be found in outcrops in the ravines beside the site. One or more edges are V-shaped, with the sides of the V being smoothed by abrasion. On all five examples, the abrasion extends less than 1 cm back from the edge. On one example, the edge appears to have been chipped to shape, with the abrasion smoothing off the chipping scars. In Figure 3.23 the cutting edges are all at the top.

Chunkey Stones (n=12; Figure 3.24, top two rows, Figure 4.26)

These carefully formed, biconcave discs are believed to be stones used in a game of chance which DeBoer (1993) has argued was dominated by Mississippian elites. At Shiloh the stones have two distinguishable forms. One has a small central concavity on otherwise slightly convex faces, illustrated in the top row of Figure 3.24. The other, illustrated by the pair of fragments in the same figure, has entirely concave faces (the two fragments come from different originals, despite their similarity). This is the shape Perino (1971:112–116) refers to as the "Cahokia" style, although this does not necessarily mean the two fragmentary examples at Shiloh came from Cahokia. The nearly flat disk in the lower left of Figure 3.24 also has the overall shape of a chunkey stone, though its raw material, coquina, is extremely unusual for such items.

Discoidals (n=2)

These are crudely formed stone discs. One is bi-pitted, as if it were a poor imitation of a chunkey stone; it also has two parallel lines incised on one face, but these appear modern and are likely shovel scars.

Figure 3.23. Saw blades (top left, SHIL 08358; top right, SHIL 06944; bottom left, SHIL 08415; bottom right, SHIL 08822)

Pentagon (n=1)

A flat piece of mudstone appears to have been ground to form a pentagon barely 1 cm across. I know of no other such items from Mississippian sites.

"Drill rest" (n=1; Figure 3.24, lower right)

The label "drill rest" was applied to this artifact by the excavators in the 1930s. That is one possible function for the item—stabilizing the free end of a drill shaft that was being turned by a bow drill. The item is carefully made of red shale.

Figure 3.24. Chunkey stones (top row, A385437), chunkey stone fragments (second row, left, A385461, right, A385452), coquina disc (lower left, A385554), drilled prism (A385443), and "drill rest" (A385443)

Figure 3.25. Sandal-sole gorget from base of bluff southwest of Mound C
(A385464)

Gorgets (n=2; Figure 3.25)

One of the items classified as a gorget is a fragment of dark gray metamorphic
stone, smoothly polished with an oval cross-section and a drill hole. What the
overall shape of this ornament was is unknown.

The other gorget is intact. It is a sandal-sole shape (see Figure 3.25) with
two perforations. The provenience listed for this item in the 1933–1934 Field
Catalogue is "Surface of small house site on bottom at foot of bluff SW from
Mound C." The raw material is gray shale. Both edges are serrated for roughly
3.5 cm at the widest point of the gorget. Both holes are drilled from a single
direction. This is likely an Archaic rather than a Mississippian artifact, and
its location at (or beyond) the edge of the Mississippian site is fortuitous.

Ring of Coquina (n=1)

This is a small piece of coquina that forms one-third of a torus or ring. The
coarse nature of the material makes it difficult to assess whether this was
intended to be the final shape or whether it is a broken fragment of a full
torus; the latter is presumed. This item and the coquina chunkey stone were
found no more than 18 m apart south or southwest of Mound E.

Rectangular Prism, Drilled (n=1; Figure 3.24, third row, right)

This is a rectangular, square-ended prism of red shale with a longitudinal hole
bored through it. Whatever it was, it split down the middle, along the drilled

hole. It could have been part of a pipe stem or an atlatl weight (see Futato [1987:Pl. 30f] for a similar artifact).

HISTORIC ARTIFACTS

Description of the historic items is deferred to the chapters dealing with the excavations in which these items were found.

4   Excavations in 1933–1934

The most extensive excavations at Shiloh were conducted from December 1933 through March 1934. The project was one of the early instances of archaeology that was funded by a federal Relief agency (Lyon 1996:27–50). The crew for the excavation was provided by the Civil Works Administration, and though the size of the work force fluctuated it reached 118 men for several weeks (Chambers n.d.). The work was overseen by Frank H. H. Roberts, Jr., of the Bureau of American Ethnology, Smithsonian Institution. Moreau B. C. Chambers was his field assistant. Philip Phillips visited the excavation and may have helped oversee some of the work, but no record of how long he was there has been found (Chambers 1976:333–334; Stephen Williams, personal communication). Unlike Roberts, a westerner with a Harvard Ph.D. whose archaeological experience was entirely in the Southwest (Judd 1966; National Anthropological Archives 2000), Chambers was a Mississippian fresh out of college but who nevertheless already had extensive experience in the Southeast (see Galloway 2000:28–37). In particular, Chambers had substantial experience dealing with houses defined only by postmold patterns, having worked on such for Henry B. Collins, Jr., at the Deasonville site in 1929 and 1930 and on Mississippian mound and village sites in Fulton County, Illinois, while a student at the University of Chicago field school the summer before the Shiloh project.

As was not uncommon for such Relief projects, the need of the Relief agency to put people to work appears to have superseded the desire of the archaeologists to carry out the excavation in a logical manner. The clearest evidence of this was the fact that excavation of the site began before the project surveyor had a chance to lay out a grid system for the excavation. The archaeologists tried to make the best of the situation, however, and it is evident from the field notes that within a few weeks the excavation was proceeding smoothly.

While the excavation at Shiloh seems to have been fairly efficient in terms of moving large quantities of dirt with minimal trained supervision, the quality of the excavation and of the excavation records leaves much to be desired. In saying this I am not applying current standards to excavators in the 1930s but rather comparing the work of Roberts and Chambers with what

other excavators in the 1930s were doing. Having dealt with the records of
other excavations of that era (e.g., Welch 1991, 1994, and ongoing work with
the records of the University of Chicago field school excavations at Kincaid),
I was surprised to find that the Shiloh work did not conform to the best
standards of the day. In terms of control over artifact provenience and quality
of record-keeping, alumni of the University of Chicago field school (see Cole
and Deuel 1937:24–32; Haag 1986:65–66; Lyon 1996:61–62) were doing better
work in the early 1930s than Roberts did at Shiloh, although it appears that
Roberts significantly improved his field techniques over time (see Wilmsen
and Roberts 1978:4–16). Roberts had begun his excavation career while a student at the University of Denver, and as a Harvard graduate student he
worked on Neil Judd's Chaco Canyon project (Judd 1966; National Anthropological Archives 2000). From his appointment to the Bureau of American
Ethnology until the start of his work at Shiloh, he continued to focus on
Southwestern prehistory. Chambers, on the other hand, had extensive experience on sites in the Southeast, was a graduate of the University of Chicago
field school run by Thorne Deuel and Fay-Cooper Cole, and had also spent
a season conducting stratigraphic excavations on ancient Eskimo villages on
St. Lawrence Island (see Chambers's précis of his career in his application to
the Harvard graduate program, written during the work at Shiloh [Galloway
2000:28–29]). It is particularly surprising that the Shiloh work was not up to
the recording standards inculcated by the University of Chicago field school,
given that Chambers had been a student there the previous summer. Perhaps
some of the deficiency of the Shiloh records can be attributed to the shortage
of supervisory personnel. Having only two archaeologists to oversee the work
of a hundred shovelers is certainly less than ideal, and perhaps it prevented
the archaeologists from maintaining as tight control over the excavation as
they might have wished. This is speculation, however, and it is worth noting
that the field notes do not hint at any frustration on the part of the archaeologists.

    With only two brief published summaries (Roberts 1935; Stirling 1935),
which largely duplicate each other, the results of the excavation were all but
lost to the archaeological community. In addition to the two previously cited
brief notices that appeared in Smithsonian publications, there is a typescript
prepared by Chambers (n.d.). It amounts to four typed pages plus a site map,
and judging from its nontechnical tone the document was intended (and perhaps used) as an information sheet for visitors to the park. Other than these
three brief overviews, the only other documentation of the excavation consists of the raw field documents curated by Roberts's home institution, the
National Museum of Natural History, Smithsonian Institution. Before describing the excavations and the resulting artifact collection, it is worth de-

scribing what these unpublished documents comprise, particularly because a previous report on Shiloh (Smith 1977) understated the extent of the documentation as well as the artifact collection.

FIELD RECORDS OF THE 1933–1934 EXCAVATION

The original field notebooks, excavation drawings, and photographs from the 1933–1934 excavation are now curated by the National Anthropological Archives (NAA), Smithsonian Institution. This material is split into two separate lots, one consisting of the written materials and drawings (NAA call number: Lot 4851, which also includes much material unrelated to Shiloh) and the other consisting of the field photographs (NAA call number: photo lot 137). In June 1996, there were 115 field photographs. Based on the striking sharpness of detail in 8×10" prints, these black-and-white photos must have been taken with a large-format camera. If a log of the photographs and their subjects was kept, it has not survived, though a few prints bear annotations on the back that appear to come from either Roberts or Chambers. I have been able to ascertain the subject and viewpoint of most of the photographs, based on the topography, distinctive trees visible in several different photographs, positive match to field drawings, notes, etc. A copy of my photo identifications is on file at the National Anthropological Archives for future users of the collection.

Among the written documents, the principal resources are two field notebooks, one kept by Frank Roberts and the other by Moreau Chambers. These notebooks are both fairly informal and record information in somewhat abbreviated form. They both contain simple line-sketches of features, posthole patterns, stratigraphic profiles, and even artifacts. Roberts's notebook (1933–1934:1) commences with the following three entries:

—Arrived Shiloh evening of Dec. 19, 1933. Cold & raining. Found only very poor quarters for living. Discouraging start.
—Spent December 20 going over mound group. Discussed problem of map & plan of survey with Surveyor Williamson and asst. archeologist Chambers. Saw C.W.A. people about men for job.
—Started work on morning of Dec. 21. Began with a series of Trenches at S. end of ridge on which mounds are located. In S. of the mound designated C on Moore's plot. Not much showing on first day. Some potsherds.

Part of the reason Roberts's notebook is less illuminating than it might otherwise be is that the dates in the above-quoted entries are the only dates that appear anywhere in the notebook. Entries appear with gaps between them, but where one day stops and another starts, or where jottings about one subject or excavation area start and stop, is a matter of guesswork. The notebook kept by Chambers, by contrast, does have each entry dated.

At the end of the notebook kept by Roberts is the "Field Catalogue of Specimens." This is a sequentially numbered list, individual numbers sometimes pertaining to single items and sometimes to entire lots of items such as a sack of sherds. Nearly all the field catalogue entries have horizontal provenience (of varying specificity), and many have some vertical provenience. In some instances, the vertical provenience is specified as "top section," "second section," and the like. In some cases, the depths-below-surface of these "sections" are supplied in Chambers's notebook.

Chambers's notebook, like the one Roberts kept, contains informal jottings, sketches, and occasional information about the progress of the excavation. His entries are dated; entries were not made daily, for there are gaps of up to 10 days between entries. Unlike Roberts, Chambers allocates a fair amount of attention to the artifacts that were being found. Over a period of days, Chambers recorded the relative abundances of sherds tempered with shell and those tempered with "grit" (i.e., grog, which in the 1930s was often referred to as "clay-grit"). This analysis also made stratigraphic distinctions, tallying pottery by the "sections" mentioned in the paragraph above. Chambers also listed and described the burials encountered in Mound C, even though it appears Roberts supervised this part of the excavation. The burial information in Chambers's notebook is not as detailed as that recorded in other documents, however.

Information about burials was recorded on a set of 4½×6½" cards. Each card records one burial and includes a description of the position of the skeletal remains (sometimes including a sketch), their state of preservation, the horizontal location, and the depth below surface or other provenience information. Some of the burials were also documented by photographs.

There are a number of profile drawings of mound cross-sections, a few of which accompany plan views. With the exception of three that are very schematic and not very informative, I present all these drawings at the appropriate place in this chapter.

Unfortunately, there is no surviving map of the excavations. The lack of such a map is the single most frustrating gap in the records, and it is not clear whether there ever was such a map or whether it has been misplaced somewhere at the Smithsonian.

Roberts was forced to begin the excavation before a grid had been established. To deal with this situation, the crew was initially put to work excavating a series of east-west trenches near Mound C. Meanwhile the surveyor, whose last name was Williamson, began making a plane-table map of the site and setting out wooden stakes at 20-ft intervals. The completion of this task was noted by Roberts (1933–1934:8): "Laying out of entire site on a grid completed. Series of 20 foot square [*sic*] used. Site too large for a smaller unit. Had difficult time getting sufficient pegs for 20 foot squares."

The surveyor made 12 detailed plane-table topographic maps, each covering a section of the site measuring 220 × 160 ft. These maps show 1-ft contour lines, and plot postholes, hearths, and other features exposed by the excavation. Lamentably, these maps do not show the edges of the excavated areas. If a feature is plotted in a particular location we know that that spot must have been excavated, but in areas where no features are shown we do not know whether this is owing to lack of excavation or lack of features. There is a striking disjunction between the indications of excavation locations in the field notes and in the plane-table maps. When information about excavation locations from the written documents is juxtaposed with the plane-table maps, it is apparent that neither source of information alone comes close to revealing the true extent of excavations. The field photos reveal yet additional excavation areas, and fieldwork in 1999 showed that there are even more excavations than revealed by any combination of maps, notes, and photos. The plane-table maps, however, are particularly important in that they provide the only documentation of some remarkable buildings at the site.

At some point after the plane-table maps were drawn, a composite map of the site was prepared. This map, also of plane-table size, appears to have been scaled from the 12 detail sheets. It includes large portions of the site for which there are no detail sheets. For those portions of the map, there is no indication what the basis might be for the topographic lines that are shown. Near the edges of the site, the disparity between the map and actual topography suggests that in these areas the mapper used a lot of visual estimation. But in the central portion of the site the composite map is, for the most part, accurate. In the process of scaling the composite from the detail sheets, one significant error was made. The westernmost two detail sheets have north edges that are 20 ft south of the edges of the eastern block of detail sheets. When the composite map was prepared, this misalignment was not noticed, and topography from the westernmost sheets was incorrectly placed 20 ft north of where it should be. This had the result of shifting the apparent location of Mound G, a situation that came to light in 1998 when I found that my grid coordinates for the mound could not be reconciled with the composite map from the 1933–1934 excavation.

One unusual additional record of the excavation survives: a silent, black-and-white movie lasting about 16 minutes. Though there are shots of some of the Civil War monuments, most of the footage shows the excavations in progress. In several of the panoramic shots, the extent of excavations visible is greater than any of the other records indicate; thus the film does provide useful information about the excavation. The film is curated by the Human Studies Film Archive at the Smithsonian (catalogue no. NA-86.12.2). A copy is supposedly also at the National Archives Motion Picture, Sound, and Video Branch (catalogue no. NWDNM(m)-106.20), but the film so labeled shows excavations in the American Southwest (I suspect that the footage of Roberts excavating at Allantown, Arizona, has been switched with that of Roberts excavating at Shiloh—these items have adjacent catalogue numbers).

That completes the list of records from the 1933–1934 excavation: photos, notebooks, artifact catalogue, burial cards, profiles, maps, and a motion picture. But experience shows that even when combined, these sources of information do not reveal the full extent of the excavation.

EXCAVATION TECHNIQUES

As was reasonable for such a site and such a crew, Roberts had the excavators at Shiloh use shovels. We do not know what instructions the shovelers were given. We do know that at least initially the excavations were trenches running east-west, though later there were trenches with other orientations, and excavations of square, rectangular, and irregular shapes. Once encountered, lines of postholes were followed. Evidence from photographs and subsequent excavation in Mound N (see Chapter 6) shows that the side walls of the excavations tended to be not quite vertical, and in plan view the outlines of the excavation units also tended to be less than straight. Photographs show trenches whose walls bow inwards and outwards, sometimes gradually, sometimes abruptly. In some instances it is clear that the unit walls were curved to avoid trees and roots, but in other instances no reason for the nonlinearity can be seen.

The excavated material was not screened. Roberts and Chambers did not say this, but it is made clear from the absence of screens in the field photographs, the presence of substantial quantities of artifacts in the backfill, and the obvious selectivity of the artifact collection. The artifact collection contains remarkably few items for an excavation of this scale, very few small items, and a strikingly high ratio of rims to body sherds (196 of 1,021 sherds [19 percent] are rims). The use of screens, particularly on extensive excavation projects, was not yet a common practice in U.S. archaeology, even though large-scale screening was being used on another CWA-funded archaeological project directed by a Smithsonian archaeologist at the same time Roberts was at Shiloh: the Tulamniu Mounds site in Kern County, California (Lyon 1996:37).

As units were excavated, the dirt was usually shoveled to the side, forming a ridge along the edge of the unit. Backfilling consisted of shoveling the ridges back into the units. Many of the field photos show these ridges, and a few show the process of backfilling. In areas of the site where excavation units were too wide for the dirt to be shoveled aside, it was carted off in wheelbarrows. This was done southwest of Mound A, in the area of Mounds R–W, for the deep trench in Mound F, and for the Mound C excavations. Photos show back dirt from the excavations southwest of Mound A piled just west of the excavation area, and the movie shows the excavated fill of Mound C being dumped south of that mound, but otherwise we do not know where the wheelbarrows' loads were dumped.

One aspect of the excavation technique that has been a puzzle is the convention that was used for designating excavation units. Archaeologists in recent decades have generally used a Cartesian coordinate system with the grid axes labeled as north-south and east-west. In these Cartesian systems, once a particular corner, say, the southeast, has been adopted as the corner whose coordinates designate the excavation unit, all excavation units on the site will be designated by the same convention even if the site occupies more than one quadrant of the Cartesian plane. Chicago-trained archaeologists in the 1930s used a different, though still rectangular, coordinate system. In this system (Cole and Deuel 1937:24–26), the site was bisected by a baseline that began somewhere off the edge of the site. Location was measured from the perspective of someone standing at the origin point of the baseline: a given point was so many feet out along the baseline, and then so many feet to the left or right of the baseline. In the Chicago system, excavation units were designated by the corner that was closest to the origin of the baseline, so that "50R20" signified a unit that began 50 feet out along the baseline from the origin and 20 feet to the right of the baseline. The system Roberts used at Shiloh appears to have been a mix of these two systems of designating excavation units. Coordinates were specified in north-south and east-west terms rather than the right-left terms used in the Chicago system. But like the Chicago system, Roberts appears to have recorded the locations of excavation units in terms of the corner closest to the baseline and closest to the origin of the baseline. The baseline ran west from a notional origin off the eastern edge of the site (roughly in the middle of the river). Thus, units north of the baseline were designated by their southeast corner, while units south of the baseline were designated by their northeast corner. I say that this *appears* to be the system Roberts used, because Roberts did not explain how he designated units, and this is the interpretation that seems best to match the proveniences he recorded. All Roberts said (1933–1934:8) about the grid system and the system for recording proveniences was that "the numbers run west from a meridian east of [the] whole group and north and south of a base line."

Roberts and Chambers followed the surveyors' convention of listing coordinates in "hundreds of feet plus feet." Thus, S2+40 W4+80 indicates a grid location 240 ft south and 480 ft west of the grid origin. Except in direct quotations from the field records, I have eliminated the plus signs in the interest of brevity (e.g., S2+40 W4+80 becomes S240/W480). Unless otherwise specified, all the grid coordinates in this chapter are those of Roberts 1933–1934 grid, not of the Welch 1998 metric grid system.

In their notebooks, Roberts and Chambers often refer to excavation units by a single provenience, the designator corner. Even if the system described in the preceding paragraph correctly specifies which corner that is (NE corner for units south of the baseline, SE corner for units north of the baseline), we still have a problem understanding references to excavation units. The problem is that, if only one corner is specified, there is no indication of how large (length and width) the unit was. The notebooks sometimes mention only one corner, sometimes two, rarely all four. Where all four corners are mentioned, the units are sometimes 20 × 20 ft, sometimes 10 × 20 ft, sometimes 10 × 10 ft, and sometimes 5 ft wide with various lengths. In the field photographs most excavation units appear to be trenches 5 to 10 ft wide and of various lengths. Thus, to excavate a 20-ft-wide area, the workers may actually have dug a set of adjacent trenches, backfilling one as they dug the next. But the bottom line is that many of the excavation units are of unknown size.

When the excavators encountered features such as hearths and pits, shovels were replaced by trowels and brushes. Trowels, it seems, were in short supply, for at one point in Chambers's notebook (1933–1934:13) there is a list of how many trowels were assigned to each of four excavation crews. This bit of information, curiously enough, provides an insight into the management of the huge crew of laborers. When the information in the two notebooks is compared some overlap exists, but for the most part the two archaeologists were recording information about different parts of the site. Apparently, Roberts allocated responsibility for part of the site to Chambers and managed the rest himself. Chambers in turn appears to have divided his workforce into several crews, each with a supervisor. All we know about these supervisors are the names of some of them: Mr. Combs, Smith, Hagy, Atkins, Joe Leith (mentioned once as a cosupervisor with Atkins), and Joe Dillon. It is not clear whether all of these supervisors worked under Chambers or whether some of them may have been under direct supervision by Roberts. It is also not clear whether workmen on the part of the site Roberts himself supervised were also organized into crews the way they were under Chambers. It seems likely that this was the case, for the field photographs reveal multiple areas being excavated simultaneously (see Figure 4.1).

Figure 4.1. Work crews in area between Mounds F and bluff edge (National Anthropological Archives, Smithsonian Institution, negative no. 79-12,799)

Artifacts from the excavation were washed, but where this was done and by whom is not revealed in the documents.

ARTIFACTS

The Field Catalogue of Specimens in Roberts's notebook has 183 entries. Not all of the items listed in the catalogue are at the NMNH today, nor are all the items in the current collection listed in the field catalogue. Some of the items, especially Civil War artifacts such as "fragments of cannon balls, grape shot, minnie [sic] balls, bayonets, canteens, horse trappings, and personal equipment" (Roberts 1935:68) were turned over to the park rather than sent to the Smithsonian. The park today has no record of these items (Stacy Allen, personal communication). After the rest of the collection was received at the NMNH, Roberts apparently kept them for study in his office for several years before they were formally accessioned in 1939. Of the 183 field catalogue numbers assigned in the field, 37 are missing altogether, or missing at least one specified item, in the Accession Memorandum of 1939. In a few instances there are specific notations in the Accession Memorandum that items were discarded, but for the most part the discrepancies are not explained. Furthermore, the memorandum contains 32 lots, most with specific proveniences, that are not listed in the catalogue. Most of these lots are sacks of sherds, for which horizontal and vertical proveniences are specified. The field catalogue does contain entries for other sacks of sherds, so it is not evident why some sacks were not given field catalogue numbers. In 1996, the NMNH computerized catalogue faithfully duplicated the original Accession Memorandum, but there is one additional mystery. In the collection itself there were four boxes of material that had been given temporary accession numbers. These items are labeled as coming from Roberts's excavation at Shiloh, sometimes with specific proveniences, but the items and the proveniences do not appear in either the Field Catalogue or the Accession Memorandum. While the list of cataloging and curation discrepancies is extensive, in my experience it is comparable with other collections from the era.

Many of the terms for artifacts used in the Field Catalogue and Accession Memorandum are not as informative as archaeologists today would wish, because distinctions we recognize today were not recognized then. My reclassification of the artifact collection using a more current taxonomy is shown in Tables 4.1 and 4.2. The wide diversity of pottery and, especially, projectile points makes it clear that the bluff overlooking the river was used repeatedly by people over thousands of years, not just by Mississippian people. The oldest items are the Decatur, Kirk corner-notched, and Kirk stemmed projectile points, which are Early Archaic styles dating between 7500 to 7000 B.C., 7500 to 6900 B.C., and 6900 to 6000 B.C., respectively (Justice 1987:71–84). There is then a hiatus lasting to the later part of the Middle Archaic, represented by the Benton stemmed point, 3500 to 2000 B.C. (Justice 1987:111). The next gap in the chronological sequence of periods represented at Shiloh is the later Mississippian and (Proto-) Historic period, between the abandonment of the mound site by Native Americans and the occupation of the area by Euro-American settlers in the early 1800s (Hays 1996). No diagnostically Civil War–era artifacts remain in the collection, apparently having all been given to the park in 1934.

Despite the broad smear of periods represented by the artifacts, the majority of the chronological diagnostics come from the Late Woodland or Mississippian periods. Specifically, these are the Hamilton and Madison points and the grog-tempered and shell-tempered pottery. Collectively, these items almost certainly date between A.D. 700 and 1500. Already by the mid-1930s archaeologists thought that grog-tempered (Late Woodland) pottery was in use before, and was replaced by, shell-tempered (Mississippian) pottery. As explained in Chapter 3, while grog-tempered pottery does on the whole pre-

Table 4.1 Pottery from Shiloh in the NMNH collection

Description	Count	%
Sand-tempered (n=5)		
Baldwin Plain *var. Chalk Bluff*	1	.1
var. Miller Slough	3	.3
Unclassified sand-tempered	1	.1
Limestone-tempered (n=21)		
Long Branch Fabric-marked *var. unspecified*	10	1.0
Mulberry Creek Plain *var. unspecified*	6	.6
Unclassified limestone-tempered red-filmed incised	1	.1
Unclassified limestone-tempered	4	.4
Grog-tempered (n=477)		
Baytown Plain *var. McKelvey*	72	7.0
var. The Fork	4	.4
var. unspecified	2	.2
Mulberry Creek Cordmarked *var. Coffee Landing*	13	1.3
var. Mulberry Creek	383	37.1
Wheeler Check-stamped *var. Edmonds Branch*	1	.1
Unclassified grog-tempered	2	.2
Shell-tempered (n=528)		
Barton Incised *var. unspecified*	3	.3
Bell Plain *var. unspecified*	87	8.4
Kimmswick Fabric-impressed *var. Langston*	16	1.5
Mississippi Plain *var. Shiloh*	358	34.7
var. unspecified	4	.4
Mound Place Incised *var. unspecified*	2	.2
Moundville Incised *var. Carrollton*	1	.1
var. Moundville	11	1.1
var. Snows Bend	1	.1
Powell Plain	4	.4
Ramey Incised	2	.2
Salt Creek Cane-impressed *var. unspecified*	2	.2
Unclassified shell-tempered *var. unspecified*	16	1.5
Unclassified shell-tempered eroded	19	1.8
Unclassified shell- and grog-tempered	2	.2
Temperless (n=2)		
Unclassified plain	2	.2
Total	1,033	100.2

Table 4.2 Nonpottery artifacts from Shiloh
in the NMNH collection

Description	Count
Pottery other than vessels	
Pottery trowel	4
Pottery trowel handle	2
Shell-tempered pipe	2
Chipped stone	
Core or core fragment	4
Miscellaneous retouched piece	4
Miscellaneous biface or biface fragment	20
Axe or hoe preform	1
Hoe or hoe fragment	5
Drill base	2
Kirk corner-notched projectile point	1
Kirk stemmed projectile point	1
Decatur projectile point	1
Benton stemmed projectile point	1
Brewerton corner-notched projectile point	1
Pickwick projectile point retouched to make a drill or awl	1
Little Bear Creek projectile point	3
Wade projectile point	1
Adena projectile point	1
Bakers Creek projectile point	1
Copena pentagonal projectile point	4
Jacks Reef corner-notched projectile point	1
Hamilton projectile point	3
Madison projectile point	6
Ground stone	
Adze	1
Axes or axe fragments	15
Axe-shaped cobble	1
Chunkey stones	12
Discoidals	2
"Drill rest" (or ornament?) of red shale	1
Flaked and ground fragment	1
Gorget or gorget fragments	2
Grinding stones or mortars	3
Hammerstones	8

Continued on the next page

Table 4.2 *Continued*

Description	Count
Nutting stone	1
Rectangular prism, drilled, red shale	1
Ring or torus of coquina	1
Sharpening stones (grooved abraders)	2
Unworked stone	
Sandstone	2
Tube of groundwater concretion	1
Chert	2
Fossil coral	1
Fossil crinoid	1
Pumice	1
Hematite or red ocher	3
Galena	3
Mica	5 lots
Mica fragment adhering to *Shiloh* sherd	1
Fired clay and daub	6
Carbonized plant material	
Charred cane	1 lot
Charred maize kernels	1 lot
Bone and shell	
Antler tines, modified	3
Antler tine, unmodified	1
Split deer metapodial	1
Deer radius fragment	1
Bone pin	2
Perforated mussel shell	1
Assorted specimens of freshwater shells	1 lot
Historic artifacts	
Horse teeth	1 lot
Miscellaneous metal objects	2 lots

cede shell-tempered pottery, the possibility that they overlap chronologically is a subject that has not yet been resolved.

Because most of the sherds in the Shiloh collection have vertical as well as horizontal proveniences, one of the questions I examine in this chapter is whether the distribution of grog-tempered pottery differs from that of the shell-tempered ware. To the extent that the two wares tend to be found in different deposits, this would suggest that they derive from different components. This is not the ideal way to attempt to resolve the question of chrono-logical overlap, given that many of the deposits from which pottery was col-lected in the 1930s were deposits of fill that may contain chronological mix-tures. The best way to settle the question of whether grog-tempered and shell-tempered pottery at Shiloh are contemporary would be to obtain differ-ential (interval) luminescence dates (Feathers 1997:52) on sherds of the two wares, a project for future research.

EXCAVATION AREAS

With no surviving map that shows where the CWA crew excavated, clues to the locations of the excavation areas have to be sought in the field notes, artifact catalogue, and site photographs. Putting this information together yields a picture of extensive excavation, yet fieldwork in 1999 demonstrated that even this picture seriously understates the actual extent of the excava-tion. Each of the known excavation areas is described below. To help organize the report, I have grouped excavation areas into the following categories:

1. East-west trenches along the bluff edge.
2. Large exposure southwest of Mound A.
3. Apron west of Mound A.
4. Trenches in the plaza area.
5. House mounds.
6. Palisade and miscellaneous other areas.
7. Mound E trenches.
8. Mound F trench.
9. Mound Q excavations.
10. Mound C excavations.

The field notebooks of Chambers and Roberts state that work on the project started with the east-west trenches along the bluff edge, so I begin there. For each of the ten areas listed here, the information provided by the field notes, artifact catalogue, and field photographs will be presented, fol-lowed by a summary of what the excavations reveal about this part of the site.

East-West Trenches along the Bluff Edge (see Figure 4.2)

Because excavation at the site began at the same time the surveyor began setting in a grid, the earliest excavations could not make use of the grid sys-tem. Roberts and Chambers dealt with this situation by setting the workers to digging trenches across the bluff-top ridge that Mound C sits on. As this

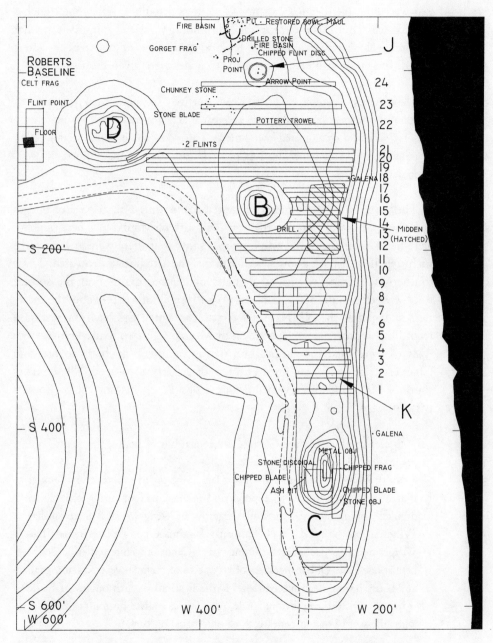

Figure 4.2. Detail of site map showing excavation trenches along bluff edge

ridge is fairly narrow, especially at its southern end, the trenches did not have to be very long; thus it would be easy for the workers to maintain a consistent east-west line. Neither Roberts nor Chambers actually say that the trenches ran east-west, but this is clear in the field photographs and is implicit in what the archaeologists said about the features that some of the trenches intersected. In lieu of grid coordinates, the trenches were given numbers.

> The trenches were numbered from 1 consequetively [*sic*] north from Mound C. All of the sacks of potsherds are so designated. The reason for this was that the surveyor had not completed laying the area off grid fashion so that sections & trenches could be numbered according to the area where found. (Roberts 1933–1934:3)

The mention of the numbering system came only after a page of entries describing what was found in the trenches south of Mound C. These trenches were never numbered, and while photos show that there were at least three such trenches I do not know whether that is the actual total excavated. These southernmost trenches yielded a "mass of charred grain" near the surface southwest of Mound C (Chambers 1933–1934:2). This is probably the material cataloged at the NMNH as A385556, for which the NMNH accession record lists a provenience "southwest of Mound C." Two maize kernels from A385556 were used for radiocarbon dating in 1997, which, as reported in Chapter 2, yielded a combined estimate of cal A.D. 1030–1160. The trenches south of Mound C also revealed evidence of an early historic cabin (Roberts 1933–1934:2):

> —In area south of Mound C found occasional bits of iron & fragments from grape shot. Also some minnie balls.
> —South of Mound C in small area a large amount of broken china, bits of iron, a knife, a spoon handle, a spoon, and an old ladle for pouring lead. China decidedly old fashioned. One type suggestive of Wedgewood. A fragment has "Virginia" on the back. Possibly an early Virginia type of pottery made like Wedgewood (?). Also located chimney base. Cabin of White settler no doubt here at one time. Oldest members of crew, two of them 80 years, do not recall any house having been placed there. No indications of such on any of battle maps or maps of army before battle. Also found a silver button at this place with [the word London beneath three plus signs] on back.

This passage is the only place in the field notes where excavation of a Historic structure is mentioned, but there may have been a second Historic house. Roberts (1935:65) wrote that "in two instances remains of white man's dwellings were discovered. These structures, log cabins with a fireplace at one end of their single rooms, had been abandoned and fallen into ruins prior to the Battle of Shiloh in 1862." Chambers's excavation notes (Chambers 1933–1934:2) are somewhat ambiguous on the number of historic structures. In his entry for December 21 we are told

Digging of trenches was started on the end of the ridge south of Mound C, revealing in two places hillocks containing quantities of broken chinaware, iron spoons, a lead pouring ladle, etc., with only a stray sherd or so throughout the area trenched.

In his record of the conversation with L. B. Philyaw (see Chapter 2), Chambers (1933–1934:46) noted that

Old log house with stick-&-mud chimney stood where house site was below Mound C. Major Reed had 4 bad women evicted from this house & it destroyed in 1899.
Jno. Wicker of Bolivar (insane) was living near Mound C at outbreak of war.

In contrast to these entries in Chambers's notebook that may indicate that there were two distinct historic structures south of Mound C, Chambers (n.d.:4) says that "bits of chinaware; case knives, lead ladles, old nails, and the like [came from] an old house site south of Mound G, beside the Brown's Ferry Road." The excavation notes and artifact catalogue do record such historic debris south of Mound C and do not record any historic debris south of Mound G, so "Mound G" is most likely a misprint for Mound C. In any case, there was at least one historic house site south of Mound C.

In addition to the historic house(s) south of Mound C, the archaeologists may have believed that there was at least one prehistoric house south of C. In the map attached to his typescript, Chambers (n.d.:5) placed two symbols for small mounds south of C, though on the plane-table map only one is shown. Excavation into this housemound was recorded in one of the field photographs, reproduced here as Figure 4.3.

North of Mound C, the trenching encountered another small mound. Roberts (1933–1934:3–4) described it thus:

Between Mounds C and B an open area with a small, low mound not indicated on Moore's map. This was given the working designation of Mound "K".—
There seemed to have been a burial at one time in Mound K. A few fragments of skull & some teeth all that were encountered. These were revealed in Trench #2 at a depth of one foot, one inch from the present surface. There were also

Figure 4.3. Excavation south of Mound C, looking northwest (National Anthropological Archives, Smithsonian Institution, negative no. 79-12,701)

some scattered bits of charcoal. The exact location of the bones is shown on the main map sheet.

—Mound K was only a simple earth structure of a homogeneous nature. All plain red dirt.

The description of Mound K by Chambers (1933–1934:4) differs in some details from that provided by Roberts:

Trench 2. This passes through the center of Mound K. Fragmentary Burial #1 comprising badly preserved portions of a skull was found at the center of the mound approx one foot below the surface. No teeth present, nor other portions of this burial. Sherds were found in this trench, of the prevailing cord-marked, grit tempered type. Disturbed area extends nearly two ft. deep. Undisturbed dirt below the mound follows approximately the present surface contour.

These descriptions of Mound K provide three noteworthy pieces of information. The most important is the presence of a human burial in Mound K, a fact not recorded anywhere else. The second is that a "main map sheet" recorded the location of the burial. No such mark appears on the surviving

Figure 4.4. Excavation trenches between Mounds C and B, looking north (National Anthropological Archives, Smithsonian Institution, negative no. 79-12,697)

maps, so perhaps a yet-undiscovered map exists that would help clarify the location of excavations. The third piece of information is the location of Trench 2, which passes through the mound. Because the mound itself is mapped, we have some confidence about the location of this trench. Several of the trenches nearest the north side of Mound B are shown in Figure 4.4, though it is not possible to tell where in the photo precisely Mound K is located.

North of Mound K there were several "depressions." The field notes mention at least three of them. Trench 4 passed through one of them. This trench encountered a small pile of mussel shells near the eastern end, and, in the lowest part of the depression, "raw gravel was found just below the humus & muck" (Chambers 1933–1934:5). Trench 5 yielded a few sherds near the eastern end.

Trench 6, said to have the "largest number of potsherds," was immediately north of a "large" depression (Roberts 1933–1934:3). Chambers adds that "a burned area near the center (immediately north of the depression previously noted) contained fire cracked stones & a few sherds. Could be traced 1 ½ ft. down."

Chambers (1933–1934:6) described Trench 7 thus: "A considerable amount of pottery was uncovered down to the depth of a foot near the highest point in the ridge. One handle sherd was uncovered. Sherds scarce near eastern end of trench."

Trenches 8 and 9 cut through the southern and northern sides of a large depression. Two cross-trenches (running north-south) were excavated, connecting Trenches 7 and 9. Other than a few "heavy" sherds, nothing was found in the depression, and Roberts (1933–1934:4) speculated that this was "the remains, possibly, of a pit from which earth was removed for one of the mounds."

At this point, on December 27, the notebooks record that the excavation was expanded to additional areas of the site. Both of the notebooks become less detailed about the locations and findings from individual trenches. No mention is made of Trenches 10 or 11, but Chambers (1933–1934:11) says of the area south of Mound B (the marginal query is his):

(salt pan?)   Hole north of Trench 12—15 ft. s. of the mound a soft area three
              ft. deep yielded an unusual amount of pottery. Two sherds were
              found here of a heavy ware bearing imprint of netting.

Several pages later, Chambers (1933–1934:18) mentioned that this "hole S of Mound B was enlargement of Trench 12" and gave a S200/W400 location for it. To the north, Trench 13 passed "just S of Mound B" (Chambers 1933–1934:18).

For the areas east of Mound B and north of the mound, Chambers (1933–1934:11–12) summarized the excavation results as follows:

—Area E. of Mound B—
A streak of soft black midden dirt extended along the bluff about half way from the base of Mound B to the edge of the bluff & parallel to the bluff edge. This lies about 20–25 ft. from the base of the mound. Depth of disturbed dirt runs about 2–2 ½ ft. deep over the entire area between Mound B & the bluff edge. The soft streak ran slightly deeper. Trenches considered: 12, 13, 14, 15, 16, 17.
Area N of Mound B—
A burial about one ft. below the ground level was found 10 ft. north of base of Mound B, in Trench 18. Flexed burial. (Probably deer bones in midden deposit. "Salt pan" sherds found here, in midden deposit—2 ft. deep.)

Two additional comments about Trench 18 must be made. First, I believe that the comment in parenthesis was added as a correction to the notion that the bones were human, because the whole paragraph was overwritten with "Deer Bones" in large letters. Second, the artifact catalogue indicates that a piece of galena was found at the east end of Trench 18.

Nothing is recorded about Trench 19, but we are told (Chambers 1933–1934:13) of two items from Trench 20: "Greenstone fleshing stone, polished. (East end of trench) Dark flint stemmed proj. pt. found 40 ft. from path." In his examination of the pottery found in various parts of the site, Chambers (1933–1934:27) gives this tally:

Middle of Trench No. 20 (Smith's crew)
—Area N. of Mound B—
Tempering: 29 grit; 21 shell; 2 indeterminate.
Decoration: 10 cord, 1 redslip; 1 rim lug. Only one of the shell tempered sherds (5/8" thick) shows traces of woven matting on exterior, the only dec. on these sherds observed.

Chambers (1933–1934:15, 18) makes several statements about Trench 21, providing information on its location as well as its contents:

Trench 21 (Smith crew) (EW) bends to south to avoid SE cor. of Mound D. About 25 ft. from base of Mound D in Tr. 21 at depth of 10 in. a neck sherd bearing a handle with 2 knobs, one above the other, was uncovered. The inner half of the ware was brick red, the outer half dark brown. Several sherds of this vessel found here.
10 ft. SW of stake W 4+20 / S 0+80 in Trench 21: Small pinkish [drawing of a small triangle] proj. pt. with sherds of large vessel [jar profile drawing] undecorated.
S-0+70   Trench 21 passes just south (with a bend) of Mound D
S-0+80   (a considerable amount of material came from here)

Chambers (1933–19344:27) also gives us a tally of sherds from Trench 21:

West end, Trench No. 21
—Area N of Mound B—
Decoration: One grit tempered sherd bears double row of cane-impressed punctations around rim. One shell-tempered "salt pan" sherd bearing net impression; a shell tempered sherd bearing below neck portions of a deeply incised scroll design; a shell-tempered sherd bearing this design [drawing of Barton Incised motif], incised; 30 grit tempered cordmarked sherds (none that are cordmarked in this lot are shell tempered). Two rim sherds with strap handles.

Little is said about Trenches 22 through 24, at least not by those designations. We know that Trench 24 passed through the south edge of Mound J,
which was fully excavated. We know that a posthole pattern was excavated
somewhere east of Mound D. Both Roberts (1933–1934:21) and Chambers
(1933–1934:20) recorded the spacings between these postholes (near-identity
of the entries and the fact that Chambers's entry is dated January 5 but
Roberts's entry is two-thirds of the way through his notebook indicates that
Roberts copied from Chambers's notes). Neither entry indicates precisely
where this posthole pattern was. The site map shows a posthole pattern west
of Mound D, but it is not the same pattern as the one shown in the notes.
One striking aspect of the pattern described in the notes is the statement,
made in both notebooks, that the central hole extended to 6 ft below the
surface. It was first seen 6 in below the surface, and its diameter tapered from
18 in at 1 ft below the surface to 12 in at the base. It was filled with charcoal
and ashes. The other holes were said to have diameters of about 11 in, but no
depths were given for them.

In the site map, I have depicted all these trenches as being 5 ft wide, because the term *trench* implies a narrow excavation and because the field photographs do not reveal wide swaths of excavation. However, we do not actually know how wide the trenches were. There are hints in the notes that some
trenches—or portions of them—may have been 10 ft or even 20 ft wide; see,
for example, the coordinates "S-0+70 S-0+80" listed beside an entry for Trench
21 (quoted earlier). We also do not know how long the trenches were. I have
shown them extending from the bluff edge to the far side of the ridge, but
in most cases this is mere conjecture.

Large Exposure Southwest of Mound A (see Figure 4.5)

The most interesting architecture found in the 1933–1934 excavations lay
southwest of Mound A. There must have been one or more initial trenches
in this area, in which postmolds were seen. Once a line of postmolds was
seen, Roberts apparently had the workers follow it. That is not stated anywhere in the notes, but the excavation photos (e.g., Figure 4.6) show a hodge-
podge of intersecting excavation trenches, at different levels, pursuing different lines of postholes. A portion of the area was exposed in a broad excavation,
but I have found no record of the boundaries of the excavated area. Several
wall trenches, alignments of postmolds, and a welter of other postmolds and
features were mapped, including a line of postmolds and a wall trench that
appear to outline a long, straight-sided, round-ended building.

The long, round-ended building was dubbed the "temple" by Roberts,
though this seems to have no basis other than the obvious fact that it is not

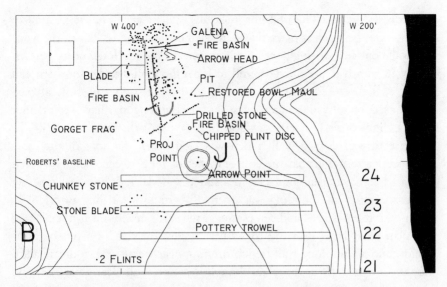

Figure 4.5. Detail of site map showing excavation southwest of Mound A

Figure 4.6. F. H. H. Roberts standing amidst excavated postmold patterns southwest of Mound A, looking southeast (National Anthropological Archives, Smithsonian Institution, negative no. 79-12,900)

an ordinary house. The building measures 4.8 m wide and at least 18 m long—it not being clear precisely where the northern end is. Part of the western wall consisted of singly set posts, but toward the south the posts were set in a wall trench that curved around to form the semi-circular southern end of the structure. A second short curved wall trench and a possibly aligned straight section of wall trench suggest that the building may have been rebuilt with a slight offset. Roberts says (Stirling 1935:396) that the outline of the short section of curved wall trench was seen below the floor of the more complete pattern and that the couple inches of fill between these two levels appeared to have been emplaced in a single episode. It is not clear whether the east side of the building was open. Roberts says (Stirling 1935:396) "a short entrance passage had been placed at the east side," but it is not clear on the plan what he is referring to. Other straight lines and clusters of postmolds, and a 10-m-long wall trench running nearly east-west, indicate additional constructions in this area, though it is not at all clear what sizes and shapes of structures are represented or what the chronological order of the structures is. In addition to the dozens of postmolds, there were three hearths and at least two pits; none of them can be securely connected to any of the structures.

Two of the hearths were circular, clay-lined fire basins of the sort Roberts found widely at the site. On the south side of one of these circular hearths—by process of elimination it must be the northernmost one shown in Figure 4.5—there was "an area of burned material suggestive of a cane mat" (Roberts 1933–1934:7). The southernmost hearth or fire basin in Figure 4.5 was described as "1 foot deep, 30 [inches] inside diameter at top, burned wall 3 [inches] thick, bowl shaped" (Roberts 1933–1934:22). The third fire basin was unusual in having a shallower extension projecting southwest from the central circular basin. The top of this hearth was 3½ ft below the surface, and the hearth itself was 2 ft 3 in in diameter (according to Chambers [1933–1934:23]; according to Roberts [1933–1934:23] it was 1 ft in diameter but this must be an error) and 18 in deep. The projecting wing was 2 ft long. Like one of the other hearths in this area, "the basin and extension were lined with a thin layer of charred matting" (Chambers 1933–1934:23). Chambers's notebook also indicates that a photograph was taken of this hearth, but I have not seen one that matches this description.

Few artifacts were recovered from this area. They include a chipped flint chisel or wedge (FS 177), which was initially catalogued as an arrowhead. A so-called maul (FS 154) consists of two adjoining fragments of a greenstone ax with an oval cross-section. The poll, which is present, is not battered, so it is not clear why this was called a maul. A "chipped flint disc" (FS 42) turns out to be a discoidal of mudstone or very fine sandstone, 2.5 cm diameter by

1.1 cm thick, bi-pitted, with two parallel incised lines crossing the center of one face. The incised lines look fresh, and I suspect they were created by an excavator's shovel hitting the stone twice, although such incised lines on crude discoidals are not unknown in the region. A "drilled stone object—frag" (FS 69) is given a provenience in this area in the Field Catalogue, but this item was not included in the formal accession of artifacts into the Smithsonian collection. Of more interest is a fragment of a gorget or pendant with an oval cross-section perforated by at least one drilled hole (FS 127). The raw material is a dark gray metamorphic of some sort. Not enough of the original object is present to determine what its overall shape was. The only other item listed in the Field Catalogue as coming from this area is a "restorable bowl."

The "restorable bowl" (FS 107) has, in fact, been restored and is shown in Figure 4.7. Because no broken edges are exposed, I am not certain what the tempering agent is; I initially diagnosed it as having fine shell, but this was mostly because of the absence of any visible temper particles. The surface color is red to orange; it does not appear to be slipped, but the underlying paste is pale gray. The shape of this vessel, with its internally constricted, broad, beveled lip, was recognized by James B. Griffin (personal communication) as the form he had christened Brangenburg Plain (Griffin 1952:117v, 118; Griffin and Morgan 1941: Pl. 49). Kenneth Farnsworth has made an exhaustive study of Brangenburg pots, documenting 306 vessels and rims from 75 sites in Illinois and adjacent states. This distinctive bowl shape occurs in Middle Woodland contexts, primarily in the lower Illinois River valley (A.D. 100–300) and a little later in the Wabash valley (ca. A.D. 300–400). Though Griffin named this pottery Brangenburg Plain, Farnsworth (personal communication) notes that "the term 'Brangenburg Plain' is a highly misleading type name for these Hopewell series vessels in that 43–44 percent of the rims from both areas [Illinois and Wabash valleys] are decorated in some fashion. Over 20 percent of the vessels are red-slipped. Others are incised or stamped (10 vessels), negative painted (30 vessels), or have petaled rim forms (12 vessels)."

Like many of its congeners, the Brangenburg bowl from Shiloh does have some decoration. One portion of the lip has engraved cross-hatching (see Figure 4.7). The cross-hatching is somewhat sloppy and also somewhat abraded and does not form any design I recognize. Chambers's (1933–1934:24) field notes give unusually specific provenience for this vessel:

—Area N of Mound J—
N-0+5′6″/W-3+41′6″
3′4″ deep (top of pit) Pit 15″ deep; diam. 1′6″ Pit contained sherds of restorable dec. vessel [here a small drawing of hatched panels and dots, which does not

Figure 4.7. Bowl with Brangenburg rim (A385501)

greatly resemble the Brangenburg pot], stone implements, broken celt, all showing signs of burning. Hole in very hard compact dirt (Below 2 ½ ft. level),
labeled *Bottom Layer.* Sherds of like kind found in this same stratum. This pit
contained charcoal & ashes & the margin showed signs of fire.

It is not terribly surprising to find at Shiloh a vessel that, on stylistic
grounds, likely has a Middle Woodland date. There are, after all, other sherds
of likely Middle Woodland date (e.g., the limestone-tempered ware) and even
Archaic artifacts. A major Middle Woodland mound center, the Savannah
site (Welch 1998a), is only 10 km away. The vessel was found in a feature
whose top was more than 3 ft below the surface, so it seems safe to conclude
that the pot was used, broken, and discarded by Middle Woodland occupants
at the site long before the Mississippian occupation that is the principal focus
of this report.

One other artifact is mentioned in the field notes as having been found in this area, though it does not appear in the Field Catalogue. Chambers's field notes (1933–1934:43) mention a "tiny bit of galena" at the "bottom of trench (E–W)," 2 ft below surface. The specified location puts the galena within a few inches of, or actually within, the east-west wall trench that runs near the northern end of the excavated area. I assume, therefore, that it is the wall trench rather than an excavation trench that Chambers's notebook refers to.

All told, this area presents us with several important items of information. First, some sort of unusually long building was present at this part of the site. It may have been rebuilt at least once. Even though there were three hearths in this area, none of them is in a position that suggests that it was inside this long building. Therefore, most likely there were other kinds of buildings here, too, at different times. Not all of the buildings in this area were necessarily of Mississippian date, for one feature contained a Middle Woodland bowl. The depth of archaeological deposits here reaches at least a meter, and pits extend even below that. Why this part of the site has an accumulation of deposits while other parts of the site clearly eroded during the Mississippian occupation (see Chapter 5) is not clear. As will be explained later in this chapter, there is reason to believe parts of the plaza area to the west had been filled in to create a more level surface. Perhaps the leveling extended this far eastward, or perhaps the apron that was built around the base of Mound A extends over this area as well.

Apron West of Mound A (see Figure 4.8)

The most dramatic consequence of Roberts's failure to report the results of the 1933–1934 excavations in any detail came in 1978, when archaeologists under the direction of John Ehrenhard sank a test excavation through Mound A to find out what was underneath it. Because they had not yet encountered deposits that appeared to be anything other than mound fill, Ehrenhard's crew continued excavating to 1.8 m below where they had expected to find the base of the mound. At that point they ran out of time and were left mystified as to why they had not found the base of the mound. What they did not know, because it had not been published, is that the level surface around Mound A is not the natural ground surface. It is an artificial apron of fill as much as 2 m thick. Roberts discovered this by excavating a set of trenches on the west side of the mound. He drew two profiles, albeit not very detailed, one east-west and one north-south, and described the stratigraphy in his notebook. Field photographs, plus the coordinates on the profile drawing, help fix the locations of the trenches.

There were at least five trenches, each 5 ft wide, excavated west of Mound

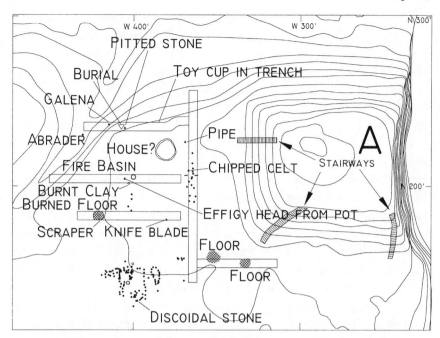

Figure 4.8. Detail of site map showing excavations west of Mound A

A. A north-south trench (shown partially backfilled in Figure 4.9) extended approximately 30–35 m along the west side of the mound, with the west side of the trench being the W372 line. Three trenches extended to the west (see Figure 4.10) and another ran east (visible at the near right of the photograph at the bottom of page 308 of the 50th anniversary issue of *American Antiquity* (vol. 50, no. 2). Two of the trenches running west apparently stopped just short of intersecting the north-south trench; in one case (the middle trench) this was because of a large tree stump in the way. During excavations in 2001, National Park Service archaeologists found what appears to be an additional north-south trench (not shown in Figure 4.8) running northward from near the western end of the middle east-west trench (Anderson and Cornelison 2001:15), though no such trench is visible in any of the field photographs. The northernmost of the east-west trenches intersected the main north-south trench with an offset to avoid a large tree, still standing until 2003, whose distinctive bark pattern helped identify the location of several of the field photographs (visible in the center of Figure 4.9 and on the near right of Figure 4.10). Profiles (see Figure 4.11) were drawn along the W372 line and along the south wall of the northernmost east-west trench. Though not very detailed, the profile drawings substantiate the uncharacteristically detailed remarks Roberts (1933–1934:28–30) wrote about what he saw in these trenches:

Figure 4.9. Trench in apron west of Mound A, 1933–1934 (National Anthropological Archives, Smithsonian Institution, negative no. 79-12,651)

At {N-2+3 / W-4+0}, the remains of a fire basin 5′ 11″ below the present ground level. This seems to be on old ground level just west of Mound A. The material above is a fill which suggests a kind of apron to the west of Mound A. The old ground level was apparently a hard yellow clay. The fill above this for 3′ 4″ consists of a grayish clay filled with bits of yellow ochre, an occasional mussel shell, some charcoal, burned pebbles etc. At the top of the stratum is a 1″ layer or streak of humus containing charcoal, bone fragments etc. This layer was apparently a surface of occupation and on the same level as the burned "pavement" around Mound A. Above this is a 34″ layer of darker earth filled with charcoal, red & yellow ochre, bits of red earth (burned clay) shell fragments, occasional bone fragments, burned rocks.

Both this stratum and the 3′ 4″ one just above the fire basin suggest a deposition occurring all at one time. The thin dark streak between is very suggestive of a level of occupation (see previous on preceding page). Possibly denotes an interval between deposition of two major strata. On this level, just S.W. from basin 3′ 3″ above the line [?] a large chunk of burned clay was 21″ by 30″ and

Figure 4.10. Excavation trenches west of Mound A, 1933–1934 (National Anthropological Archives, Smithsonian Institution, negative no. 79-12,681)

7″ thick. In the old ground level south of fire basin a number of post holes running roughly on line W-4+2 & lying between N-0+80 and N-2+0. Do not know whether they have any connection with basin.

    Basin only about half present. West side broken away.

In addition to the profile drawings, Roberts took several photographs to document the findings in these trenches. The hearth with the west side broken away (see quotation above) was photographed, and there is a close-up of the "thin dark streak" sandwiched between the two fill layers. Roberts may also have photographed the layer containing mussel shells depicted in the east-west profile, inasmuch as there is a photograph (NAA neg. no. 79-12,692) showing the wall of an excavation in which mussel shells are visible in a deep layer, but unfortunately the photo has no identifiable landmark that clarifies its location.

A part of the excavation west of Mound A that was not well documented is a roughly square cluster of postmolds shown southwest of the excavation trenches. The posts appear to form a straight-walled structure 4.3 m wide and 4.0–4.8 m long, it not being clear where the southern wall is. Immediately to

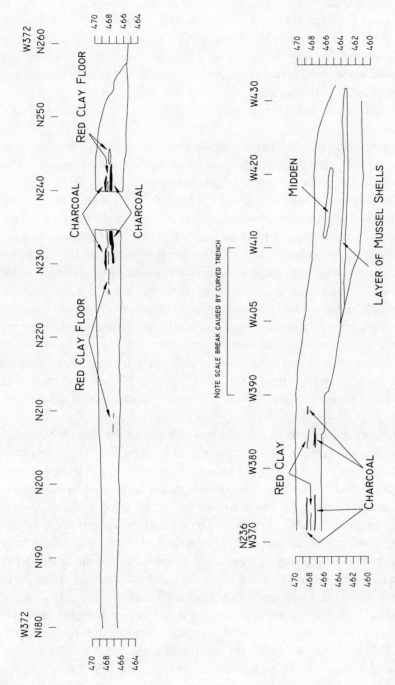

Figure 4.11. Stratigraphic profiles west of Mound A

the east of this structure is an intriguing oval pattern of postmolds, 1.3 × 3.2 m, that presumably was a granary or free-standing structure. Whatever it was, it and the square building beside it would probably have been used by particularly important people or for important activities, given the proximity of Mound A. The only artifact specifically provenienced to this area is a "discoidal stone" (actually a round hammerstone) found 15 inches below surface at the edge of the postmold pattern. Whether it is actually related to the structure(s) is not clear, because the depth of the floor of the building is not known.

Despite being among the best-documented excavations at the site, there are a couple of puzzles about what was found in the apron excavations. The site map (see Figure 4.8) shows a rough, double-line circle of 3.4 m diameter west of the north-south trench. I have labeled this "House?" because the double line looks like the convention Roberts used to draw wall trenches. However, the notes do not mention such a feature in this location, and the field photographs do not show any excavation at this location. It may be that Roberts interpreted a topographic rise here as the remains of a house, but this is a guess. The site map also shows four postmolds in a rough line between the middle and southern trenches west of the north-south trench; these are likely the "post holes running roughly on line W-4+2" mentioned in Roberts's notes (1933–1934:29). The field photographs do not reveal any excavation at the location of these postmolds, nor are they in the location of the possible north-south excavation trench seen during the 2001 NPS excavation, so here as in other portions of the site the true extent of excavations remains unknown.

The deep excavations in this apron of fill around the base of Mound A provided a substantial sample of pottery, most of which has depth provenience. The depths were recorded as surface, top section, and second section. The distinction between top and second section is specified in Chambers's notebook in terms of feet below surface (the actual number of feet declines to the west, as does the slope of the apron's surface) and appears to correspond to the apron's upper and lower fill episodes. Unfortunately, the artifacts from the premound soil apparently were not distinguished from the lower part of the apron, so the second section counts may include some of the deposits beneath the apron. The pottery counts are tabulated in Table 4.3. The relative abundances of different types of pottery in the two sections are strikingly similar, and both layers of the apron have predominantly shell-tempered pottery. This clearly demonstrates that by the time the apron was built, shell-tempered pottery was the dominant ware, at least among the people who discarded broken pottery in the location from which the apron's fill was dug. It is worth emphasizing that this does not necessarily mean that shell-tempering

Table 4.3 Pottery counts by depth, apron west of Mound A

Type variety	Surface	Top section	Second section	Total
Mulberry Creek Plain			2	2
Baytown Plain var. McKelvey		2	6	8
Baytown Plain var. The Fork		2	1	3
Baytown Plain var. unspecified		1		1
Mulberry Creek Cordmarked var. Coffee Landing			1	1
Mulberry Creek Cordmarked var. Mulberry Creek	5	6	6	17
Unclassified grog-tempered var. unspecified			1	1
Mississippi Plain var. Shiloh	4	64	60	128
Mississippi Plain var. unspecified	4			4
Moundville Incised var. Moundville	3	1	2	6
Barton Incised var. unspecified			2	2
Kimmswick Fabric-impressed var. Langston		2	3	5
Bell Plain var. unspecified		8	5	13
Unclassified shell-tempered var. unspecified		1		1
Unclassified shell-tempered eroded		1		1
Unclassified grog-&-shell temp var. unspecified			1	1
Unclassified temperless var. unspecified			1	1
Total	16	88	91	195

precedes the construction of Mound A itself but merely the construction of the apron. This is of particular interest because ground-penetrating radar (see Chapter 7) suggests that the apron may have been added after Mound A was built.

Other artifacts from the excavations west of Mound A include a shell-tempered elbow pipe (FS 106), undecorated; a perforated mussel shell (not in Field Catalogue; SI Acc. No. A385480); an abrader or sharpening stone (FS 166); a piece of fossil coral (FS 164); one piece of Tuscaloosa chert, one piece of sandstone, and a piece of fired daub from bags that supposedly contained only sherds; two lumps and some tiny fragments of galena (FS 159) weighing 24 g; a fragment of a greenstone ax head with a rectangular cross-section (FS 56; see Figure 3.22, lower right); a chert hoe made of banded red, gray, brown chert (possibly Tuscaloosa or weathered Ft. Payne chert); and two adjoining fragments of a large blade made of white chert (FS 58; see Figure 4.12).

One other artifact from the excavations west of Mound A is worth illustrating. It is an effigy head from the rim of a shell-tempered bowl (FS 130; see Figure 4.13). I do not know what animal is represented by this endearing "button-eared" effigy.

Before leaving the subject of artifacts from the Mound A apron, mention

Figure 4.12. Knife blade of white chert from west of Mound A (A385396)

Figure 4.13. Effigy head from shell-tempered bowl, west of Mound A (A385505)

must be made of a "toy cup" that was catalogued as coming from "W. of Mound A" at N212'6" W335. That grid coordinate is actually north and a little east of the mound. Realizing that this must have been an error, Roberts later drew a mark to indicate that the northing and westing had been reversed, and the Accession Memorandum lists the item as coming from N335 W212'6". However, that location is on the northwest corner of the summit of Mound A, where there is no record of excavation. The artifact probably did actually come from west of Mound A, because N212'6" is right in the middle of the northernmost east-west trench west of Mound A. However, W335 cannot be correct; the correct coordinate must be something between W360 and W425. So the "toy cup" probably came from somewhere in that trench, but we do not know where. The item itself is a small (5 cm diameter), crude, hemispherical pinch pot with a rim adorno that amounts to nothing more than a small knob of clay.

There is one more aspect of the excavation west of Mound A that needs to be described. In the northernmost of the east-west trenches, a human burial was encountered. The burial dates before the construction of the apron, though there is no way of knowing how much earlier it is. Chambers (1933–1934:50) recorded it as follows:

W-407 / N-235   5 ½ ft. below surface
Burial in deep trench W. of Mound A

Skull to E, damaged in discovery; flexed on left side, left leg tightly flexed against chest, right femur at rt. angles to axis of torso, heels against hips in each case. Left arm closely flexed, hand extended near left ear. Right fore-arm folded across breast, rt. hand clenched under left wrist. Skull in nearly vertical position, slightly tilted to left side. Apparently buried in shallow pit. Scattered layer of clam shell passes obliquely about a foot above the bones.

The burial card for this interment duplicates this description verbatim but adds that "this burial was in the best condition of any skeleton found during the excavations." Probably the relatively good bone preservation is due to the chemical effects of the overlying mussel shells. The NMNH Accession Memorandum for the Shiloh collection states that this skeleton was accessioned with the collection and transferred to the Division of Physical Anthropology. One of the papers documenting this transfer lists the skeleton as male, and because the paper is signed by T. Dale Stewart—a highly competent biological anthropologist—we can have reasonable confidence in this assessment. Incidentally, this was the only human skeletal material that Roberts sent to the Smithsonian, and Dorothy Lippert (personal communication) of the

Table 4.4 Mollusk species identified from Shiloh

No.	Original identification	Current taxonomy
1	*Actinonaias carinata orbis* (Morrison)	*Actinonaias ligamentina* (Lamarck), mucket
4	*Campeloma ponderosum* (Say)	*C. decisum* (Say), pointed campeloma
1	*Cyclonaias tuberculata granifera* (Lea)	*Cyclonaias tuberculatum* (Rafinesque), purple wartyback
1	*Dromus dromas* (Lea)	*Dromus dromas* (Lea), dromedary pearlymussel
4	*Lithasia salebrosa* (Conrad)	*Lithasia salebrosa* (Conrad), muddy rocksnail
1	*Lithasia verrucosa* (Rafinesque)	*Lithasia verrucosa* (Rafinesque), varicose rocksnail
3	*Obovaria retusa* (Lamarck)	*Obovaria retusa* (Lamarck), ringpink
1	*Plethobasus cicatricoides* (Frierson)	*Plethobasus cicatricosus* (Say), white wartyback
*	*Pleurobema cordatum* (Rafinesque)	*Pleurobema cordatum* (Rafinesque), Ohio pigtoe
1	*Pleurobema plenum* (Lea)	*Pleurobema plenum* (Lea), rough pigtoe
1	*Pleurobema pyramidatum* (Lea)	*Pleurobema rubrum* (Rafinesque), pyramid pigtoe
6	*Pleurocera canaliculata* (Say)	*Pleurocera canaliculata* (Say), silty hornsnail
2*	*Quadrula metanevra* (Rafinesque)	*Quadrula metanevra* (Rafinesque), monkeyface

*The box labelled *Quadrula metanevra* has two shells of obviously different species, one of which is probably the missing *Pleurobema cordatum.*

NMNH Repatriation Office has confirmed that it is still in the collections there.

The NMNH Accession records also include a list of mollusk shells from the Shiloh site identified by the Division of Mollusks, U.S. National Museum. Shells were found in several areas of the site, but apparently the most extensive deposit of them was the "layer of clam shell" mentioned as overlying the burial beneath the apron west of Mound A. The sample sizes, original species identifications, and current taxonomy from Parmalee and Bogan (1998) and Turgeon et al. (1988) are listed in Table 4.4. The species listed generally favor medium to strong currents, firm sand and gravel bottoms, and depths ranging between 3 and 24 ft.

The excavations west of Mound A revealed several important pieces of information about the site. First, the surface around what appears to be the base of Mound A is in fact an artificial apron as much as 2 m thick. At some unknown time before the apron was constructed, at least one human burial was placed west of Mound A. There was also a clay-lined hearth, possibly associated with a building, on the premound surface. The apron itself was built in two separate stages. Shell-tempering was already the predominant way of making pottery by the time the earlier stage was built. That stage had several (not necessarily contemporaneous) buildings atop it, as shown by the two separate fired floor areas encountered southwest of the mound. This surface was occupied long enough for a humic horizon and a sheet midden to accumulate. The later stage apparently also had at least one building, a square or rectangular structure at the southwest corner, and possibly another, the puzzling double-line circle drawn on the site map. It therefore is clear that the surface of the apron was not open space but was intensively used. This is just one of the ways in which the current, vacant appearance of the site belies its appearance in the occupation's heyday.

Trenches in the Plaza Area (see Figure 4.14)

This section of the report lumps together a large number of excavation areas that, for the most part, are poorly documented. The portion of the site under discussion is essentially the area lying between the park road and a line drawn between Mounds D and E (trenches in Mounds E and F will be described elsewhere). Throughout this area the field notes refer to far fewer excavation units than the field photographs reveal. The site map shows only the excavation units specifically mentioned in the field notes or Field Catalogue, and these units are drawn as 20-x-20-ft squares unless the records indicate other sizes or shapes. I have made no effort to show on the site map all the excavations evident in the field photographs because of the difficulty of determining precisely what their coordinates are. Furthermore, test excavations in 1999 revealed that there were even more excavation trenches than the field photographs reveal. Given the poor-to-nonexistent documentation for so many units, it seems pointless to attempt a unit-by-unit description of the work. Instead, this section of the report summarizes what we know about this large portion of the site. My discussion will move counterclockwise starting near Mound E.

South of Mound E there was a long trench more or less on the N200 line. The qualifier "more or less" is required because photographs reveal that the trench was not completely straight, and there are mentions of excavations both north and south of this line. There may have been more than one trench in this area. Southwest of Mound E, the trench cut through a deep deposit that Roberts (1933–1934:10) called a "small mound . . . composed largely of clay, burned sand, charcoal." A patch of burned floor 2.7 m wide clearly indicates the presence of a building there.

Farther to the southwest, roughly halfway between Mounds E and F, excavations revealed a scatter of postmolds. No clear building outline is recognizable, but the 1933–1934 composite map shows a house mound at this location as well as a string of others between Mounds E and F.

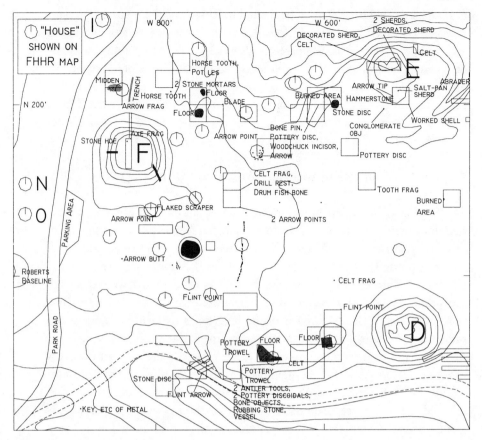

Figure 4.14. Detail of site map showing excavations in the plaza area

North of Mound F the excavators found burned floors, a trench of dis-turbed dirt 9 m long (the field notes do not say whether this was thought to be prehistoric or recent), and a midden deposit that Chambers (1933–1934: 21) said was deepest along the N220 line at W850. Apparently quite a lot of the area north of Mound F was excavated, but unfortunately none of the field photographs show this portion of the site. The land surface north of Mound F slopes to the north, and the depth of deposits here may represent either accumulating wash off the mound or perhaps intentional fill deposits such as are present elsewhere in the plaza area.

Southwest of Mound F, the area of the current parking lot was completely excavated. No artifacts were catalogued from this area, and the character of the deposits here was not described by either archaeologist.

South and southeast of Mound F there was a great deal of excavation, as revealed by the field photographs (e.g., Figure 4.1). Roberts refers to "series of trenches" in this area, and the field photographs reveal at least three and probably four trenches running east-west. The 1933–1934 composite map does not have any features plotted in this area but does have several house mounds indicated. It is a little puzzling why so much effort was expended in this area, given the dearth of noteworthy results.

It is much more obvious why a great deal of excavation was carried out west of Mound D, because there the archaeologists encountered deep and complex deposits. Regrettably, these deposits are not described very clearly. Running west from Mound D, there is a slightly elevated ridge which, it turns out, is not natural. The ridge is composed of deposits as much as 3–3.5 ft (1 m) deep. Some of the deposits consist of the collapsed remains of a series of houses, at least some of which burned so intensely as to fire their clay floors over wide areas. Roberts (1933–1934:6) describes these houses as follows:

> Series of house floors running East to West in area west of Mound D. Large chunks of burned plaster at house sites show imprints of poles. Also find fragments of burned cane. Floor areas seem to run in roughly circular form but can't be too sure of this. One or two suggestions of a corner but nothing real definite.
>
> On two of floors found some pieces of mica. Edges show cutting by native methods.

Chambers tells us that the burned floors were found at depths around 10 in (Chambers 1933–1934:11) and that the mica was found on the "floors of first and second structures west of Mound D" (Chambers 1933–1934:16). Whether the first and second structures are the two whose burned floors are shown on the site map, or whether there are additional structures west of Mound D, is not known.

To the west of the structures, deep trenches revealed artificial fill deposits, commencing with a ridge of clay:

> In this area in one trench a number of fossil horse teeth were found 2 feet below present ground level. They were in made earth. No other fossil bones. The teeth must have been picked up and carried in by Indians. In this area one trench cut through a bed of white clay. Trench bottom [?] hard, potsherds in bottom of trench beneath hard-packed clay. Clay in definite ridge outline, (Photo), possibly a dyke of some sort. (Roberts 1933–1934:5)

Profile drawings of two trenches through the "made earth" west of Mound D do indeed support the interpretation that these deposits are artificial. For both trenches, all four walls were profiled, and the drawings are presented in

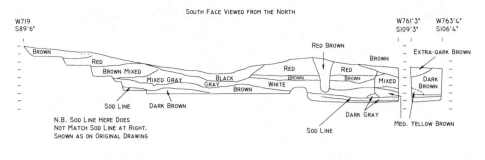

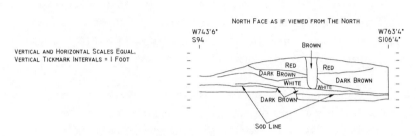

Figure 4.15. Vertical sections of excavation trench I west of Mound D

Figures 4.15 and 4.16. These trenches are visible on the site map (lower center of Figure 4.14) as the two parallel trenches diagonal to the site grid. Trench I is the longer, northern trench and II the southern one. The profiles of both trenches show multiple layers of deposits atop the "sod line." Chambers (1933–1934:29) noted that "mixed dirt found at E end of trench extends to depth of 4 [ft] 8 [in]" and "sherds found chiefly at bottom of this mixed dirt." Some of the layers have level surfaces with features that are the size and shape of postholes or wall trenches, which suggests that deposits were laid down at this periphery of the plaza in order to create level surfaces for structures.

One last detail about the deposits west of Mound D needs mention. Some human teeth and "faint traces of additional bone fragments" were found in an oval pit somewhere west of the mound (Roberts 1933–1934:13). No more precise provenience is given, nor is there any mention of the size of this oval pit. Roberts's conclusion was that "Nothing of consequence of of [sic] sufficient character to indicate burial" (1933–1934:13).

Continuing on the counterclockwise journey around the plaza area, we come to the area north of Mound D. Field photographs reveal multiple trenches here, but the excavation notes are largely silent about what was found. The Field Catalogue does not list any artifacts from this area, either.

Finally, out in the center of the plaza between Mounds D and F, the com-

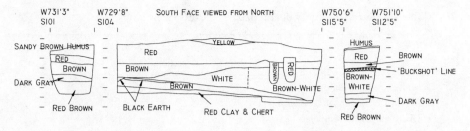

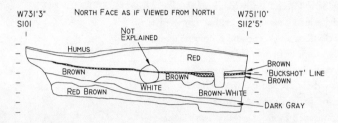

Figure 4.16. Vertical sections of excavation trench II west of Mound D

posite site map shows a line of postmolds running north-south. Because all the field photographs show that trenching in this area generally ran east-west, it is likely that an unrecorded east-west trench intersected this line of post-molds somewhere and that the excavators then followed the line. The notes do not mention this alignment, so we do not know what the size and spacing of the posts were. The line extends 21.5 m, and there is no indication of any parallel line. Thus, it does not appear to be part of a building but is instead a fence of some sort. Perhaps it enclosed the site at an earlier, smaller stage of development, or perhaps it was a screen to enclose a portion of the plaza. Other scenarios can be proposed, too, but at this point I have insufficient information to choose among them.

Roughly half the artifacts recovered from the site came from the plaza area, as that term is used here. The distribution of pottery by depth is presented in Table 4.5. Most of the sherds in that tabulation come from trenches south of Mound E. It is not clear what depth measurements correspond to the "top section" and "second section" designations. One possible answer comes from Chambers's (1933–1934:42) mention on February 5 that "Joe Dillon has been marking for Hagy's crew as follows: -Top or first layer, surface to 12 or 18 in.; Second layer, 12 or 18 in. to 3 ft.; below 3 ft, the sacks have depth indicated." A month before that notebook entry, Hagy's crew had been in this general part of the plaza, but unfortunately there is no record whether it was Hagy's crew that excavated the trenches south of Mound E from which

Table 4.5 Pottery counts by depth, plaza area excavations

Type, *var.*	Top section	Second section	Other	Total
Mulberry Creek Plain	1	2		3
Baldwin Plain *var. Miller Slough*	2			2
Unclassified sand-tempered		1		1
Baytown Plain *var. McKelvey*	11	39	1	51
Baytown Plain *var. The Fork*	1			1
Mulberry Creek Cordmarked *var. Coffee Landing*	4	6		10
Mulberry Creek Cordmarked *var. Mulberry Creek*	81	233	2	316
Unclassified grog-and-limestone tempered		1		1
Unclassified sand-grog-and-limestone tempered	2			2
Mississippi Plain *var. Shiloh*	42	52	2	96
Moundville Incised *var. Moundville*		2	1 (3.5 ft)	3
Moundville Incised *var. Snows Bend*		1		1
Barton Incised *var. unspecified*			1	1
Kimmswick Fabric-impressed *var. Langston*	1	5		6
Bell Plain *var. unspecified*	3	22	2	27
Mound Place Incised *var. unspecified*		2		2
Powell Plain			4	4
Ramey Incised			2	2
Unclassified shell-tempered *var. unspecified*		9	1	10
Unclassified shell-tempered eroded	2	15		17
Unclassified grog-&-shell temp *var. unspecified*		1		1
Total	150	391	16	557

most of the pottery comes. Given the uncertainty about absolute depths, we will continue to employ the terms "top section" and "second section."

The striking thing about the sherds tallied in Table 4.5 is the predominance of grog-tempered pottery. In the Mound A apron fill, only a few tens of meters to the east of where most of these sherds were found, about one-sixth of the pottery was grog-tempered, but here about two-thirds is grog-tempered. The percentage of pottery that is grog-tempered increases slightly with depth, 66 percent in the top section and 71 percent in the second section, but given the sample sizes this change is probably not important.

The Powell Plain and Ramey Incised sherds (see Figure 3.2), along with a nondiagnostic fragment of an eared projectile point of white chert, were found in a 20-x-40-ft block west of Mound D, but the field notes give no further details about the provenience of these items.

Other artifacts from the plaza area include one Kirk corner-notched point, a Kirk stemmed point, a Brewerton corner-notched point, two Hamilton points, two Madison points, an unmodified fossil crinoid stem, the butt end of a dark gray metamorphic ax head with an oval cross-section, a pottery trowel (see Figure 6.7), and two chunkey stones (top two in Figure 2.4). There are also two items made of coquina, one a fragment of a ring or torus, the other a chunkey stone or discoidal with slightly concave faces (lower left of Figure 2.4). Two other items of ground stone have no known function. One is a piece of unidentified very dark red stone (shale? hematite?) that had been shaped to a rectangular prism, then drilled longitudinally. The item split down the longitudinal hole, and only one-half was found (second up from bottom right in Figure 2.4). This was originally catalogued as an "arrow straightener" but could be a fragment of an atlatl weight, a fragment of a stone pipe, or something else. And finally, there is an artifact catalogued as a "drill rest" made of red shale (bottom right of Figure 2.4). For a drill rest, it is very nicely made of a fairly soft stone, but I can offer no other conjectures about its function.

Based on the excavations in the plaza area, it is clear that the apron around the base of Mound A is not the only part of the site in which fill was deposited to build up or to level areas. With this information in hand, one notices, while walking around the plaza, other areas where the surface has suspiciously abrupt changes of topography and areas where the general slope toward the bluff is reversed. It may well be that there was a *lot* of filling in and around the plaza. We know that massive fills were deposited to expand or level plazas at Cahokia, Etowah, and Moundville, and though Shiloh is quite a bit smaller than those sites we should not dismiss the possibility that the visible mounds are not the only artificial deposits at the site. That the plaza area is as uneven as it is may indicate that abandonment of the site occurred before the leveling project was complete.

The other major point to be made about the plaza excavations is that we clearly do not know where all the excavations were. Much of the plaza area has been excavated, but which parts are intact and which are not will have to be assessed by remote sensing or test excavations. The 1933–1934 records simply do not tell us enough about the locations of units.

House Mounds (see Figure 4.17)

Roberts did not use the term *house mounds,* which I have adapted from Nash's "residence mound" (Nash 1968). However, Roberts did recognize that there were numerous small mounds at the site, each containing the remains of a house. His excavation trenches had intersected several of them, and it looks

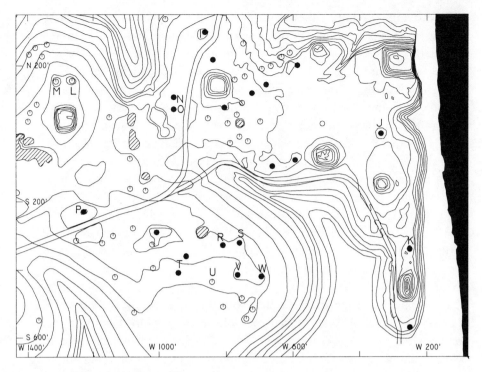

Figure 4.17. Detail of site map showing excavated house mounds (solid circles)

as though he later dug into several more to verify that these mounds did indeed usually contain houses. In Figure 4.17, I have placed small solid circles on all the small mounds Roberts is known to have dug into. The documents show that Roberts excavated into mounds I, J, K, O, P, Q, R, S, V, W, a mound that may be T, and several that were not assigned letters. It is possible that he excavated into all 16 mounds to which he assigned letters (H–W). Mounds J, P, R, S, and W were apparently excavated completely; the rest may only have had trenches excavated into them. Only Mounds I, J, and P had plan maps drawn. Profiles were drawn for Mounds I, V, and R. The area of most intensive excavation of house mounds is the arm of land on the far side of the ravine west of Mound C (see Figure 4.18).

One of the few aspects of the 1933–1934 excavations that Roberts's brief publications described well were the houses. The field records substantiate nearly all the details provided in the published description of houses:

The houses were found to have been round in outline, with walls of wattle and daub construction. This was evidenced by the fact that there were large quan-

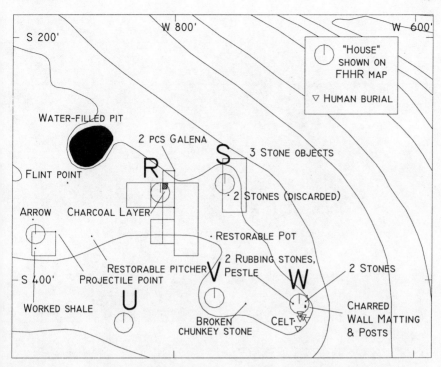

Figure 4.18. Detail of site map showing excavations in vicinity of Mounds R–W

tities of burned clay bearing the impression of poles and cane and even, in some cases, small sections of cane walls in the debris removed from the floors of a number of houses which had been destroyed by fire. The wall of each house was supported by a series of heavy posts, 2 to 3 inches in diameter, placed at intervals of approximately 4 feet around the periphery. The spaces between these upright timbers were filled by panels of cane strips [see Figure 4.19]. The latter, averaging ½ inch in width and 3/16 inch thick, were placed side by side in vertical position. In most cases they touched along their edges. The vertical strips were reinforced by a series of horizontal canes spaced approximately 1 foot apart and extending from post to post. The horizontal and vertical pieces were not interwoven, and there was nothing to show how the horizontal ones were held in place, although indications were that they had been on the outside of the wall. The canes were covered with a thick coating of mud plaster. Where indications of an entry or doorway were present they were invariably on the east to southeast side. Two of the structures had had a passageway leading to the doorway. The only interior feature noted was that of a shallow, circular fire basin in the center of the hard-packed floor. A few

Figure 4.19. Panel of charred cane strips from wall of burned house in Mound W (National Anthropological Archives, Smithsonian Institution, negative no. 79-12,710)

examples had a raised rim of mud plaster, but most of them were merely depressions in the floor. The average house was 16 feet in diameter and, judging from burned posts in a number of those uncovered, the walls were approximately 8 feet high. The floor was on or slightly below the ground level. Where depressed, this was no doubt due to constant sweeping of the area. There was no indication of a pit dwelling. The mounds covering the sites of many of these structures were merely the result of debris accumulating around the fallen walls and roofs. Practically every small mound had a depression near the center. This feature was due in part, no doubt, to the fire basin, but was sufficiently pronounced to suggest that there was a opening in the roof above the fireplace. (Stirling 1935:395)

Although nearly every element of this description is substantiated by the field records, there are a few discrepancies. By "entrance passage" Roberts apparently meant straight, parallel-sided passageways protruding orthogonally from the doorway. Though he says two instances of such passages were found, the field records document only one of them, in Mound P. A floor plan of Mound P was drawn and is reproduced here as Figure 4.20. The passageway, only one wall of which is evident, is clearly on the west side, not on the south or southeast.

The plan of the Mound P house also clearly shows that a portion of the wall was built by setting posts in a wall trench. Other segments of wall trenches were mapped elsewhere at the site. Thus, the implication that all house posts were individually set is not accurate, though it appears that in most instances they were.

Another, minor quibble is that it is not clear that all houses were round. The postmold pattern southwest of Mound A (see Figure 4.8), for example, clearly has three straight walls and two clear corners.

As for the house floors being at or slightly below ground level, the reality is more complex. Near the end of his field notebook, Roberts (1933–1934:30) observed that "House mounds in most cases seem to be at high points of ground. Houses built on rises in each case (?)." This would seem to imply that the floors were above the general level of the surrounding ground. Vertical profiles across Mound R (see Figure 4.21) show the floor clearly, and the floor of this house appears to be at about the level of the surrounding ground. On the other hand, the floor of the house in Mound I (see Figures 4.22 and 4.23) appears to be pedestalled above the surrounding surface. And in Mound V (see Figure 4.24), it is not clear where the floor is. The relationship between house floors and the surrounding surface is discussed in greater detail in the next two chapters, and here it suffices to say that the relationship is not uniform.

The only house floor that was completely exposed and photographed was Mound J, near the bluff south of Mound A. There is no photo of Mound J before excavation began, so we do not know how much overburden was removed, but the floor appears to be at about the level of the surrounding ground surface. What is shocking about the floor, however, is how uneven it

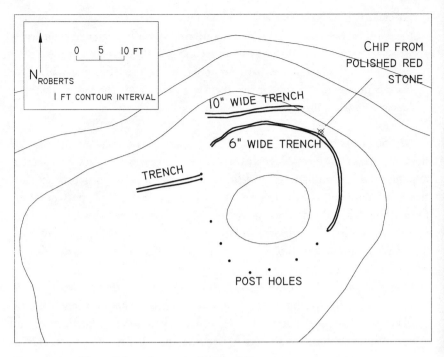

Figure 4.20. Plan of floor features of Mound P

is (see Figure 4.25). That surface is shown in half a dozen photographs, including several with men in suits posed beside it, so this clearly was the "finished product" rather than merely a moment of unevenness during the excavation. I know of no other Mississippian house floors that are so uneven, except possibly the one we partially excavated in Mound N in 1999 (see Chapter 6). Neither Roberts nor Chambers comments in his notebook about floors being even or uneven, so it is not clear whether Mound J is representative of floors elsewhere at the site.

Only one of the artifacts found during excavations of house mounds is noted to have been found on a floor. This is a bi-pitted sandstone nutting stone, found on the floor of Mound S. Excavations in and around the houses from Mound W to south of Mound Q turned up 14 other artifacts, only 6 of which have vertical provenience. A Mill Creek chert hoe, which was catalogued as a "stone axe," came from a depth of 12 in, on or beside a house mound south of Mound Q. A broken chunkey stone, made of quartzite, was found in the "First Layer" between Mounds V and W. This probably means it came from no more than 12 to 18 in below surface. Four complete chunkey stones were found in Mound R 36 in below surface "lying in a row running to east from [or form?] line at bottom of mound" (Roberts 1933–4:10). The

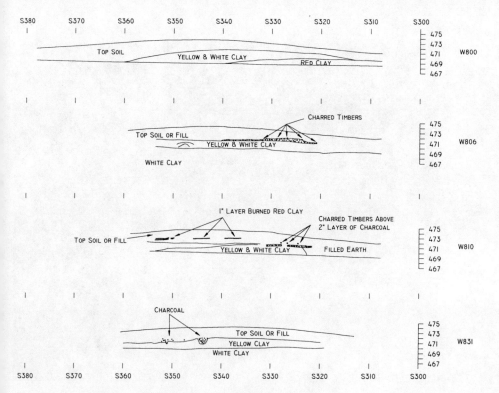

Figure 4.21. Vertical profiles north-south across Mound R

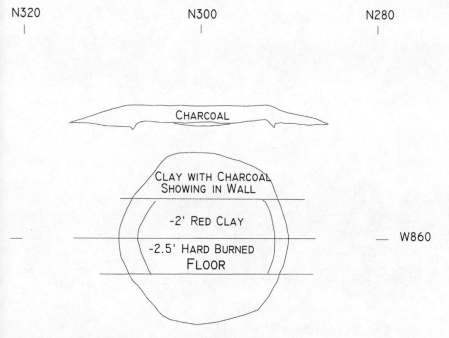

Figure 4.22. Vertical section and plan of Mound I

Figure 4.23. Vertical section of Mound I, looking northeast (National Anthropological Archives, Smithsonian Institution, negative no. 79-12,648)

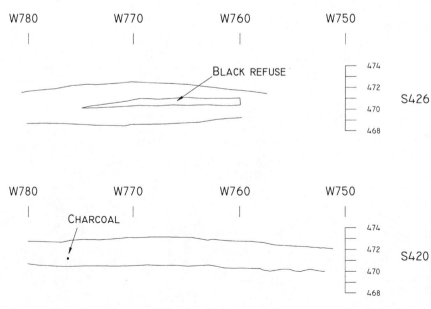

Figure 4.24. Vertical sections of Mound V

Figure 4.25. Floor of Mound J, looking northeast (National Anthropological Archives, Smithsonian Institution, negative no. 79-12,686)

four stones are similar in form and size (see Figure 4.26), have pits at the center of both sides, and are all made of quartzite. A depth of 36 in would put these artifacts below the floor in Mound R, but if they were not on a surface it is an interesting question how they came to be lying in a row.

The other artifacts found in the Mound R–W vicinity are a miscellany of chipped and ground stone. One ax head (catalogued as a "scraper") is made of greenstone and has an oval cross-section; another is made of light gray metamorphic stone and has a rectangular cross-section. The projectile points include one Madison and one Decatur point, the latter an Early Archaic type. The Madison point is made of a gray chert or agate, the Decatur point of Tuscaloosa chert. Another item, originally catalogued as a "projectile point," is an expanded base for a drill or awl. And there is a fragment of the blade of a projectile point made of a medium gray chert with white flecks; the blade edge has beautifully flaked tiny serrations. The only other artifact from this area is a piece of worked red ocher, found with Burial 2 in Mound W.

It is not uncommon to find burials under and around Mississippian houses in the Southeast. Roberts did find several burials at various locations across the site, and several may be inside or beside houses (e.g., in Mound K, west of Mound D). One example is a burial that Roberts (1933–1934:32–33) says was found in Mound "P" at So10/W421. This grid location is hundreds of feet away from Mound P, and there is no other indication of excavation at that grid location, so either the grid location or the letter designation is erro-

Figure 4.26. Four chunkey stones from base of Mound R (A385439)

neous. In any case, the burial may have been in a house mound and is described in the following terms:

> Very fragmentary leg bones tightly flexed. Fragments of long bones from arms.
> Remainder missing. Roots of an old tree, long removed from mound, passed
> through bones, may have been responsible for disappearance of skeleton. Posi-
> tion of leg bones suggested an East placement for head. Only 1 foot beneath
> present surface.

The most clear-cut instance of burials in a house mound comes from
Mound W. This was a house mound where a structure had burned so in-

tensely that the floor was fired red. Six skeletons were found, two of them buried together. The following information is duplicated from the Burial Cards (grid locations apparently are coordinates for the skull):

Mound W Burial #1

Lying on back. Head to the east. Knees flexed upwards slightly inclined towards the south. Lower legs tight against femurs. Upper arms extended along sides of thorax, position of lower arms not determinable. Skull smashed. Ribs & vertebrae missing. Adult male. No pit, just in earth on red surface above undisturbed yellow. 1 foot below surface of ground. Located S-4+40, W-6+96.

Mound W Burial #2

Head to the east. Lying practically on back, just slightly tilted toward left side. Skull smashed in. Adult ♂, knees tightly flexed towards S.W. 1 foot beneath surface. Body lying on hard burned floor as in case of #1. Right arm along body, left arm across chest. Located W-6+91′6′, S-4+30′3″ [a piece of worked red ocher is catalogued as being found with this burial, but is not mentioned on the burial card]

Mound W Burial #3

Too fragmentary for determination of position. Just portions of long bones. Located S-4+32′6″, W-6+88′6″

Mound W Burial #4

Adult. Head to east. Very tightly flexed. Bones in poor shape. Lying on floor. 18″ below present surface. Knees flexed to the north. Lying on left side. Located S-4+31′6″, W-6+94′3″

Mound W Burials 5 & 6

Double burial, one adolescent, one young woman, approx 20 yrs. Young woman lying on left side, face to S.E. head to E. Very tightly flexed. Bones not in good state of preservation.

Smaller individual, on north side, head to the east, apparently buried on back, knees very tightly flexed pointing toward the north. Located just 1 foot south from post of house. Bones not well preserved. Both skeletons 18″ below surface, lying on top of burned area. No charcoal, no ash, nor burned clay above bones. Located S-4+28 W-6+94 (point between skulls).

The intriguing aspect of these burials is that the bodies apparently were buried lying on the house floor but only after the building burned. It is clear from the details provided for Burials 5 and 6 that none of the burned debris of the structure lay on top of the bodies despite the bodies lying on a floor that was elsewhere covered by burned debris. It is reasonable to suspect that the six people buried here had some connection with the house, perhaps as former residents. But clearly the house burned before the people were buried.

Aside from the one piece of red ocher, there were no preserved burial goods with the Mound W burials. Where such goods are present (with some of the burials in Mound C, for example), they are usually listed on the Burial Cards and are otherwise listed in the Field Catalogue. The ocher is the only item listed for the Mound W burials.

The final point to be made about the houses excavated at Shiloh also involves an absence of artifacts. In only one of the excavated house mounds, or floors exposed by trenching operations, did the excavators find an artifact lying on the floor. In a number of instances, burned floors provided unambiguous surfaces that the excavators could hardly miss seeing (and in fact did not miss), so had there been, say, smashed pots lying on the floor the excavators would have found them. They did note the discovery of every restorable pot, and in all three cases the pot fragments were found in pits rather than on floors. Given the large number of floors encountered, and especially the large number of burned floors, it is striking that all but one of these houses appear to have been cleaned of artifacts before being abandoned or burned. Removing usable artifacts before abandoning a house is not unusual. But for all the examples of burned houses to have been cleaned out before the fire suggests that most of these instances of burning were intentional, post-abandonment fires rather than accidental conflagrations.

Palisade and Miscellaneous Other Areas

Most excavating at the site was carried out in the rectangle formed by the park road, the river bluff, and the ravine edges north of E and south of D. The only known excavations outside this rectangle are several house mounds (discussed above), trenches in Mound Q, excavation of a portion of the palisade, and several other scattered locations for which excavation is mentioned.

Roberts says (Stirling 1935:396) that the palisade was "trenched in several places for a distance of several hundred feet, and the molds made in the earth by the posts of the palisade were clearly in evidence." He goes on to mention "indications of bastions or watchtowers," but the only additional description of the palisade he provides is several sentences about how a palisade goes across a small ravine. The palisade actually goes across several ravines, some of them quite large; Roberts apparently was not aware of the full extent of the palisade. The field notes do not state locations of the "several trenches" he excavated; in fact, the field notes do not mention the palisade at all. The plane-table site map shows the line of the palisade, and along that line a series of dots extends for a length of 120 m (400 ft). The most likely interpretation is that this line of dots is supposed to represent the portion of the palisade that was excavated. The dots, spaced at intervals of 1.5 to 3 m, are surely schematic representations rather than an actual representation of all the individual postmolds. The plane-table map does not show any bastions along this portion of the palisade, even though two are visible today along this same stretch. A photograph (NAA Neg. no. 79–12,668) shows some of the palisade excavation, and Figure 4.27 shows the line of dots juxtaposed against the line of the palisade and bastions as mapped with a high-precision GPS receiver in 1999.

Another excavation far away from the central plaza area is indicated by an entry in the Field Catalogue. Specimen #73 was described as "Piece ore. S. Mound F. W-9+40/W-9+60—S-8+0/S-8+20." When the artifacts were formally accessioned into the NMNH collection, this specimen was omitted with no explanation. The provenience is written very clearly in the Field Catalogue, so unless the provenience is wholly erroneous it appears that Roberts put an isolated excavation 100 m south of the excavations of Mounds W, R, and S.

Mound E Trenches (see Figure 4.28)

Precisely what parts of Mound E were excavated is impossible to tell from the surviving records. Several excavation units are mentioned in the field notes, and there are three profile drawings (bold east-west lines in Figure 4.28). None of the profile drawings is on an edge of an excavation unit mentioned in the notes. The field photographs (e.g., Figure 4.29) show multiple, closely spaced parallel trenches rather than large block excavations implied by the grid corners mentioned in the notes. It is possible that the baulks between some or all of these trenches were later removed, creating the larger blocks implied by the notes. Fortunately, the structure of the mound is a little clearer than the structure of the excavation.

Two of the profile drawings are well south of the mound's high point, but the third profile is nicely centered. Unfortunately, this is the shortest profile, extending across the top of the mound but stopping short of the mound's sloping sides. But the profile (see Figure 4.30) clearly shows the mound to have been built in at least two stages. At the base of the mound, presumably on the premound surface, there is a red clay floor. Whether the red color is the result of firing or is the color of the raw clay is not stated. The field notes sometimes use "red clay" interchangeably with "burned clay" in describing floors, but excavations on Mound A in 2001 revealed floor and mound surfaces made of unfired, bright red clays (Anderson and Cornelison 2001). In

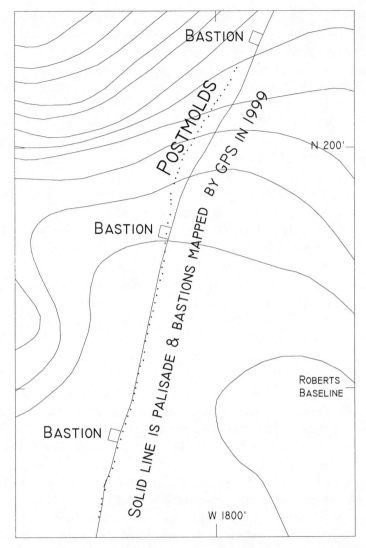

Figure 4.27. Detail of site map showing schematic representation of palisade posts

light of the findings in Mound A, it seems reasonable to assume that "red clay" usually means naturally red clay, unless the surface is also described as being burned or fired. Above the red clay floor is 3 ft (1 m) of red sandy clay, atop which is another floor. This second floor is also "red clay" and is 1 in thick. One or possibly two post holes (one is called a "refuse hole" but is the same size and shape as the post hole) originate at this level, and there is a fire basin between them. Three other post holes originate at higher levels and penetrate through the second floor. Above the second floor there is almost 4

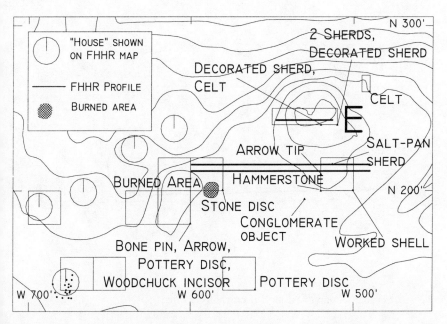

Inside the figure (map labels):

N 300'

"HOUSE" SHOWN ON FHHR MAP

—— FHHR PROFILE

BURNED AREA

2 SHERDS, DECORATED SHERD

DECORATED SHERD, CELT

CELT

E

SALT-PAN SHERD

ARROW TIP

HAMMERSTONE

N 200'

BURNED AREA

STONE DISC

CONGLOMERATE OBJECT

WORKED SHELL

BONE PIN, ARROW, POTTERY DISC, WOODCHUCK INCISOR

POTTERY DISC

W 700'   W 600'   W 500'

Figure 4.28. Detail of site map showing excavations in Mound E

Figure 4.29. Excavation trenches on Mound E, looking west with Mound F in background behind figure (National Anthropological Archives, Smithsonian Institution, negative no. 79-12,684)

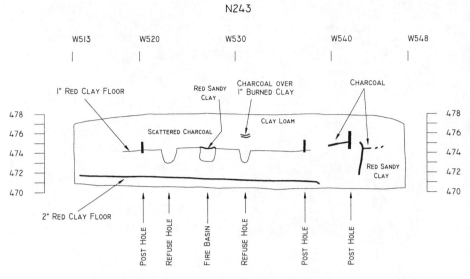

Figure 4.30. Vertical section of Mound E on the N243 line

ft (1.2 m) of clay loam containing scattered charcoal. No features are shown originating at the modern surface; bioturbation and leaching probably would have rendered them invisible had any originally been present.

The other two profiles (see Figure 4.31) are more than twice as long and, despite superficially greater complexity, tell much the same story. At the base and presumably resting on the premound surface there is an extensive "red clay floor," in one place specifically described as burned and in another place said to be 1½ in thick. Though the floor is interrupted in places, no features are drawn originating at this level. Above the red clay is a patchy deposit of "midden" and then red clay, with the red clay forming a nearly level surface 25 ft (7.5 m) wide, 2.5 to 3 ft (0.75 to 1 m) above the basal red clay floor. The wide, level surface of the upper red clay is perhaps too regular to be just an accident of the mound-building process and instead is probably the upper surface of the first mound stage. Even though the two long profiles are only 4 ft apart, the red surface is 25 ft wide in the northern profile but only 11 ft wide in the southern profile, suggesting that the southern profile is very near the edge of this red clay surface. Above this surface is another 2 ft of fill, containing no features other than a slanting lens of charcoal (in the northern of the two profiles, only). Thus, these profiles document two episodes of mound construction, just like the northernmost of the three profiles across Mound E. And like the northernmost profile, the premound surface had a red clay surface, as did the surface of the first mound stage.

Even though all three profiles reveal two episodes of construction, it is not

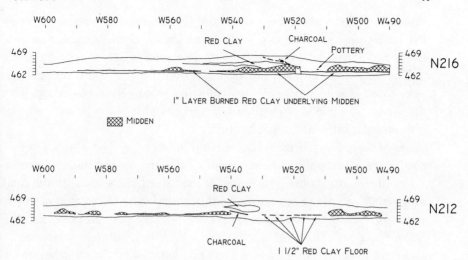

Figure 4.31. Vertical sections south of Mound E on N212 and N216 lines

completely certain that the same two episodes are shown in the northernmost profile as in the two southern profiles. We could easily conclude that the episodes were the same if the absolute elevations of the red clay floors and surfaces matched. Explicit elevations relative to an unknown arbitrary datum are written for points on the two southern profiles, showing that the surfaces do match. However, I have not been able to match these relative elevations with the surfaces in the northernmost profile, which uses absolute elevations in feet above sea level. It is possible that the basal red clay floors in the various profiles might not all be the same, for it lies 5 ft below the surface in the southern two profiles, but only 6–7 ft below the surface in the northernmost profile. According to the topographic map, the surface is 2–4 ft higher at the northern profile than in the south. Making the necessary mathematical calculations, this means that the lower red clay floor in the south is 0–3 ft lower than the lower red clay floor in the north. In other words, it might all be the same surface, or it might not. If not, the surface is higher in the north, which if true would suggest that the red clay floor there does not lie directly on the premound soil but instead on a low platform. However, there are too many uncertainties in this chain of inference to have any confidence in such a conclusion.

Few artifacts were recovered from the Mound E excavations. The pottery consists of one Moundville Incised *var. Moundville* jar rim, one Barton Incised *var. unspecified* jar rim (Figure 3.4, lower right), two Bell Plain *var. unspecified* body sherds, and an unclassified, buff-colored, shell-tempered rim sherd with broad-line incisions forming a four-line running scroll on the shoulder of a burnished, short-neck bowl (Figure 3.11, lower right, profile at left of Figure 3.12). The two Bell Plain sherds include one sherd from a gadrooned bottle and a body sherd with a notched or beaded appliqué fillet.

The only other artifacts provenienced from Mound E are two ground stone tools. One is a greenstone ax head with a rectangular cross-section. The other is an adze made of medium gray metamorphic stone; its cross-section is rectangular but with rounded corners.

Six of these seven artifacts have vertical provenience. The Moundville Incised sherd was found in the fire basin on the first mound stage, shown in the northernmost profile. The Barton Incised sherd, the sherd with the running scroll, and the ax head came from near the center of the mound in the upper fill layer. Both Bell Plain sherds came from the same area but from the "second section." This may signify the lower fill layer, but there is no specific statement to that effect. Given the very small sample size, there is not much to be said about this vertical distribution, except that, insofar as the short-neck bowl form and the running scroll motif may be later than the other pottery diagnostics at the site, it is gratifying to find this sherd in the upper fill layer of the mound.

Mound F Trench (see Figure 4.32)

The trenching of Mound F was a substantial operation. It commenced with a north-south trench that nearly spanned the mound summit. Initially 6–8 ft wide, at a depth of roughly 5 feet it was stepped down to half the initial width. Dirt from the excavation was initially shoveled onto piles lining the sides of the trench. After the trench was stepped down, a narrow cut was extended out the north side of the mound so that dirt could be carted out in wheelbarrows (see cover photograph). When finished (see Figure 4.33), the trench was 20 m long and exposed on its east side a vertical face roughly 3.5 m high.

The trench profile (see Figure 4.34) reveals that Mound F was built in three stages atop a previously occupied surface. The premound sediment contained shells, pottery, and charcoal, and it was penetrated by two lines of postholes at more or less right angles. The profile drawing also indicates that there was a fire basin in or on this premound soil at the south end of the trench. In addition to these features, there was a shallow, roughly rectangular basin filled with dark earth, roughly 60–80 cm wide and of undetermined length, extending less than half a foot into the premound soil. A field photograph (NAA negative no. 79–12,674) shows one of the lines of postmolds at the bottom of the photo, several isolated postmolds, and the large basin filled

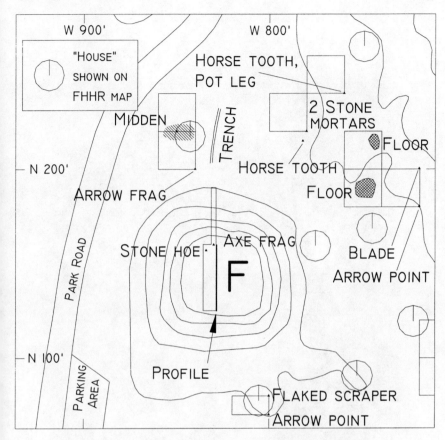

Figure 4.32. Detail of site map showing excavation trench in Mound F

with dark earth beyond the vertical wooden stake. Unfortunately, no map of these features survives.

The first episode of mound building here created a mound 3 ft high (1 m). It was not very wide (7.6 m maximum, unless the southern part of it was later dug away), most of the summit being south of the end of the deep excavation trench. The mound fill was white clay, and at the south edge of this first-stage summit the profile drawing shows a posthole 1 ft wide by 1½–2 ft deep. Having no other clues, it is impossible to tell what kind of architecture was on this first-stage summit.

The second episode of mound building raised the mound an additional 3–3½ ft, to a total height of 6 ft. Dark yellow clay fill was deposited directly over the first-stage summit, and after the 6-ft height was reached this surface was expanded to the north with a deposit of yellow clay. It looks like the

Figure 4.33. Trench in Mound F, looking north (National
Anthropological Archives, Smithsonian Institution, negative no.
79-12,676)

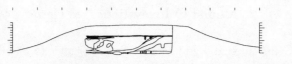

LOCATION OF PROFILE IN MOUND (MOUND SLOPES SCALED FROM TOPOGRAPHIC MAP)

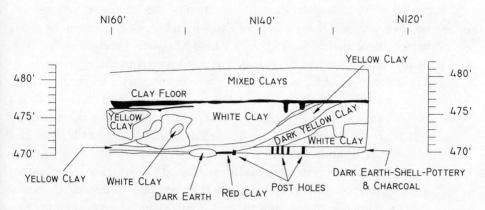

Figure 4.34. Vertical section north-south of Mound F

lateral expansion occurred only after an appreciable interval. The profile drawing shows the premound midden to be intact under the portion of the mound covered by the dark yellow clay but eroded away north of the edge of this deposit. In any case, at some point after the dark yellow clay surface had been built, yellow clay was added on the north flank of the mound, extending the mound northward 2–3 ft. Then the mound was extended at least 26 ft (8 m) farther north, maintaining the 6-ft level. On top of this expanded surface, a building or buildings were constructed, indicated by the notation of a "clay floor" and two postmolds in the profile. The clay floor, incidentally, was red, unlike the white surface of the first mound stage.

The final episode of mound building added 4 more feet of "mixed clay" fill, thus creating a mound platform 10 ft (3 m) above the premound soil. No features are indicated in this uppermost layer of fill. One of the only two artifacts from this mound came from the uppermost mound fill: a hoe blade chipped of limestone. The other is the bit end of an ax head made of dark gray igneous or metamorphic rock. Neither of these two artifacts gives us any clue as to the date of any of the mound construction episodes.

Mound Q Excavations (see Figure 4.35)

Both Cadle (1902:218) and Moore (1915:224) refer to Shiloh as having seven mounds, as shown on Moore's 1915 map (see Figure 2.5), and this has become the conventional wisdom about the number of mounds at the site (not including the house mounds). Moore (1915:224), however, also mentioned "various low humps and knolls of aboriginal origin, one of which, comparatively low and of very irregular outline, is sometimes described as an eighth mound." No information is given about the location of this possible eighth mound, but I suspect it is the one now labeled Mound Q. Excavation in 1933–1934 demonstrated that Mound Q, with a height between 1 and 1.5 m, is a built mound rather than a natural knoll. The profile (see Figure 4.36) shows 2½ to 3 ft (.75 to .9 m) of fill atop a layer described as midden. Because no sod line or other explicit indication of the premound surface is marked, it is not clear whether the midden layer is itself a fill deposit or whether it is the premound surface. If the former, the mound is at least 4 ft tall and was built in two construction episodes.

Few excavation units are recorded on Mound Q, but there are an unusually large number of point-provenienced artifacts here. These include one of the few restorable vessels from the site, a Bell Plain *var. unspecified* narrow-neck bottle or carafe (see Figure 4.37). Two small loopy strap handles were attached at the top of the neck, though one has broken off. The pot is 21.5 cm tall, about 18 cm in maximum diameter, and has a mouth of 4.7 cm diameter. It was found in a pit; Chambers (1933–1934:43) confusingly says that it was "18 [inches] below ground level" and then immediately afterward "depth 2 ft." In any case, it is clear the pit was intrusive from the surface into the mound fill.

There are three other pieces of pottery from Mound Q. Two are sherd discoidals, one made of a fragment of Mississippi Plain *var. Shiloh* and the other made of a fragment of a Bell Plain *var. unspecified* red-filmed vessel. Another sherd of Mississippi Plain *var. Shiloh* was found with a piece of mica adhering to it; the mica was still on the sherd in 1996. Mica flakes were found at three locations. Several loose fragments of mica were found within a few inches (horizontally; no depths are provided) of the mica-lined sherd. Of the other two mica locations, one was 18 in deep, and the other is listed as 8' deep, but that is almost certainly a misprint for 8".

Together with the mica-lined sherd and the restored bottle, the excavators recovered several fragments of charred cane. One of these cane fragments provided the sample for the Beta 113782 radiocarbon assay (cal A.D. 1215–1285) reported in Chapter 2. It is not clear whether the mica and the charred cane

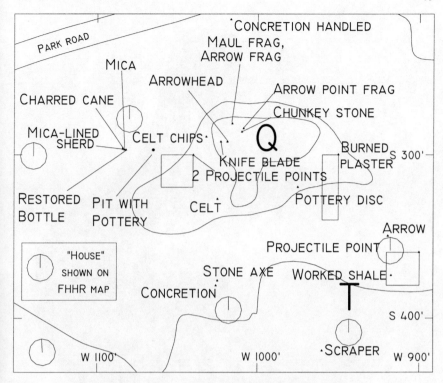

Figure 4.35. Detail of site map showing excavations on Mound Q

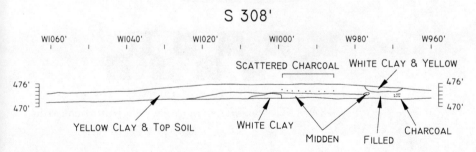

Figure 4.36. Vertical section east-west of Mound Q

were in the same pit as the restored bottle or whether these items were merely very close to the pit.

The mound fill contained several items of distinctly pre-Mississippian origin. A Jacks Reef corner-notched projectile point, a Middle Woodland type, was made of Ft. Payne chert. A Little Bear Creek projectile point, a Late Archaic type, was made of an unidentified chert. There were also four non-

Figure 4.37. Restored Bell Plain *var. unspecified* narrow-neck bottle from pit in Mound Q (A385502)

diagnostic bifaces or biface fragments, including one long, thick serrated blade made of Tuscaloosa chert and a crudely flaked knife with an expanding stem, also made of Tuscaloosa chert.

Two ground stone items were found in the fill of Mound Q. One is a portion of an ax head with an oval cross-section, made of medium gray metamorphic rock. The other is also an ax head, rectangular in cross-section, made of a light gray metamorphic rock.

Of the other two items recovered from Mound Q, only one is artifactual. That consists of several fragments of fired daub ("burned plaster" in the Field

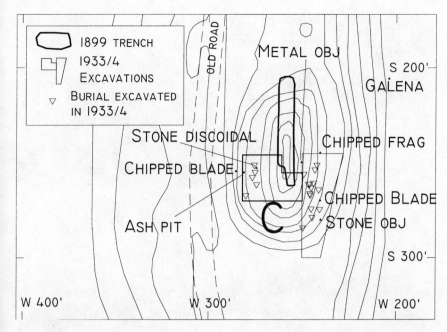

Figure 4.38. Detail of site map showing excavations in Mound C and locations of burials (open triangles)

Catalogue). The other item is a natural tubular concretion, such as are found not infrequently in the Tuscaloosa Formation. This item bears no evidence of modification or use.

Mound Q is definitely a built monument rather than a natural topographic rise. It probably had one or more structures on it, but any evidence of that would now be obliterated by bioturbation and leaching, not to mention an undetermined amount of archaeological excavation in 1933–1934. The radiocarbon assessment on cane indicates a date somewhere in the thirteenth century, but whether this is an ante quem or a post quem date depends on whether the cane was in an intrusive pit or loose in the mound fill.

Mound C Excavation (see Figure 4.38)

Like Cadle in 1899, Roberts excavated a portion of Mound C, probably because he thought that this strategy would be most likely to reveal additional burials with exotic accompaniments. Roberts did find additional burials, but the only preserved burial goods were some lumps of white clay near the heads of several burials, and a few grains of charred maize on or beneath the pelvis of one burial. During the excavation, Roberts encountered the trench excavated by Cadle three and a half decades earlier. Roberts found that Cadle's

Figure 4.39. Excavation on southeast side of Mound C (National Anthropological Archives, Smithsonian Institution, negative numbers by rows: 79-12,612, 79-12,613, 79-12,615, 79-12,617)

work had uncovered only a portion of the wooden-roofed burial chamber, so Roberts documented the remaining portion of the tomb.

Roberts excavated two portions of the mound. On the southeast side (see Figure 4.39) he removed somewhat less than one-quarter of the mound but may have left a number of low blocks unexcavated beneath burials. On the west side he cut a wide block out of the center of the mound (see Figure 4.40), nearly all of which was cut down to or below the premound surface. The only parts of the original mound now present are a wedge-shaped portion on the southwest side and that portion of the northern half outside Cadle's trench.

Information from the burial descriptions and profile drawings permit the reconstruction of the mound's history, though some details are not entirely clear. The first event must have been the deposition of a low mound of yellow clay, only a foot or so high. A pit 12 in deep, 7 ft long, and 33 in wide was dug into this low mound, with the long axis oriented north-south. Both Cadle (1902:220) and Roberts (on the burial card) mention that the bottom of the pit was on the premound ground surface. A number of flexed bodies

Figure 4.40. Excavations on west side of Mound C (National Anthropological Archives, Smithsonian Institution, negative no. 79-12,657)

and bundled skeletons were placed in the pit. Cadle (1902:220) reports finding the remains of three bodies, either buried in "sitting position" (i.e., flexed) or as bundled reinterments. In the portion of the burial pit that Cadle did not excavate, Roberts found the "bunched long bones of two or three individuals." Thus, remains of at least five bodies were placed in the pit, and at least some of these remains were bundled reinterments. With one of these bodies there was a shell ear ornament and, at about the center of the pit, lay the carved stone figurine pipe. The pit was then roofed with "large logs" (Cadle 1902:220) about 8 in across by 3 ft long (burial card and Chambers 1933–1934:48). Chambers (1933–1934:48) says the wood was either chestnut or cypress; the burial card lists walnut as a third possibility. Then white clay was piled over the roofed pit and initial mound. No clear stratigraphic demarcation between the initial mound and the white clay cap is visible in the photographs, nor is any clear boundary mentioned in the field notes or shown on the profile drawings (Figures 4.41, 4.42). Thus, it is doubtful that much time elapsed between the building of the initial mound and its capping with white clay. All of this work, in fact, may have taken place as a single and obviously extremely important event in the life of the Shiloh community.

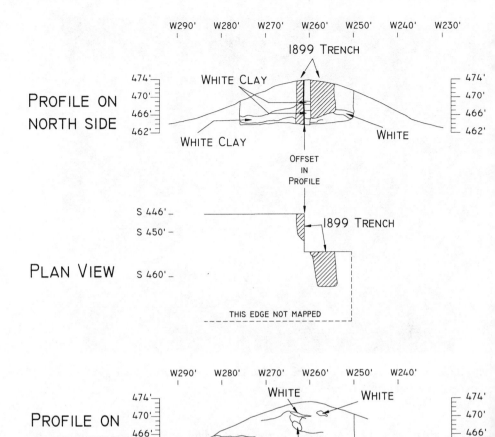

Figure 4.41. Vertical sections on west side of Mound C

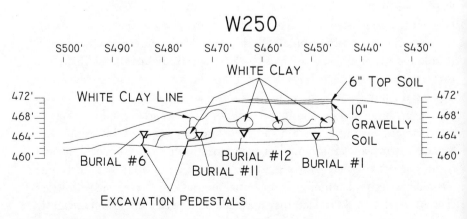

Figure 4.42. Vertical section on southeast side of Mound C

It is not clear whether the white clay cap over the initial mound ever formed a finished mound surface. From the irregular upper boundary of the white clay visible in photographs (e.g., at the level of Chambers's right hand in Figure 2.3) and the profile drawings (Figures 4.41 and 4.42), it appears that the source of fill dirt changed erratically from white clay to yellow clay, with no pause in construction. At least 20 additional flexed or bundled burials were added to the mound, 19 excavated by Roberts and the other by Cadle. These were added either during the construction or afterward; grave pits were noted for fewer than half these burials. It is also possible that the white clay cap did form a finished surface but that the intrusion of multiple, sometimes intersecting, grave pits so disturbed the mound stratigraphy that excavators in the 1930s could not discern any consistent surface for the white clay. Based on the ability of Roberts and Chambers to discern stratigraphy elsewhere at the site, I think it likely that the top of the white clay was never a finished surface.

After the building of the mound was finished, the mound stood 3 m above the premound surface and covered an oval area about 25 m long by 16 m wide. The long axis of the mound has the same orientation as the roofed tomb at the center of the mound. This may have been due to the topographic constraints of the ridge on which the mound was built. However, given that the mound seems to have been built in a single episode, it is reasonable to conclude that the similarity in orientation was intentional.

There are two sources of information about the 19 burials that Roberts encountered in the mound outside the central tomb. Chambers described the burials in his field notebook and duplicated these entries on a set of cards. Roberts also recorded descriptions of many burials on cards. The descriptions by Chambers and those by Roberts sometimes differ in slight details. Consequently, in the burial descriptions in Table 4.6, both sets of information are presented.

In addition to being in Mound C, one thing these burials have in common is their flexed body position. The side on which the body is flexed, the direction in which the head lies, and the direction in which the head faces are all variable. The variation does not have any spatial pattern. Several of the burials had masses of white clay near their heads. It is puzzling that the burial cards only mention this for two burials, when Chambers (1933–1934:31) says such masses were "usually" found near burials. No other burial goods were found. The people buried in the mound are said to include adults, subadults, and children and both males and females. However, it is not clear how much we should trust these assessments given the usually poor condition of the skeletal remains. There is no explicit statement of the disposition of the skeletal remains at the end of the excavation. In the absence of evidence to the contrary, I presume the bones were reburied when the mound was rebuilt over them.

Table 4.6 Descriptions of burials in Mound C

Burial #	Chambers's description	Roberts's description
1	W242 – S451 At level of 5'9" below stake W250 S450 Skull crushed, mandible broken on left side. Flexed on left side, head to west, knees at right [angles] to body, heels drawn up near hips, left arm extended along body, right forearm across stomach. Buried on sloping surface, head one foot higher than feet. Overall length of burial 3'6". Photographed. (Left as permanent exhibit.)	[none]
2	W245'9" – S461 At level of 5' below W250 S460 Skull to east, badly crushed; lower leg bones tightly flexed to S.W.; right arm extended along side. Flexed on back on left side.	Located skull {W245'9" S461} 4'0" below level of stake below W250 S470 Only fragments of skull in white clay.
3	W245'6" S466'8" At level of 4'2" below W250 S470 (Skull when found was in good condition, but was damaged by visitors during our absence.) Female. Head to south, legs flexed, heels to hips, knees to west. Buried on left side. Skull in vertical position, facing west. Crowded against west edge of burial pit let into hard yellow clay. Rather poorly preserved. One hand against face.	Located at skull {W245'6" S466'8" 4'2" below {W250 W470} Body in very poor state of preservation. Head to south, face toward west. One arm flexed with hand in front of face. Bones too far gone for definite position determination. Skull in good shape but before it could be removed it was crushed by a visitor. Legs lightly flexed point toward west. Right arm probably flexed across body. Hand at knees. Buried in oval pit in hard clay.
4	W243 S453'6" At level of 4'9" below W250 S470 Loosely flexed on right side, head to north, facing south. Skull crushed. Bones very poorly preserved.	Located skull at {W243 S453'6"} 4'9" below W250 S470 Adult. Loosely flexed adult. Lying on back head to north. Lying on back. Legs loosely flexed knees to the west. Right arm extended along side. Few vertebrae. Most of thorax bones decayed. Skull smashed. Face toward south. –in pit in yellow clay –in same pit as no. 3

5 W245 S474 At level of 3'8" below W250 S480 (measurements taken at pelvis)

Rather tightly flexed on left side, knees toward west. Portion above pelvis entirely missing, except for part of radius or ulna. A few grains of charred corn were near the pelvis. Bones poorly preserved. Unattached femoral epipheses [sic]; length of femur, 18" [below this a drawing of long bones]

Pelvis and legs only, was buried on left side. Legs tightly flexed. Knees pointing to the west. Right leg overlaps left [drawing]. Adult young male lower epiphesis [sic] not occluded. Upper portion of body possibly removed during digging for another burial. Bones not present during excavation.

Located pelvis at {W245 S474} 3 3/8 feet below W250 S480

Some kernels of charred corn at pelvis. Few chips & potsherds. In soft dirt on clay.

6 W249'6" S484 At level of 4' below W250 S480

Head to east, flexed on right side. Left femur, tibia and fibula, originally tightly flexed against body, settled after burial over on right side, while right femur, etc., loosely flexed, when found was at right [angles] to shaft of left femur, and touching the head of the left femur and the distal ends of the left tibia and fibula. Very poorly preserved.   [drawing]

Located at {W249'6" S484} 4 feet below W250 S480

7 W244'6" S478'6" At level of 5'3" below W250 S480

Skull damaged in finding. Loosely flexed on right side, head to north. Bones almost completely decayed. Left humerus extended along body, right humerus extended toward knees. Face crushed. Teeth well worn.

Located {W244'6" S478'6"} 5'3" below W250 S480

Adult

Skull crushed by mattock in digging. Bones on old surface. Partially in cut in clay center of mound. Small pit possibly (?) On right side, head to north, knees slightly flexed to west. Left arm along body, right toward knees. Bones almost completely decayed. Face crushed, teeth worn. No caries present.

8 W243'9" S460'6" At level of 5'9" below W250 S460

Skull badly crushed. Tightly flexed on back, knees at west of skull; overall length 22". At western edge of burial pit let into hard yellow clay.

Located skull {W243'9" S460'6"} 5'9" below W250 S460

Bones of adult. Skull crushed down on rest of bones. Head apparently to the south. Knees tightly flexed. Bones give impression of sitting burial with upper portion crushed down onto lower. In yellow earth at west edge of burial pit.

Continued on the next page

Table 4.6 *Continued*

Burial #	Chambers's description	Roberts's description
9	W245'9" S446 4'3" below W250 S450 2 ft. below surface Closely flexed on right side, head to east. Poorly preserved. Knees drawn up against right side, heels to hips. Skull faces north.	Located {W245'9" S446} 4'3" below W250 S450 2 ft. below surface Lying on right side. Head to east. Knees flexed toward north.
10	W246'6" S461 5'9" below W250 S460 Flexed on left side, head to south, knees to west. Bones in good condition. Skull crushed. Buried in hard, dry clay. Femora, tibiae, and fibulae broken. Feet nearly gone, though traceable. Pelvis poorly preserved. Lower legs drawn up tightly against hips. Left arm flexed, hand clenched beneath chin. In yellow clay deposited earlier than burial pit. Mass of white clay against skull.	Located W246'6" S461 Was 5'9" below W250 S460 Head to south. Flexed on left side, knees to west. Bones in good condition. Skull crushed. Buried in hard dry clay. Pelvis poorly preserved. Lower legs tightly drawn up against femurs. Left arm flexed, hand clenched beneath chin. Buried in yellow clay deposited earlier than burial pit. Mass of white earth against skull. No offerings.
11	W240'6" S474'3" 1'9" below W240 S470 Very poorly preserved. Head to SE, skull crushed. Flexed on left side, head 6" lower than knees, heels drawn up to hips, knees at rt. [angles] to torso. Approx. one ft. above base of mound. Arms probably extended along sides. Male (?). In soft dirt.	Located W240'6" S474'3" Was 1'9" below W240 W470 Head to SE. Skull crushed. Flexed on left side. Head 6" lower than knees, heels drawn up to hips, knees at right angles to body line. Approx 1' above base of mound. Arms extended along sides (male?). Buried in soft dirt.
12	W245 S463 6.4 ft. below W250 S460 Elev. 465 above sea level Skull to west, legs flexed to right, heels to hips, knees at right [angles] to torso. Skull on only slightly higher [level] than feet. Right arm folded across breast. Skull vertical, maxilla shoved over orbit. Teeth contain caries. Buried in soft, dark earth on hard yellow clay.	Located W245 S463 6.1 ft. below W250 S460 In hard yellow clay.
13	W241 S464 Elev. 464.8 above sea level Tightly flexed on right side, facing NW. Skull to NE, 6" lower than feet. Heels flexed to hips, femora parallel to torso. Knees	[none]

14 W274'3" S461'3" 4'6" below W270 S470 [none]

Skull damaged in finding. About 2' below surface soil. Skull to east, flexed on right side, femora at right angles to torso. Strata of white clay about 6" below burial.

15 W275'6" S451 4'9" below W270 S440 [none]

Skull to NE, flexed on left side; in very poor condition. 2 ft. below ground level.

16 W275 S454'9" 1'6" below W280 S460 [none]

Skull smashed in finding. Skull to east, flexed on right side. Heels drawn up toward hips. Teeth well worn, bones slight. Presence of pre-auricular sulcus is female sex characteristic. Mass of white earth at base of skull, a larger mass one foot north of face.

17 W 280 S467 3.3 ft below W280 S470 [none]

Leg bones of a burial; heads of the femurs point N.

18 W249 S455'9" 7'4" below W250 S450 [none]

Buried in hard whitish clay on base of mound. Rather closely flexed.

19 W276'6" S451'6" 1 ft. below S460 W280 [none]

Traces of lower leg bones, extended NW-SE

Although no artifacts were found with the burials, six items were recovered during excavation of the mound. One is a small metal spoon of historic origin. A fragmentary blocky preform of Ft. Payne or Dover chert and a section of a biface made of agate are not very informative. A fragment of a Mill Creek chert hoe and fragments of two chunkey stones are at least diagnostically Mississippian. One of the fragmentary chunkey stones is sandstone, the other ferruginous sandstone. Perhaps the most interesting item from this portion of the site, however, is a small cube of galena, or lead sulfide. This very dense crystalline mineral has a dark gray, metallic appearance and produces a glittery, dark gray powder when abraded. It was used widely throughout the Southeast by Mississippian people, apparently being esteemed for its unusually great weight, its glittery appearance, or both (Walthall 1981:15–18). Of those fragments that have been traced to their geological sources, most come from the upper Mississippi Valley source region (adjoining portions of northwestern Illinois, southwestern Wisconsin, and Iowa) and the southeast Missouri source region a few tens of kilometers southwest of Cahokia (Walthall 1981:41–42). The Field Catalogue gives this Shiloh artifact an improbable provenience, W-2+4/S-4+6, that is part way down the river bluff. It is likely that the provenience should have been written W-2+40/S-4+60, which would put the galena within the area excavated on the southeast side of the mound. Galena is certainly known from Mississippian burials elsewhere and was found elsewhere at Shiloh. If the correct provenience really was Mound C, it is not terribly surprising that the galena was not found with a burial, because there was so much digging of graves on the southeast side of the mound that several graves were disturbed by later graves. The galena may initially have been in a grave and may have been moved by the digging and filling of a later grave.

The color white was evidently of symbolic importance to the people at Shiloh. In addition to the use of white clay to cap the initial roofed burial pit, "irregular shaped masses of white clay were usually found near burials, often close to the head" (Chambers 1933–1934:31). Color symbolism was highly significant to later Southeastern Indians (Hudson 1976:235–239), and it is not uncommon to find mineral pigments with Mississippian burials elsewhere in the region. Mound C, or the burials in it, appear to have been associated with the color white.

CONCLUSION

As anyone who has waded through this chapter will appreciate, the excavations in 1933–1934 were extensive. We know the general areas where excavation was focused, though we often do not know precisely where the limits of excavation were. Substantial numbers of artifacts were picked up by the workmen and were usually given at least horizontal proveniences. Samples of pottery—hundreds of sherds—were collected by stratigraphic unit in several parts of the site, giving us some tantalizing hints at the chronology of these parts of the site. Mounds E and F were trenched and the profiles drawn, giving us information about the constructional history of these monuments. A large fraction of Mound C, the burial mound, was excavated, exposing 19 burials and a remnant of the central, log-covered tomb from which Cadle had removed the figurine pipe in 1899. Mound Q was trenched, revealing it to be artificial rather than a natural topographic rise. Portions of a few dozen houses were excavated, revealing the domestic construction techniques used by the Shiloh occupants. An enigmatic long building with at least one round end was exposed near Mound A. It is clearly some kind of "public" building, but its precise use and significance eludes us. The ground surface around Mound A was revealed to be an artificial apron up to 2 m thick, showing us that Mound A is actually a lot taller than it appears to be. Portions of the plaza area were revealed to have sheets of fill, probably deposited in an effort to make the plaza more level. A fence or wall extending across part of the plaza area was revealed. Over 100 m of the palisade line was excavated. The scale of this work is staggering, by the standard of today's typically more intensive excavations.

Unfortunately, the documentation of these excavations is not concomitantly extensive. The field notebooks are terse; they were not updated daily and often record relatively unimportant details while remaining silent on more important details. Most devastatingly, the detailed topographic map of the site that was made for the project did not record the locations of excavations. This has left us uncertain as to which parts of the site still contain intact deposits and which parts have already been excavated. The 1933–1934 excavation units I have depicted on the site map are not necessarily accurate indications of the actual excavation edges, and there were many additional units excavated that cannot be shown on the map because I do not have coordinates for them. But none of this signifies that the records of the 1933–1934 excavations should be written off as useless or that the artifact collection must be treated as merely a large, biased surface collection.

One piece of wisdom that has emerged from the preparation of this chapter is that any archaeologist who plans to excavate at Shiloh needs to spend a long time going through the records from the 1933–1934 excavation. Even though I have worked with these records for several years now, I am not confident that I have yet wrung from them all that there is to learn. Even given the brevity of the field notes, by comparing the written records, photographs, and drawings, pieces of the excavation puzzle can be put together.

For example, computer imaging and analysis of the photographs may permit the derivation of coordinates for some of the excavation units not otherwise recorded. Several of the field photographs have not yet been identified, but it may be possible for their locations to be ascertained one day. Intensive remote sensing studies may help clarify ambiguities in the field notes. Certainly, when Frank Roberts turned his attention away from Shiloh before writing a final report, much information was irretrievably lost. But his work at Shiloh can be at least partially reconstructed, and we know enormously more about the site as a result of his work than we would otherwise.

5   Queens College Fieldwork in 1998

Excavations in the 1930s were extensive, but the picture I could draw from them was lacking in many of the details that concern archaeologists today. The only way to acquire such details was new excavation. The park, agreeing that a "generic" picture of the occupation was not as desirable as a more specific and detailed picture, consented to have me excavate two of the house mounds. Though conceived as a single project, the excavation would be split between two seasons: one house would be excavated in the summer of 1998, the other the following summer. The 1998 excavation was conducted in accordance with the provisions of Federal Archeological Permit SHIL 98-001.

The specified goals for the first season were:

1. Relocate the grid monuments from Gerald Smith's 1976 project, to use in recording proveniences.
2. Take small-diameter soil cores from house mounds near the periphery of the site to locate one or more houses that had burned. Locations of all cored house mounds would be recorded.
3. Excavate one of the burned houses, screening all deposits through ¼-in mesh (or finer), taking flotation samples from the floor and hearth, and recording provenience of all artifacts to 1-×-1-m grid squares (or, for artifacts on the floor, piece-plotting).

There were two reasons I wanted to excavate a burned rather than an unburned house. The primary one was that burned houses frequently contain artifacts that were stored or were in use within the house at the time it caught fire; during an accidental conflagration the residents do not always have time to remove all their belongings. By contrast, houses abandoned intentionally usually have most or all the belongings removed by the departing residents. Emptied houses reveal little more than their size and shape, whereas it is much easier to ascertain what activities were conducted inside a house if artifacts are left within it. The second reason for focusing on a burned house was that wooden parts of burned buildings sometimes char without combusting, so that identifiable details of the structure remain in charcoal form. Unless turned to charcoal, the wooden parts of buildings decay, so that inferring the details of an unburned building's construction is difficult. Excavations in the 1930s encountered several burned buildings, giving me some reason to expect that I would be able to locate others. Those excavations also recorded some of the architectural details revealed by the charred timbers, so the recovery of architectural details was a less important goal than the recovery of evidence for activities inside the structure.

Incidentally, my research design also called for excavation of a ring several meters wide around the house. Particularly during hot southern summers, many household activities probably took place outside the house rather than inside it. A good picture of the household's activities would have to include these extramural activities. As it turned out, however, I did very little excavation outside the house, in part because the deposits outside the house were considerably eroded and in part because I ran out of time.

The rest of this chapter presents in detail the work done and results obtained relevant to the three goals listed.

ESTABLISHING THE EXCAVATION GRID SYSTEM

The initial three days on site were occupied in establishing a grid system and selecting a house mound for excavation. I sought to relocate the metric grid-system monuments set in the site in 1976 by Gerald Smith (1977:1–2) but eventually concluded that the markers were either too deeply buried to be located without excavation or have been destroyed by the park's mowers.

During the search for the grid monuments, a Park Service employee's use of a metal detector for about two hours led to discovery of several twentieth-century shell casings, a pair of sunglasses frames, and a fragmented 1935 TVA benchmark. Other than the date and enough lettering to indicate that it was a TVA benchmark, the recovered fragments have no other identifying features. Though the benchmark had clearly been hit and thrown by a mower, we nevertheless recorded the location where the fragments were found. Except for these fragments, the metal items were discarded.

Failing to find Smith's grid monuments, I set up a new metric grid system. This grid, like Smith's and Roberts's, is oriented to magnetic north. In June 1998, the declination at Shiloh was −0°34′E compared to +2°17′E at the time Smith made his grid and +4°23′E for Roberts's grid (National Geophysical Data Center 2002). I sought to place our N0 E20 grid point approximately on Smith's N250 E650, though it appears that my stake missed Smith's point by several meters. For purposes of leveling across the site, I arbitrarily defined the ground surface at this point (N0 E20) as an elevation of 50 m (note that true amsl elevation is close to 146 m). The choice of numbering for this three-dimensional coordinate system was driven by a desire to make the grid system visibly different from Smith's coordinate system, so that there would be little chance that anyone reading my site records would confuse the two coordinate systems. To tie the grid system into permanent markers, I obtained grid coordinates for the vertical posts supporting two of the Civil War tablets on the site, and in the following season a high-precision GPS receiver provided UTM coordinates for points on our grid.

CORING HOUSE MOUNDS

To select a house mound for excavation, three crew members combed the wooded area between Mound G and the palisade embankment with a soil corer. One or more cores were pulled and soil profiles recorded from each of 25 locations (numbered 1–23, 25–26, number 24 was not used; see Figure 5.1). As we gained familiarity with the topography of the site, we reassessed five of these locations as tree-falls or other natural features (nos. 1, 4, 23, 25, 26) instead of house mounds, and three others (18, 19, 20) were later realized to be part of the palisade embankment. Thus, 17 apparent house mounds were cored. The goal of the coring was to locate a burned house, which should be visible in the core as a layer of burned daub and charcoal. No such deposit was seen in any of the cores.

Nearly all the cores had to be terminated at 20–25 cm below surface, at which depth we encountered a deposit so hard it was initially believed to be tree roots. Eventually, however, the ubiquity of the hard material at such a consistent depth led us to suspect we were hitting either a hard-packed structure floor or a naturally formed hardpan. To resolve the nature of the hard material at the depth of 20–25 cm, we excavated a single 30-cm-diameter shovel test in each of two house mounds (both tests screened through ¼-in mesh, with no artifacts found). In neither case was a stratigraphic break indicative of a structure floor seen. Rather, the hard material had the appearance of a slightly argillic B-horizon with small quantities of pea-sized sesquioxide concretions ("buckshot"). This sediment was dry, unlike the overlying material, for there had been no rain for three weeks prior to the two days of rain that heralded the start of our coring operation. Because of the small diameter of the shovel tests and the consequently poor visibility of their profiles, I would not conclude that structure floors were *absent* from the tested mounds but merely that we did not observe any in our shovel tests.

All the core locations were marked with numbered pin flags. Locations of the flags were measured later in the season, either by triangulation from known points or by taping distances along compass bearings from known

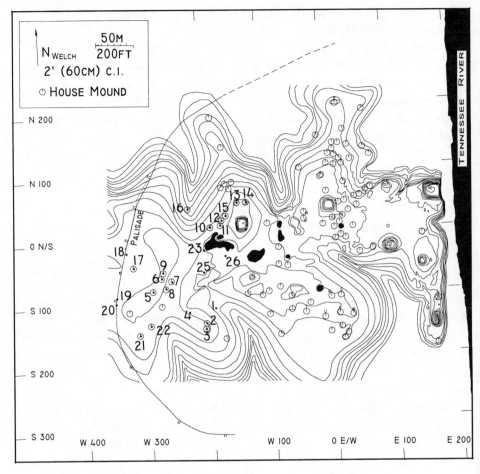

Figure 5.1. Locations, shown by numbers, of house mounds cored in 1998 season

points. In most cases, the resulting location error is probably no greater than the diameter of the house mound itself.

Though five of the cored house mounds (6, 11, 14, 17, 18) yielded sparse flecks of charcoal and another (13) yielded one small piece of possibly fired clay, none of the cores yielded the quantity of charcoal and fired clay expected in a burned structure. Lacking a demonstrably burned structure, I selected for excavation a well-defined house mound (#7 in our coring tests) that had no large trees on it that would complicate excavation. The mound selected appears to be one of those indicated on Roberts's 1933–1934 site map. It is located at approximately S251 W1655 in terms of Roberts's grid in feet, at approximately N171 E375 in terms of Smith's grid in meters, and in terms of my metric grid is centered at S66.5 W255.

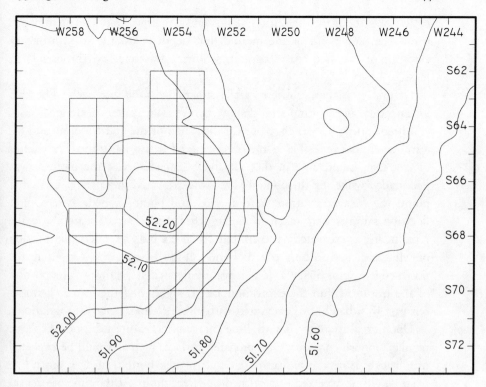

Figure 5.2. Excavation units on house mound 7

EXCAVATION

The house mound was cleared of brush and gridded in 1-×-1-m squares. Elevations were shot at each grid corner and a topographic map prepared (Figure 5.2). I designated as baulks to be left in situ a 1-m-wide line of squares running N–S and another line running E–W across the highest point of the house mound. These baulks provide N–S and E–W vertical sections (profiles) across the house mound, such that the excavated area consists of four quadrants around the mound's center.

Excavation proceeded mainly by 10-cm arbitrary levels within 1-×-1-m units. These arbitrary levels are defined in terms of depth below "datum", which in turn was defined as the highest point of the mound (2.26 m higher than the ground surface at our original site-grid datum, No E20). Thus, levels such as "20–30 cm b.d." have the same absolute elevation in all excavation units. Naturally, excavation units located off the higher parts of the mound might not have a "0–10 cm b.d." or "10–20 cm b.d." level if the ground surface in that unit was below such an elevation. On excavation forms and in all notes about the excavation of this house mound, "b.d." refers to depth below the high point of the mound, not depth below the 50-m arbitrary elevation at No E20. All excavated sediment was screened through ¼-in mesh.

Natural stratigraphy, when visible, superseded arbitrary levels. The two instances of such natural stratigraphy involve (1) a scatter of charcoal, ash, and fired earth at ca. 20 cm b.d. near the center of the house mound and (2) a soil-color change visible in the outer ring of excavation units. The scatter of charcoal, found only in the NE and SE quadrants of the mound, was pedestalled while the surrounding area was excavated to 30 cm b.d. At that point, the excavation units were cleaned and photographed. Two 20-liter flotation samples were taken from the pedestalled charcoal scatter, and the remainder was excavated to 30 cm b.d. At 30 cm b.d., a semicircular portion of what appeared to be a charcoal-and-ash-filled basin was seen along the north edge of unit S68 W255. This was designated as Feature 1. The portion of the feature within the excavation area (roughly half the feature is under our east-west baulk) was excavated with all fill (9 liters) saved for flotation.

Upon excavation, we saw that the charcoal in Feature 1 did not display a regular, smooth contact with a prepared surface, such as would be expected of a hearth. Instead, the feature had an irregular bottom surface, much like what would be expected of a burned-out tree stump. At the time of excavation, this produced considerable uncertainty in my interpretation of the feature. One possibility was that the feature was indeed a hearth, and the scatter of charcoal around it was the remnants of the burned roof of the house. The other possibility was that the feature was a burned tree stump, and the scatter of charcoal constituted charred pieces of the tree that fell away from the stump. This latter possibility would easily account for the morphology of the feature and was the interpretation I favored until I got an analysis of the charcoal inside the feature. Before revealing the results of that analysis, however, it will help to describe the rest of the excavation.

As mentioned, we attempted to excavate stratigraphically a soil color change seen in the outer ring of excavation units. The color change consisted of a redder sediment containing slightly more clay underlying a pale yellow sediment of nearly pure silt. The contact between these two sediments was gradual rather than abrupt, at least in the excavation units near the periphery of the house mound. As we attempted to follow this contact zone in toward the center of the mound, however, we found it impossible to follow and were forced to revert to arbitrary excavation levels. The principal difficulty was that in some places the pale yellow silt appeared to bifurcate, with redder sediment above the upper band and below the lower band. At other locations, the pale yellow silt overlay a darker brown sediment instead of the redder sediment seen elsewhere. In hindsight, the difficulty we experienced was caused by the interaction of pedogenesis, bioturbation, and erosion on an actual stratigraphic distinction. This became clear only after we had excavated well below the level of the central feature and surrounding charcoal scatter.

After removing the contents of the portion of Feature 1 that lay inside the excavation unit, we expanded the excavation into the northwest and southwest quadrants of the house mound. Confounding my expectations, the pale-yellow-over-redder stratigraphy I expected to see was absent or very weakly developed in these quadrants. The scatter of charcoal seen around Feature 1 in the eastern quadrants did not extend into the western quadrants. Excavation in the western quadrants proceeded by arbitrary 10-cm levels, with all units taken down to 30 cm below the top of the mound. The most noteworthy finds in the western half of the mound were a smashed medicine bottle and several metal harness buckles, most likely of Civil War date.

Despite a careful lookout for such features, no postmolds or wall trenches were seen in any of the excavation units. Thinking that perhaps the lack of such architectural features merely meant that we had not yet excavated deeply enough, units in the eastern half of the mound were taken down to 40 cm below datum—roughly the level of the surrounding ground surface on the downslope side of the house mound. Several units were excavated farther, to 50 cm below datum, and the unit in which Feature 1 had been found was excavated to 80 cm below the top of the mound. No additional features were seen, nor was a distinct house floor visible anywhere.

At this point, the end of the excavation season was only a few days away, and the house mound remained a puzzle. Rather than finding a distinct house floor rimmed with wall posts or wall trenches, what I had found was a charcoal-filled, irregular basin in the center of the mound. This basin was surrounded by a scatter of charcoal, but no floor surface was visible. What made this feature particularly puzzling was that, in relation to the topography of the surrounding ground surface, the feature and the charcoal scatter was almost 20 cm above what appeared to be the natural ground surface. Regardless of whether the feature was a burned tree stump or the central hearth inside a house, why was it 20 cm above the surrounding ground surface? The answer to this question became clear when the vertical profiles of the excavation baulks were cleaned and inspected.

The charcoal scatter around Feature 1 lies at the top of a buried soil (see Figure 5.3; all soil terminology follows definitions in USDA [1998]). The paleosol begins with the 5–10-cm thick 2A horizon (brown sediment) and proceeds through a 12-cm thick leached (albic) 2E horizon that grades into a progressively redder and more clayey 2B horizon. At 25–30 cm below the top

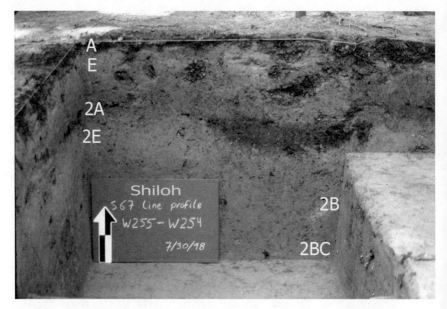

Figure 5.3. Vertical section through Feature 1, with soil horizons labeled

of the 2B horizon, sesquioxide (iron and manganese) concretions begin appearing, marking the transition to a pale 2BC horizon. The top of the paleosol is 20 cm above the surrounding ground surface, and Feature 1 intrudes through the 2A horizon into the leached 2E horizon. This paleosol is much better developed than the modern soil at the top of the mound, indicating that the modern weathering profile (the one starting at the current surface) is of much more recent origin. The fact that the top of the paleosol is perched some 20 cm above the ground surface around the house mound suggests that the surrounding surface eroded by 20 cm after the formation of this paleosol. Because the sediment atop the paleosol contains Mississippian artifacts, the paleosol must antedate the Mississippian occupation, and therefore the top of the paleosol must have been the ground surface at the time of the occupation.

If this interpretation of the soil profile is correct, then the soil profile off of the house mound ought to display a truncated profile in which a shallow A horizon overlies a relatively thin and weak E horizon that grades directly into the middle of the B horizon seen below Feature 1. To test this idea, I excavated a shovel test unit of roughly 50 cm diameter several meters northeast of the mound, at S50 W252. The soil profile seen there consisted of a weak A horizon only a couple centimeters thick, below which there was an E horizon roughly 8 cm thick. Below that there was a redder, illuviated B horizon 20–22 cm thick, with the pale, concretion-bearing BC horizon beginning

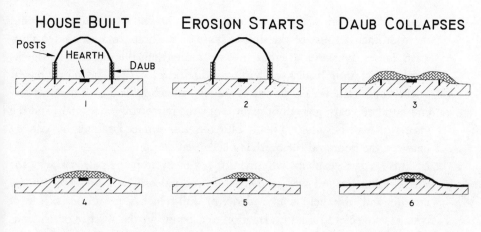

Figure 5.4. House mound erosion model

at 32 cm below the present ground surface. This profile matches the test expectations: an A horizon 2–3 cm thick rather than 5–10 cm thick, an E horizon only 8 cm rather than 12 cm thick, a B horizon only 20–22 cm thick instead of 25–30 cm, and the top of the BC horizon at 32 cm rather than 52 cm below the top of the A horizon. The ground surface around the house mound has been eroded roughly 20 cm below the top of the paleosol preserved in the mound.

The next questions, of course, are: when did the erosion occur; why was the paleosol preserved in the mound; and what is the sediment lying atop the paleosol in the mound? I explored but rejected a number of possible explanations because they demonstrably did not fit the facts and have found only one scenario that appears to answer all these questions satisfactorily. It is illustrated in Figure 5.4. A wattle-and-daub house with a basin-shaped central hearth (Feature 1) is built atop the original ground surface. Foot traffic outside this house and the several others nearby denudes the ground surface. The barren soil surface, which here slopes gently toward the river, suffers sheet erosion (a phenomenon that park personnel confirm as a problem in areas of high foot-traffic). The sheet erosion leaves the house standing atop a pedestal (see Figures 4.21 and 4.22 for an example of a pedestalled floor). A similar phenomenon can be seen throughout the South even today, where the uneroded ground surface under a house built on piers is noticeably higher than in the adjacent eroded yard. In the hypothetical scenario for Mound 7, after the house is abandoned it burns, accidentally or on purpose, resulting in a scatter of charcoal in the center of the floor and collapsed daub all around the wall line. Because of the steeper slope of the house mound's sides, rainwash causes the slopes to erode inward (rather than the top eroding downward; see Schumm [1966] and Kirkby and Kirkby [1976]). The inward retreat of the slopes removes the postmolds or wall trenches. And over the next several hundred years, growth of plant roots, the burrowing of animals, and the effects of frost heaving gradually blur the near-surface stratigraphic contact between the floor and the overlying collapsed daub.

This scenario explains why there is sediment atop the paleosol, why the surrounding ground was eroded while the paleosol was preserved in the mound, and why there is no evidence of wall trenches or wall posts. It is, of course, convenient for an explanation to account for the absence of evidence of its key component, in this case the wall posts of the hypothetical wattle-and-daub house. It is certain, however, that *something* capped a portion of the ancient ground surface and protected it from the sheet erosion of the surrounding terrain, but was it a house? Although this could be tested by soil chemistry analysis, I had not collected the necessary samples (the unexcavated baulks, of course, could provide such samples). I did, however, have large flotation samples containing charcoal from inside and around Feature 1.

There were three possibilities for the origin of the charcoal in Feature 1: charred material such as typically found in the central hearth of a house; the charred superstructure of a burned building; and the charred remains of a burned tree stump. Charred material from hearths typically includes assorted species of wood charcoal, plus by-products of edible plant foods, including nutshells and maize cob fragments. In contrast, the burned superstructure of a building would consist of charred roof supports or fragments of the wattle of the walls. Assuming the building was like those found in excavations of burned houses in the 1930s, the superstructure elements would have fairly small diameters (<8 cm) and might include more than one species. Finally, if Feature 1 was a burned tree stump and there never was a house here, all the charred material would consist of charcoal from a single species of tree, and much of the material inside the feature would have the cellular structure of roots rather than trunk or limbs. After processing the flotation samples from in and around Feature 1, I sent the charred material to C. Margaret Scarry of the University of North Carolina with an explanation of the problem and a request that she identify the charred material.

Scarry's analysis of the charred material from inside Feature 1 shows that it is not typical of hearth materials, and neither is it consistent with a charred tree stump. No food remains or by-products were found, and the wood charcoal comes from at least two species of tree (at least one species of hickory and at least one member of the white oak group). None of the identified

Table 5.1 Radiocarbon assays of samples from 1998 excavations

Lab number	SHIL catalog number	Conventional ^{14}C age	Calibrated* date ranges for combined samples	
Beta-143848	SHIL 06106	860 ± 50**	1σ :	AD 1160-1225, AD 1230-1240
Beta-143849	SHIL 06107	870 ± 50***	2σ :	AD 1040-1090
Beta-143850	SHIL 06543	820 ± 60****		AD 1120-1140
				AD 1150-1270

*   Calibrations were obtained using OxCal v. 3.4 (Bronk Ramsey 2000)
**   Measured ^{14}C age of 890 ± 50 adjusted for –26.8 o/oo δ^{13}C
***   Measured ^{14}C age of 870 ± 50 adjusted for –24.6 o/oo δ^{13}C
****   Measured ^{14}C age of 860 ± 60 adjusted for –27.1 o/oo δ^{13}C

fragments has the cellular structure of roots. Few of the charcoal pieces appear to come from timbers of more than 10 cm diameter. Instead, most of the charcoal fragments—and this is true for the material around the hearth as well—come from sticks 2–4 cm in diameter. Such sticks are at the small end of the range of 1.5–2.5 in (4–6.5 cm) reported by Roberts (1933–1934:26–27) for the superstructure of houses at Shiloh. Thus, the contents of Feature 1 and the charcoal around it match reasonably well with what is known of the (burned) wooden superstructure of houses at Shiloh. The basin-shaped feature may originally have been a cooking hearth, but if so, like the rest of the (hypothetical) house, it apparently was cleaned out before the house burned so that the only remaining macroscopic evidence of the house is the charred wattle.

The age of the charred material from in and around Feature 1 is also relevant. If the charcoal dates to a period distinctly earlier or distinctly later than the A.D. 1050–1400 period indicated for the Shiloh occupation, then the hypothetical scenario illustrated in Figure 5.4 would fall apart. Three samples were submitted for radiocarbon assessment, one from inside Feature 1 and two from the material around its mouth. Two of the samples (Beta 143848 and Beta 143849) consisted of fragments of small sticks, to avoid the "old wood" problem. The radiocarbon assessments are shown in Table 5.1. All of the age estimates overlap at one standard deviation. Because the three samples are believed to provide three independent estimates of the age of the wattle of the burned house, they were combined prior to calibration to yield a single estimate (see Figure 5.5) for the date of the wattle used in this house.

The radiocarbon assessments lie in a time range during which the tree-ring calibration curve fluctuates, offering multiple possible calibrated ages. The most probable calibrated age range, however, is cal A.D. 1160–1240, right in

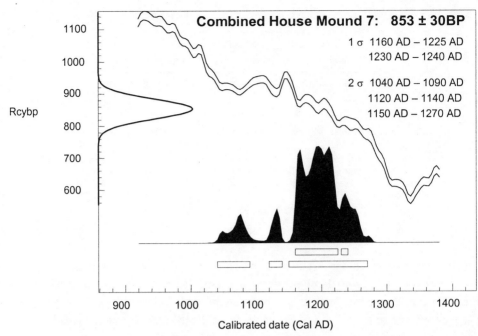

Figure 5.5. Calibration of combined radiocarbon assays from House Mound 7

the middle of the estimated span of occupation at Shiloh. This dating assessment is consistent with the expectation derived from the hypothesis that the charred material is the remains of a wattle-and-daub house rather than a burned tree stump.

Based on the pedological, botanical, and radiocarbon data, I believe Mound 7 is the remains of a wattle-and-daub house that burned after the interior hearth and floor were cleaned out. The hypothesis of sheet erosion leaving the house pedestalled is consistent with all the available data. It also explains the observation of Roberts (1933–1934:30) that "House mounds in most cases seem to be at high points of ground. Houses built on rises in each case." Having established this, we can move on to examine what can be said about the activities in and around this house.

HOUSE FEATURES

Given the absence of wall features—postmolds or wall trenches—it is difficult to say much about the size, shape, or construction of the house that stood at this location. All that we know is that there was a central fired, basin-shaped feature (probably a hearth), a wooden superstructure that contained many sticks of 2–4 cm diameter, and daub on the walls. According to

Chambers (n.d.), the roofs of houses at Shiloh may also have been daubed (see Lewis [1995] for evidence of daub on roofs in eastern Tennessee). In the vertical sections through the house mound (see Figure 5.6), the buried 2A horizon extends 4.5 m north-south, which indicates that the roof of the house must have been at least this wide. The scatter of charcoal extends over an irregular area whose longest dimension is about 4.3 m. These dimensions compare well with Roberts's statement that "the average house was 16 feet [4.9 m] in diameter" (Stirling 1935:395).

The distribution of fired clay, presumably fired daub, coincides with the scatter of charcoal. None of the fired clay pieces was sufficiently large or unweathered to preserve indications of the material (if any) on which the daub was supported. Because of the quantity of sediment atop the remains of the house—a deposit as much as 20 cm thick—the walls must have been thickly daubed. In this regard, it is noteworthy that Roberts (1933–1934:29) mentions finding "a large chunk of burned clay" that was 53-X-76-X-18 cm (21-X-30 in X7 in thick) on the first surface of the apron west of Mound A. If walls were coated with 18 cm of daub, this would account for the depth of sediment atop the floor level in House Mound 7.

Given the absence of large timbers in Mound 7, and the absence of holes for large interior roof-support posts, this house must have been constructed with a bent-pole technique. This must also have been the technique used in the structures excavated in the 1930s. Roberts (1933–1934:27) found charred wall posts as long as 2.64 m (8 ft 8 in), but these poles averaged only 5 cm (2 in) in diameter. The wall poles were spaced 1–1.2 m (3–4 ft) apart. In at least one of the houses Roberts excavated, the gap between these widely spaced posts was filled by a solid sheet of vertically oriented split cane strips. Crossing the vertical cane strips were horizontal strips of split cane spaced approximately 30 cm (1 ft) apart. Daub coated the outside of the cane sheet. A charred section of such a wall from Mound W is illustrated in Figure 4.19.

Nothing in House Mound 7 suggests where the doorway was located. Roberts reported that "where indications of an entry or doorway were present they were invariably on the east to southeast side" (Stirling 1935:395). However, the only house (Mound P) for which there is a complete map of wall and doorway features shows the door unambiguously on the west or west-southwest side. Roberts also tells us that "two of the structures had had a passageway leading to the doorway" (Stirling 1935:395). Any evidence of a door or passageway on the south-to-southeast side of House Mound 7 would have eroded away long ago.

A conjecture about the likely location of the house outline can be made from the evidence from the vertical sections and the distribution of charcoal. The conjecture is illustrated in Figure 5.7. The house, 4.3 m in diameter, is

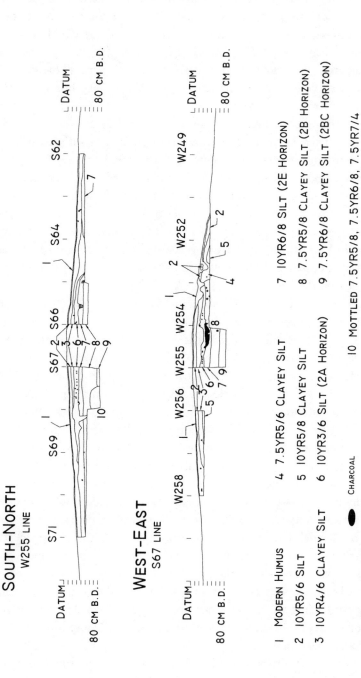

Figure 5.6. Vertical sections through House Mound 7

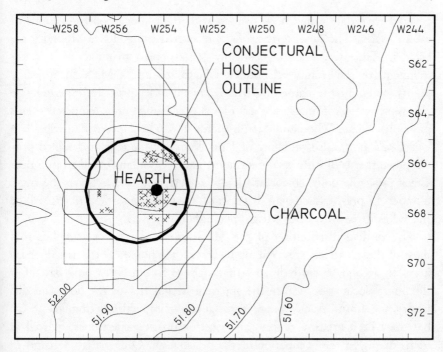

Figure 5.7. Conjectural structure outline for House Mound 7

shown with the hearth off-center. This is because the hearth does not appear to be concentric with the preserved 2A horizon that is interpreted as underlying the floor. The conjectural house wall does encompass nearly all the charcoal scatter, and accords reasonably well with the topography.

ARTIFACTS AND ACTIVITIES

Before we can infer what activities took place in and around the house, we need to assess whether the recovered artifacts in fact date to the occupation of the house or whether they derive from periods earlier or later than the house. The house appears to have been cleaned out thoroughly before it burned, inasmuch as there were no pottery vessels and few stone tools lying at the level of the floor. The mixing of the above- and below-floor strata, to be expected from bioturbation of these near-surface deposits, prevented us from making a clean distinction between above-floor and below-floor deposits. Thus, we have artifacts from arbitrary 10-cm-thick levels, and we must assess whether to consider these artifacts as preconstruction, post-abandonment, or contemporary with the use of the house.

Reassuringly, the majority of the chronologically diagnostic artifacts recovered have date ranges that overlap with the radiocarbon indications of ca. A.D. 1200. The prehistoric artifacts recovered from House Mound 7 are listed in Table 5.2. The diagnostically Mississippian materials include 214 fragments of shell-tempered pottery, 1 Hamilton and 3 Madison projectile points, and 2 hoe-resharpening flakes. Several other prehistoric periods are also represented by small numbers of items: 3 eroded grog-tempered sherds probably of Late Woodland date; 8 sherds of sand-tempered Baldwin Plain *var. Chalk Bluff,* also probably of Late Woodland date; 3 unclassified grit-tempered sherds of unknown date (most likely Woodland); and 1 Little Bear Creek projectile point characteristic of Late Archaic times. Given the small numbers of pre-Mississippian diagnostics, the nondiagnostic artifacts will be treated as if they are all of Mississippian date.

The vertical distribution of the Mississippian diagnostics suggests that most of these artifacts are contemporary with the house. The house floor lay between 20 and 30 cm b.d., so artifacts above 20 cm b.d. would date after the house occupation. Given the apparent irregularity of the floor and difficulty in defining exactly where it was at any point, artifacts from 20–30 cm b.d. may be a mixture of pre- and post-occupation specimens, as well as items dating to the occupation of the house itself. Only 20 (10 percent) of the Mississippian diagnostics were found above 20 cm b.d., indicating that few items were discarded at this spot after the house burned.

Assessing whether the other 90 percent of the Mississippian diagnostics are contemporary with or antedate the house is not easy. The problem is that *inside* the house everything below 30 cm b.d. should antedate the house, but *outside* the house deflation of the surface has (at least potentially) jumbled together artifacts of ages from modern to pre-house. In some of the excavated units, the modern surface was lower than 30 cm below datum. Thus, if we add together all the artifacts from excavation levels below 30 cm, such a total would conflate "sealed" pre-house deposits from inside the house with chronologically mixed lag deposits from outside the house. To avoid such conflation, we can restrict the scope of our analysis to the four grid squares (S66/W255, S68/W255, S68/W254, S69/W255) that are (nearly) entirely inside the conjectural house outline.

The only chronologically diagnostic artifacts from the four grid squares inside the house are 43 shell-tempered sherds (4 are sufficiently unweathered to be classified Mississippi Plain *var. Shiloh*). Of these, 8 (19 percent) are above the floor level, 33 (77 percent) are from the 20–30 cm b.d. level that could include pre- and post-house materials, and only 2 (5 percent) are from definitely below the floor level. Though conclusions based on such a small sample might be erroneous, these data do not support the notion that substantial quantities of Mississippian materials were discarded at this location

Table 5.2 Prehistoric artifacts from House Mound 7

Description	Count	%
Pottery		
Sand-tempered (n=8)		
Baldwin Plain *var. Chalk Bluff* (medium sand)	8	3.5
Grit-tempered (n=3)		
Unclassified grit-tempered	3	1.3
Grog-tempered (n=3)		
Unclassified grog-tempered	3	1.3
Shell-tempered (n=214)		
Mississippi Plain *var. Shiloh*	10	4.4
Unclassified shell tempered eroded	204	89.5
Total pottery	228	100.0
Chipped Stone		
Core	3	0.3
Shatter	793	80.1
Flake, cortical	10	1.0
Flake, noncortical	129	13.0
Flake, biface retouch	41	4.1
Flake, hoe resharpening	2	0.2
Preform	4	0.4
Biface	1	0.1
Drill	1	0.1
Graver	1	0.1
Little Bear Creek projectile point	1	0.1
Hamilton projectile point	1	0.1
Madison projectile point	3	0.3
Total chipped stone	990	99.9
Ground Stone		
Abrader	1	100.0
Unworked Stone		
Chert, heat altered	593	17.3
Chert, not heat altered	1,134	33.1
Metaquartzite, indeterminate heat alteration	116	3.4
Unspecified metamorphic	2	0.1
Orthoquartzite	5	0.1

Continued on the next page

Table 5.2 *Continued*

Description	Count	%
Fossil crinoid	2	0.1
Sandstone	13	0.4
Limestone	2	0.1
Shale	1	<0.1
Chalk	1	<0.1
Conglomerate	1,010	29.5
Concretions	546	15.9
Total unworked stone	3,425	100.0

before the house was built. Tentatively, then, it appears that most of the Mississippian artifacts from the excavation derive from the occupation of the house itself, with small numbers of items being discarded here after the house collapsed.

Accepting the interpretation, then, that most of the recovered artifacts are contemporary with the occupation of the house, what do the artifacts indicate about activities at this location? The apparent emptying of the house before its conflagration hampers my ability to answer that question. The artifacts that were recovered are mostly small fragmentary items that would have accumulated along the edge of the wall or been trampled into the surface (see Hally 1983; Schiffer 1987:62–63). In all likelihood, this sort of artifact collection drastically underrepresents the diversity of activities carried out at this location. Only activities that produce small durable debris are likely to be represented; other activities, no matter how frequently performed or how important to the occupants, are unlikely to be represented. This is a common, though frustrating, problem in archaeology: we suspect that some evidence is missing but do not know what it is.

The available evidence consists entirely of pottery fragments, pieces of chipped stone, and one piece of ground stone. The pottery is badly weathered, with eroded surfaces. All but one of the shell-tempered sherds appear to be body sherds, with the exception being a fragment of a jar handle too incomplete to yield width-thickness or other potentially informative measurements. About the only thing the sherds reveal is that fragments of some broken pots accumulated here.

The one ground stone artifact is a piece of sandstone with an artificially smoothed surface. With no visible traces of mineral pigments or other material, I cannot say what was ground or abraded on this tool.

With the chipped stone, fortunately, I can begin to be more specific about activities in and around the house. There are not only several classes of tool present but also by-products of tool manufacture and maintenance. The raw materials for nearly all the tools are chert and quartzite pebbles from the Tuscaloosa Formation (Marcher and Stearns 1962). The Tuscaloosa gravels underlie the site and are exposed in the ravines that form the north and south edges of the site. The ready availability of the raw material led the knappers to an exploitation strategy that may have been efficient in terms of time but was highly inefficient in terms of use of this raw material.

The method of working these pebble cherts appears to have been to heat quantities of the pebbles in a fire. This improves the flaking quality of the chert, as well as changing the yellow-to-tan raw material to a deep red (Bond 1981:15–16; Ensor 1980, 1981:19–28). Of the 1,727 intact pebbles of Tuscaloosa chert, 593 (34.3 percent) are visibly heat-altered. During the heating, some pebbles shattered, as seen by nonconchoidal fracture surfaces and "potlids." After the heating, stoneworkers sorted through the material to find pieces—either whole pebbles or fragments—suitable for knapping (see Ensor [1981: 300–306] for a full description of this reduction strategy used on Tuscaloosa chert at another site). The heat treatment was not very thorough or perhaps not very well controlled. Many pieces displayed visible heat alteration near the exterior surface but not in the interior. Because of this heterogeneity in the effects of the heat treatment, I did not record presence/absence of heat treatment on shatter or other knapping products. Impressionistically, however, the vast majority of shatter displays some evidence of heat treatment.

The quantity of Tuscaloosa chert shatter (produced by either heat or knapping) is surprisingly small, only 793 pieces. That there were fewer than half as many pieces of shatter as there were intact pebbles indicates just how profligate the use of raw materials was. Most of the intact pebbles are far too small to be of use for knapping, which indicates that the stoneworkers did not bother to sort the raw material before heating it.

The lack of selection of the materials that went into the fire is also indicated by the presence of quartzite pebbles and shatter. The Tuscaloosa gravels contain quartzite pebbles as well as chert, but the quartzite fractures unpredictably and is not nearly as workable a material as the chert is. While the House Mound 7 assemblage contains quartzite pebbles and shatter, it does not contain flakes or tools of this material.

Three artifacts were identified as remnant cores. Two of these are Tuscaloosa chert, the other is a cream-to-tan-colored material that may just be a variant of the Tuscaloosa chert. All three cores were flaked in random fashion, producing flakes rather than blades.

In addition to the intact pieces of raw material, the shatter, and the core remnants, knapping is revealed by the presence of 84 flakes of Tuscaloosa chert. Of these, 9 (10.7 percent) are cortical flakes, 59 (70.2 percent) are non-cortical, and 16 (19.0 percent) are biface-retouch flakes. These quantities of knapping debris are inadequate to account for the two finished tools made of Tuscaloosa chert: a miscellaneous biface and a graver. Either most of the knapping debris produced here was cleaned away, or else some of the chipped stone tools used by this household were made elsewhere.

In addition to working Tuscaloosa chert, the residents of this household made or modified tools of other, in some cases nonlocal, materials. Some of these materials are identifiable, such as Dover, Ft. Payne, and Mill Creek chert, but several other materials are present for which I do not know the source. The unidentified materials include dark tan, tan, and creamy tan cherts that may just be variants within the Tuscaloosa chert, though unlike the typical Tuscaloosa material they are slightly translucent. Some of these pieces may be Cobden chert from southern Illinois. Most of these variously tan-colored pieces are noncortical flakes and shatter, though there is one core (previously mentioned) and a preform made of the creamy tan chert.

Among the raw materials whose source(s) I have not identified is a distinctive gray-speckled flint. Though the fracture surfaces are smooth, the material looks rather like a blend of coarse salt and pepper grains. It may be fossiliferous Ft. Payne, which Futato (1987:146) described with the same salt and pepper simile. There are pieces of shatter, noncortical flakes, and biface-retouch flakes of this material, as well as two finished tools. One of the finished tools is a Late Archaic, Little Bear Creek projectile point, probably attached to a spear. The other is a Madison point, likely an arrowhead.

The identified nonlocal materials include Ft. Payne, Dover, and Mill Creek chert. The Ft. Payne source is not very distant, cropping out only a few dozen kilometers upriver at Muscle Shoals, Alabama, as well as in the hills in eastern Hardin County, Tennessee. Dover flint comes from a little farther away, downriver in the neck of land between the Tennessee and Cumberland rivers. Mill Creek chert, by contrast, is a more distant material, coming from southern Illinois. All three of these cherts are represented mostly by shatter and noncortical flakes. The assemblage includes a crude preform, a graver, and a Madison projectile point made from Dover chert. There are also Mill Creek and Dover hoe-resharpening flakes (one each), with distinctive "hoe polish" on the dorsal surface. Both of these raw materials were extensively exploited for hoe manufacture during Mississippian times, and the hoes were widely traded across the Midwest and Midsouth (see, e.g., Brown et al. 1990; Cobb 2000). The presence of the resharpening flakes indicates the use of such hoes by the occupants of the house, even though the hoes themselves were not recovered.

Among the items made of unidentified, nonlocal materials are an amorphous biface, a drill, and a Hamilton projectile point. The biface is broken, has a plano-convex cross-section with an excurvate blade edge, and is made of a chert having shades of cream, white, and pink. The drill, or awl, is an elongate, narrow, bifacially flaked cylinder with an incurvate, ground base. The raw material has a white surface, though this color may be due to patination rather than the inherent coloration of the raw material. Because of the apparent surface patination and the ground, incurvate base, I suspect this is a spear point reworked into a drill or awl long before the Mississippian use of the Shiloh site. The Hamilton point, most likely used as an arrowhead, is rather crudely chipped from a gray chert. The point was snapped off, perhaps during manufacture. The knapper was not successful in thinning this tool, for a series of thinning flakes had hinged out, leaving a large lump projecting from one face.

These chipped stone items represent, directly or indirectly, a set of activities engaged in by the users of the house. These activities include acquisition and heat-treatment of local Tuscaloosa chert; manufacture of chipped stone tools from local chert; acquisition and knapping of several nonlocal cherts (Ft. Payne, Dover); use and resharpening of chert arrowheads (both local and nonlocal raw materials); use of a graver (for engraving or scratching lines on some hard substrate); importation of at least one Mill Creek chert and one Dover chert hoe, along with hoe use and resharpening; and use of a biface for some unidentified task(s). To this we can add the grinding of some unidentified material, as represented by the abrader. This is not a very extensive list of activities. In particular, woodworking is conspicuously absent from the list. Items of wood, cane, and other plant materials were prominent among the tools and utensils described for Historic Southeastern peoples (Swanton 1946:439–608), and the working of wood presumably required stone cutting or grinding tools. Yet no axes or adzes were found, nor any by-products of the manufacture or use of such tools. This may be due, of course, to the relative durability of such tools, their relatively high value, and the low rate of discard that both of these factors engender.

The spatial distributions of the unworked and the worked stone differ, though the distance between their centers of concentration is only a few meters. That distance, however, translates into a difference between the inside and the outside of the house (or, perhaps, in the center of the floor rather than along the walls). Pieces of conglomerate (see Figure 5.8) and unchipped Tuscaloosa chert pebbles (see Figure 5.9) are most numerous in the center of the house mound, i.e., in the center of the house. In contrast to the distribution by count, the distribution by weight shows that while these materials are most numerous near the center of the house, the largest pieces are found outside the house: conglomerates on the east side (see Figure 5.10) and un-

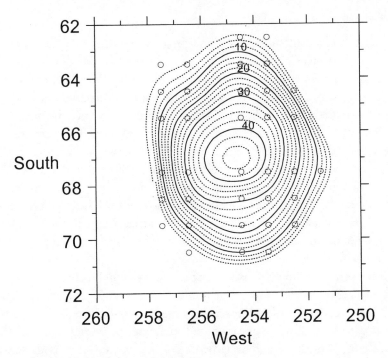

Figure 5.8. Spatial distribution of conglomerates, by count

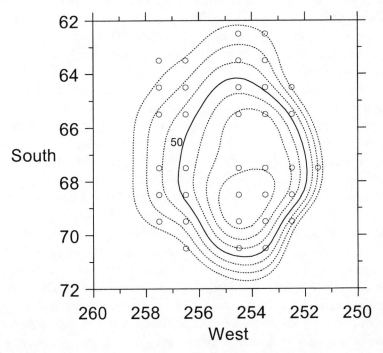

Figure 5.9. Spatial distribution of unworked Tuscaloosa chert, by count

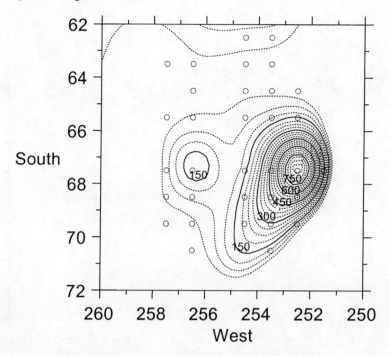

Figure 5.10. Spatial distribution of conglomerates, by weight

worked Tuscaloosa chert on the west side (see Figure 5.11). Like these larger chunks of raw material, knapping by-products are found mostly along or outside the walls. This can be seen in the distribution of shatter (see Figure 5.12), cortical and noncortical flakes (see Figure 5.13), and biface-retouch flakes (see Figure 5.14); all are most numerous along or outside the southeast side of the house. These distribution patterns can be summarized simply: large and sharp pieces of stone were not left in the middle of the floor. Indeed, the only surprising aspect of the distribution of stone is that so many small pebbles—many with a diameter smaller than a dime—were left in the center of the floor.

That so many pebbles of Tuscaloosa chert were found close to the hearth suggests that the hearth may have been where chert was heat-treated. Though it is an obvious conclusion to draw, I would be surprised if it were true. During the heat treatment, a significant number of pebbles explode. If the chert undergoing this treatment is not contained somehow, e.g., in a pit, the treatment process results in sharp pieces of hot chert whizzing through the air. This would be rather dangerous to occupants of the house. Given that there was a large amount of open space inside the site's palisade, it seems far more likely that heat-treatment would have been carried out somewhere out-

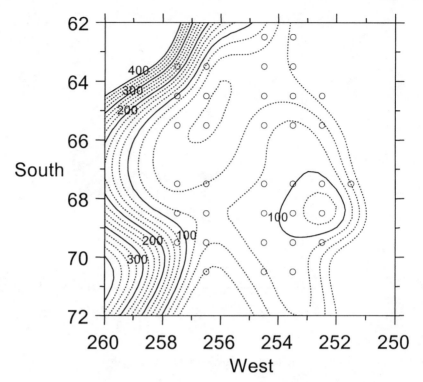

Figure 5.11. Spatial distribution of unworked Tuscaloosa chert, by weight

doors. Yet, if the chert was not treated inside the house, I have no good
explanation for the large numbers of small pebbles inside the house.

While the focus of the excavation was the prehistoric material associated
with House Mound 7, during the excavation a few Civil War–era items were
recovered. Accounts of the battle (e.g., Allen 1997a, 1997b; Sword 1988) show
that relatively little fighting took place within the confines of the prehistoric
site. During the first day of the battle, Union troops were mostly west of the
site, notably along the line of the "Sunken Road." By the time that position
collapsed, the Confederates had already come around the Union left flank
and passed west of the site, moving to pinch off the retreat from the Sunken
Road. At the end of the day—after the surrender of the Sunken Road—units
under Clanton, Chalmers, and Jackson formed up in line east-west across the
prehistoric site and advanced north into Dill Branch ravine. Because of the
steepness of the ravine slopes, the heavy Union defenses on the opposite crest,
and the approach of darkness, this advance soon stalled and the Confederate
command called the troops back. The troops retreated several miles to the
west to spend the night, with only a squadron of cavalry under Nathan
Bedford Forrest occupying the mound site overnight (Allen 1997b:14). In the

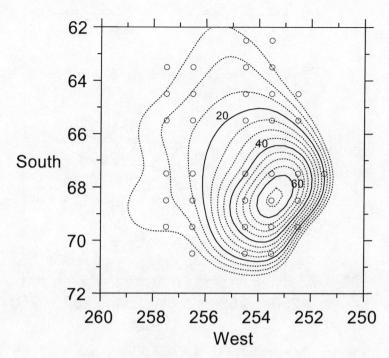

Figure 5.12. Spatial distribution of shatter, by count

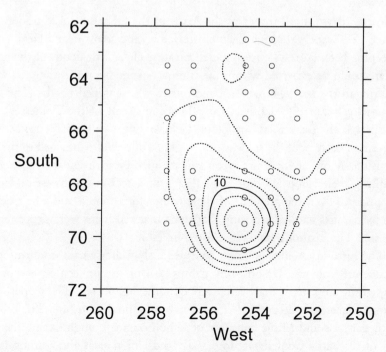

Figure 5.13. Spatial distribution of cortical and noncortical flakes, by count

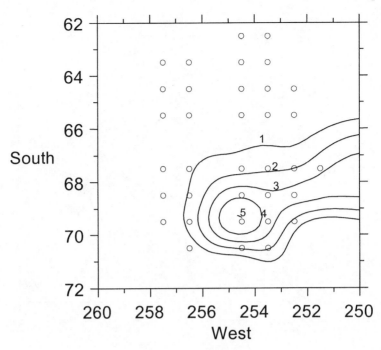

Figure 5.14. Spatial distribution of biface-retouch flakes, by count

following dawn, fresh troops of the Army of the Ohio advanced unopposed across Dill Branch, through the prehistoric site, and across Cloud Field, easily sweeping back Forrest's outnumbered cavalry. Thus, little debris of the battle itself should be expected within the confines of the prehistoric site.

Prior to the battle, however, Union units were camped nearby. The 17th Kentucky Infantry (3rd Brigade, 4th Division, Army of the Tennessee) was camped at the eastern end of Cloud Field, only 195 m from House Mound 7. Mann's Battery, of the 1st Missouri Light Artillery (also attached to the 4th Division, Army of the Tennessee), was camped even closer; the monument marking their camp is inside the palisade line, 100 m southwest of House Mound 7. Given the presence of these camps for a month and a half before the battle, it is hardly surprising that some material items were deposited on the site. The historic artifacts are listed in Table 5.3.

The historic assemblage has a conspicuously military cast, confirming its derivation from the Union army camps. All of the projectiles, except the grapeshot, are rounds that were dropped rather than fired. The grapeshot is strongly faceted, indicating that it came from a fired munition. The bullets, both flat-base and Minié balls, are of Union origin (though during the first day of the battle Confederate forces salvaged Union arms and ammunition).

Table 5.3 Historic artifacts from House Mound 7

Description	Count
Bullets and other munitions	
Flat base bullet, .54 caliber, 2-ring, unfired	3 complete
Flat base bullet, .58 caliber, 2-ring, unfired	1 complete
Minié ball (conical base), .58 caliber, 3-ring, unfired	1 complete
Musket (round) ball, .45 to .47 caliber, unfired	1 complete
Grapeshot, faceted	1 complete
Buckles, iron, square D-shaped, with roller,	5 complete,
for 1½" belt or strap	4 roller fragments
Key, iron, for a chest or locker	1 incomplete
Nails, iron, wrought or cut	4 incomplete
Staple or mounting bracket, iron, wrought or cut	1 complete (?)
Unidentifiable corroded iron	5 fragments
Window glass	6 fragments
Medicine bottle	1 (29 fragments)

The flat-base bullets and the round ball are consistent with infantry weapons, perhaps from the 17th Kentucky Infantry camped nearby. The Minié ball, however, is a curiosity, for in this caliber such a round indicates either a Burnside or Sharp carbine, which were not common this early in the war and were primarily cavalry rifles (Stacy Allen, personal communication; John Cornelison, personal communication). No Union cavalry are known to have camped or to have maneuvered in this area. The iron buckles closely match some on display in the Park Visitor Center, especially those on a bag used by Union artillerymen. This would be consistent with an origin in Mann's Battery, camped nearby. However, such buckles are not very diagnostic; I have a (modern) belt with a nearly identical buckle. The only other item in Table 5.3 that is chronologically diagnostic is the medicine bottle.

Medicine bottles are common nineteenth-century artifacts. This one was found smashed into 29 fragments, all but 3 of which were found in a single 1-×-1-m grid square and within a single 10-cm arbitrary level. The other three pieces were found in adjacent units or levels. The glass is clear, with a light green cast. The base bears a pontil mark, but on the interior of the base and on the sides the seam of a two-piece mold is clearly visible. The seam extends up the neck to near the lip, which was finished by hand. A molten bead of glass was attached to the neck, stretched out, cut, then folded inside and smoothed. The bottle would have had a cork stopper. Because this combination of hand-work and mold techniques was used during much of the nineteenth century, the bottle is not definitely of Civil War origin. However, given the military character of the rest of the assemblage of historic artifacts, it is reasonable to assume that this bottle, too, was left by one of the soldiers who camped or fought here.

EVALUATION OF THE INVESTIGATION

The excavation of House Mound 7 produced less information about prehistoric lifeways than I had hoped for when the research design was prepared, yet it did produce unexpected insights into the nature of this archaeological site. The most striking finding was that the house floor at this house mound, and possibly many of the others, is elevated above the level of the current surrounding ground surface. This finding is important primarily for its implications for any future excavation or other disturbance at the site. If sloping areas of the site have been stripped of 20 to 30 cm of sediments, we should not expect sheet midden in these areas. In these areas, prehistoric features that were shallow may no longer be present, but on the other hand the bottom portions of originally deep features would now be near the surface. If there are human burials in such eroded areas, for example, the skeletons and funerary objects might be very close to the surface. Thus, even though sloping portions of the site may not have extensive prehistoric deposits, care should be taken to avoid even shallow disturbances to the modern surface.

Another implication of the prehistoric erosion of some parts of the site is that other parts of the site may have been zones of accumulation. Such colluvial accumulations might be present, for example, in the pond area southwest of Mound G. If there are such deposits in these or other ponds at the site, it is even conceivable that waterlogging and deoxygenation of the deposits may have preserved organic materials (recall the "humus & muck" Chambers [1933–1934:5] recorded in a small pond north of Mound K). Thus, the pond deposits should not be disturbed without careful testing to ascertain whether they contain sensitive deposits.

Turning now to the House Mound 7 area specifically, one significant finding is that there is very little grog-tempered pottery at this location. The excavation collection from 1933–1934 contains a nearly even mixture of grog-tempered and shell-tempered pottery, which naturally has led to questions about possible chronological overlap of grog-tempered and shell-tempered pottery at this site. At House Mound 7, however, the data show that little, if any, grog-tempered pottery was in use by A.D. 1200. Several possibilities arise from this observation. It is possible that the eastern portion of the site near the bluff had substantial occupation prior to the A.D. 1200 date of House Mound 7, at a time when both shell- and grog-tempered pottery were being used. Alternatively, perhaps there was no overlap, and instead the eastern portion of the site was the location of a Late Woodland occupation that was abandoned before the advent of shell-tempered pottery. Data from the House Mound 7 excavation do not help discriminate between these two alternatives, but the data do constrain any chronological overlap to the period before A.D. 1200.

Initially I had planned to excavate a burned building in the hope that it might contain many artifacts that the occupants did not have time to remove while the house burned over their heads. At the time House Mound 7 was selected for excavation I did not expect that it contained a burned structure, but the multiple species and uniformly small size of the charred wood in and around the central hearth suggest that a building probably did burn here. This building—if that's what it was—appears to have been cleaned out before the fire. So, even though I apparently did excavate a burned building, I did not find out as much about the activities of the occupants as I had hoped. It is particularly frustrating that no subsistence remains were encountered, for the recovery and analysis of charred plant materials are now much more sophisticated than was the case in the 1930s. Yet the excavation does tell us some things about what people did here.

The occupants of House 7 made some of their chipped stone tools from the Tuscaloosa chert pebbles that are available at the edges of the site. Quantities of these pebbles, apparently not even sorted by size, were heat-treated and the resulting material examined for usable pieces. These pieces were fashioned into at least one cutting tool (a biface) and a graver. Other raw materials were also used, including Ft. Payne, Dover, and Mill Creek cherts, plus an assortment of other raw materials not yet identified. Unlike the Tuscaloosa chert, however, these raw materials came to the site in the form of finished tools (e.g., Mill Creek hoes) or at least as preforms or cores from which cortex had already been trimmed. Tools of both local and nonlocal materials were (re)sharpened just outside the house, most notably at grid square S70 W255; one-quarter of all biface-thinning flakes were found in this grid square, including a Mill Creek hoe-resharpening flake. If Roberts is correct that doorways were mostly on the east to southeast side of houses, we can imagine a knapper sitting just outside the door of the house, working sharp edges onto a set of stone tools.

This picture of a knapper working just outside the doorway assumes that the retouch flakes are found where they were produced. However, it is also possible that the knapping was done inside the house, with the uncomfortably sharp by-products swept out the door. It seems unlikely that such sweeping was done frequently, for there is no evidence of the floor surface being lowered by repeated sweeping.

The small quantity and poor preservation of the shell-tempered pottery prevents firm conclusions about the nature of the vessel assemblage used in this household. The only vessel form demonstrably present is a handled jar, but this apparent exclusivity may easily be a result of preservation biases. Had larger numbers of rims been present and in better condition, we could have compared the kinds and sizes of vessels used at House 7 with those used elsewhere on the site, a kind of analysis that has yielded interesting results at other Mississippian sites (e.g., Blitz 1993; Maxham 2000; Welch and Scarry 1995). Similarly, the absence of preserved subsistence remains forestalls analyses like those done by Jackson and Scott (1995a, 1995b; Welch 1991:77–103) and Scarry (Scarry and Steponaitis 1997; Welch and Scarry 1995). Thus, several of the kinds of analysis for which House 7 data had been anticipated are simply not possible.

Finally, it is worth noting that Mound 7 is one of a cluster of five such mounds. Several other such clusters are present at the site. It is a reasonable conjecture that such clusters represent the buildings used by a single family, perhaps an extended one. Hudson (1976:213) summarized the ethnohistorical literature and pointed to a worthy goal for future archaeological research:

Eighteenth-century Creek, Cherokee, Chickasaw, and Choctaw households typically consisted of clusters of buildings. At a minimum these consisted of a summer house and a winter house, and large households in some places added a third or even a fourth building for storage or other uses. The extent to which this pattern of multiple houses extends back into Mississippian times is not definitely known.

6 Queens College Fieldwork in 1999

For the second season of fieldwork I again tried to locate and excavate a burned house. With the first season's efforts directed to a house near the edge of town, the second season's attention was directed to the center of town. The reason for shifting the focus was to find out whether there were differences between households in the different parts of the site. Funding for the second season was obtained from NPS sources by the park superintendent, Woody Harrell. Also during this second season, an archaeological crew from the Southeast Archeological Center of NPS spent several weeks at the site mapping, remote-sensing, and conducting test excavations to help resolve issues important to the preparation of this report.

Unlike the 1998 season, when we spent several days trying to find a previous excavation grid system, in 1999 we found that our original datum stake and a half dozen others were still in situ. We therefore had no difficulty re-creating the 1998 grid system and using it for the 1999 excavations. The NPS fieldwork in 1999 also used this grid system, so all proveniences recorded in 1998 and 1999 use the Welch 1998 grid system (as does the National Park Service excavation on Mound A that began in 2001).

CORING HOUSE MOUNDS

As in 1998, we began by extracting small-diameter soil cores from house mounds, inspecting the cores for charcoal and fired clay. Actually, coring of mounds near the center of the site began at the end of the 1998 field season, with 17 mounds sampled. At the start of 1999, two of these were re-cored, and an additional six mounds sampled (with multiple cores each). Again as in 1998, coordinates for the cores were obtained by taping from known points, or in some cases recording taped distances along bearings taken with a Brunton compass. Locations for all these cores are shown in Figure 6.1, with the numbers continuing at the end of the 1998 sequence shown in Figure 5.1. Only one of the cored mounds, number 44 in Figure 6.1, displayed a layer of

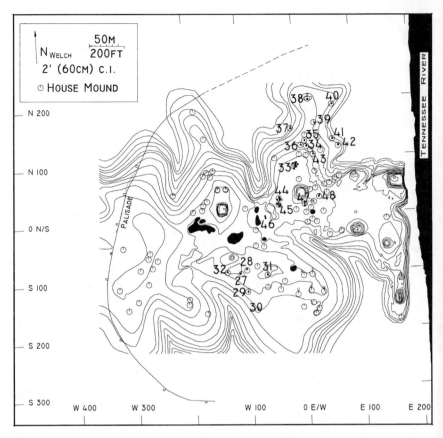

Figure 6.1. Locations of house mounds cored for 1999 season

charcoal and fired clay, and this was the one that had been labeled Mound N by Roberts in the 1930s. Because we knew at the time that we cored it that this mound had been designated "N", we used this appellation consistently in the field records.

We took four cores from Mound N. These were labeled the North, East, South, and West cores, though as shown in Figure 6.2 the East core is almost directly between the North and South cores. The only core that contained fired clay was the East core, in which the deposits between 46 and 68 cm below surface consisted of chunks of apparently fired red and dark brown clay. The South core penetrated only to 29 cm below surface, and the North core only to 30 cm below surface, so we were not disturbed that they failed to display the same fired clay deposit as the East core. We interpreted the core results as indicating that there was a burned structure whose floor was buried beneath 68 cm of overlying deposit. This being the only house mound we

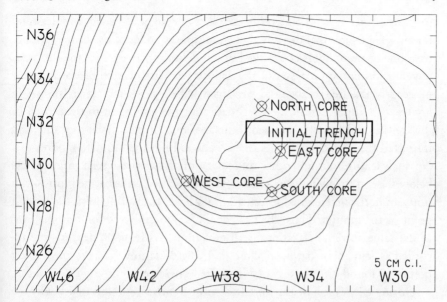

Figure 6.2. Mound N topography, core locations, and initial excavation trench

found with evidence of a burned structure, we chose it for excavation despite the greater than expected depth of the overlying deposit.

Incidentally, at the time of the 1999 fieldwork, I was not aware of Bellomo's (1983) unpublished master's thesis, in which he reported extracting cores from Mound N and finding charcoal and fired clay (see Chapter 2). As it turns out, this was not the only work on Mound N that had remained unpublished and of which I was consequently unaware.

EXCAVATION

In the previous season, the floor of the burned structure we excavated had been only 20–30 cm beneath the mound summit. A floor this shallowly buried does not take a great deal of time to expose. At Mound N, it appeared that we would have to excavate 68 cm of overburden, including 22 cm of burned structural debris. Because the 1999 field season was twice as long as 1998's, I thought we could expose the floor below Mound N despite the greater amount of overburden. As it turned out, this decision was overly optimistic because the floor was deeper than expected. This was not the only, or even the biggest, surprise that Mound N gave us.

With the soil core showing 46 cm of deposits atop the burned structural debris, it was obvious that the overburden was not simply collapsed daub. Such a depth of deposit clearly indicated intentional deposition of fill atop the burned structure. Though the core had not suggested such, I understood that it was possible that there might be multiple episodes of use of the mound, with one or more floors above the burned debris. To make sure the stratigraphy and formation processes of the deposit were understood before we commenced broad-area excavation, we began with a 6-×-1-m trench (shown in Figure 6.2) running from the west margin of the mound in to the center. In the trench, and in all subsequent units, we first sliced off the root mat and inspected the surface for evidence of features from the ultimate mound use. No such features, or any other soil color differences, were seen immediately below the sod in any unit. As in the 1998 excavations, we excavated in 1-×-1-m units, in horizontal aligned 10-cm arbitrary levels measuring from the highest point of the mound. Thus, the base of the 10–20-cm level, for example, was at the same absolute elevation in all grid units. As in 1998, depths were recorded as "cm below datum" ("cm b.d.") where "datum" refers to the highest point of Mound N. All excavated deposits were screened through ¼-in mesh.

During excavation of the initial 6-×-1-m trench, we found that below the sod there was a leached (E) soil horizon, and below the zone of leaching we found that the deposits were a jumble of patches of different colors and textures of sediment. These mixed sediments included chunks of fired clay and charcoal, and artifacts. Clearly, this deposit was fill, which was what we were expecting.

The first unexpected finding was two small, perfectly circular, vertical holes that had been filled with clean sand. These appear to be two 2-in-diameter (5 cm) sediment cores whose holes were intentionally filled with sterile coarse sand. Later in the season, we encountered two more such features. All four of them were excavated as features (Features. 1, 2, 4, 5), with their contents removed in 10-cm arbitrary levels and screened through fine (1/8 in) mesh. None of the features contained anything but sand and very small quartz pebbles. The fact that the core holes were intentionally filled with sterile sand suggests that the cores were the work of archaeologists rather than, say, road crews. It was only months later that the origin of the cores was discovered in the field notes of Randy Bellomo (Bellomo 1981), who had extracted the cores in connection with his master's thesis (Bellomo 1983).

At 40 cm b.d. in the eastern end of the initial excavation trench, we encountered a puzzling feature: an L-shaped band of homogeneous silt along the north and east sides of the N31 W32 unit. Inside the homogeneous silt zone there was one circular patch of charcoal. I interpreted this as the remains of a charred post in a wall-trench and labeled the L-shaped silt deposit Feature 3. Because there had been no indication of a floor west of this presumed wall-trench, I believed that this must be part of a structure lying east of

Mound N. By the next day, however, we were beginning to suspect that things were not as we had thought.

At 50 cm b.d., a narrow band of homogeneous silt was visible along the north edge of units N31 W34 and N31 W35. By 60 cm b.d. it was clear that the homogeneous silt formed a continuous band along, and almost exactly parallel with, the north side of our excavation. At the eastern end of our excavation, the homogeneous silt in this "feature" turned a right angle and ran south, forming an L-shaped band along two sides of our excavation trench. At the depth where the core indicated we ought to be encountering burned debris, we continued to find mottled fill. The L-shaped band of homogeneous silt had a not-quite-vertical face that was expanding into our excavation trench as we went downward. Thus, it became clear that the L-shaped band was not itself a feature but rather that it was the undisturbed matrix around a large rectangular feature whose edges almost coincided with our excavation trench. A large straight-sided feature running east-west from the edge of the mound into the center sounded, in fact, remarkably like the archaeological excavation we ourselves were conducting, and thus we began to suspect that this might be an undocumented excavation unit from 1933–1934.

To ascertain whether we had been digging inside an old excavation trench, we expanded the excavation to the north, west, and south. In unit N32 W37, at 10 cm b.d., we found the north edge of the old excavation trench, and we traced this northern edge an additional 2 m to the west by excavating several additional shallow units. On the east side of the mound, in unit N30 W32, we found the southeast corner of that trench about 1.2 m (roughly 4 ft) from the northwest corner. With the edges of this east-west rectilinear feature visible within 10 cm of the modern surface, it was clear that the feature must be recent. So the feature is a recent, straight-sided, right-angled feature over 7 m long but only 1.3 m wide, with an east-west orientation rotated a few degrees clockwise from our 1998 grid. No artifacts of 1930s vintage were found in the fill of the trench, and nothing in the field records from 1933–1934 indicates any excavation in Mound N (there is record of excavation in Mound O, just to the south of N), but given the size, shape, and orientation of the feature (the 1933–1934 grid was based on a magnetic declination about 5 degrees clockwise from our grid's declination), it is almost certain that we had excavated our initial 6-×-1-m trench precisely inside a similar trench excavated by Roberts. The outline of the old trench, at the depth where it first became distinguishable, is shown in Figure 6.3.

Once it was clear what had happened, it was also clear that we could obtain a vertical profile through the mound by cleaning the side of the old excavation trench. The south side of the old trench was offset about 30 cm

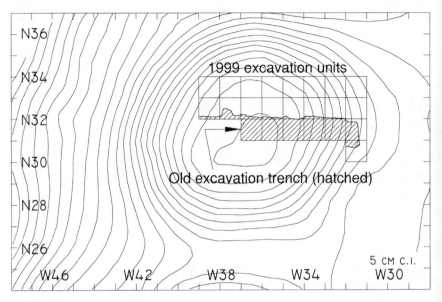

Figure 6.3. Outline of old excavation trench, Mound N

from our existing 6-×-1-m trench, while the north side of the old trench almost perfectly coincided with our trench. Thus, it would take far less work to expose the profile along the north side of the old trench, which is what we did. The northern profile is shown in Figure 6.4.

As had been hoped, the profile along the north side of the old excavation trench displayed a deposit of fired clay and charcoal roughly 50 b.d. In some places, the base of this deposit appeared to be a 1–2-cm-thick band of fired clay that could be a burned floor surface. This band lay atop a pale ashy homogeneous silt (the deposit we had initially labeled Feature 3). The sediment above the zone of fired clay and charcoal was clearly fill, at least up to the base of the leached E horizon. From the base of the E horizon upward, any stratigraphy that might have been present would have been obliterated by bioturbation and leaching. Thus, Mound N appeared to have 45–50 cm of fill deposited above the remains of a burned structure, whose floor appeared to be at 50–55 cm b.d. We attempted to excavate that portion of the burned structure lying in the 6-×-2-m block of units north of the initial 6-×-1-m trench.

During the excavation of the 6-×-2-m block, we found that the leached E horizon extended deeper than it had in the backfill in the old trench, corresponding to the difference between 700 or 800 years of weathering on the intact mound and 65 years weathering on the backfilled 1933–1934 trench. Under the leached zone, the sediments consisted of patches of a variety of

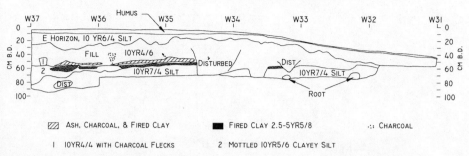

Figure 6.4. Vertical section along north wall of old excavation trench, Mound N

textures and colors—fill, as expected. We began to encounter lots of fired clay and scattered charcoal in grid square N33 W36 around 35 cm b.d. and at depths between 40 and 50 cm b.d. in adjacent squares. It is not clear whether all of this material is debris from the burned structure, for we were not able to make any clear distinction between this and the overlying fill. Most of the fired clay, though sometimes bright orange or red, was finely comminuted rather than consisting of solid chunks. This made it impossible to see any impressions of organic wall materials on the fired clay. We continued removing the fill and burned material until reaching the level of the fired clay band that was visible in the profile at ca. 50 cm b.d., which we had interpreted as the floor of the burned structure.

Upon exposing the fired clay band visible in the profile, we found that Mound N had surprised us again. The fired clay band was clearly not a burned floor but instead was a discontinuous band of fired clay rubble. That is, rather than being a smooth surface, the band actually consisted of multiple fragments of fired clay. Though the vertical profile suggested that the band was lying on a fairly smooth surface, no such surface was visible as we excavated down through the band. To complicate matters, a den or burrow (groundhog-sized) had run on a slight slant down through the fired clay deposits in squares N32 W34–37, disrupting the integrity of the deposits in most of these three squares. Nevertheless, it eventually became clear that even though the fired clay rubble lay mostly between 50 and 65 cm b.d., the floor of the house lay 15–20 cm below that. Unlike the house excavated in 1998, which had been built directly on the natural ground surface, the house beneath Mound N had been built in a shallow basin so that the floor was 15–20 cm beneath the ground surface outside the house. True to the archaeological maxim that important discoveries usually occur in the last week of the field season, there was only a week left in our season when we discovered that the floor was 15–20 cm deeper than had been expected. With so little time left,

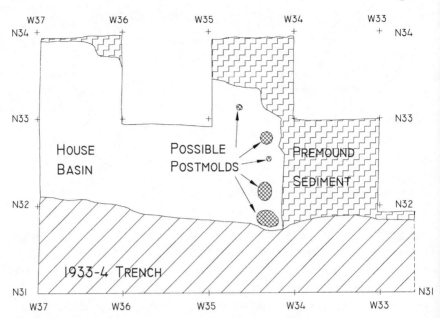

Figure 6.5. House basin and possible postholes beneath Mound N

we were able to expose only a small portion of the floor and define only a portion of the outline of the house basin. The basin outline and several features that may be holes for wall posts are shown in Figure 6.5.

So little of the house basin is exposed that it is difficult to tell whether the structure is circular or rectangular. The postmolds, if that is what they are, are 10 to 20 cm in diameter, which is consistent with the small-diameter, bent-pole building supports seen in excavations in the 1930s. Roberts (Stirling 1935:395) reported that wall support poles were spaced approximately 4 ft (1.2 m) apart, while the possible postmolds beneath Mound N are much more closely spaced. Whether this indicates a different construction technique is a question best left unanswered until more of the house basin has been exposed and a clearer picture of the structural details obtained.

Some of the burned structural debris lay as much as 20 cm above the house floor. This of course raises the question of whether the burned debris is in fact related to the floor, or whether it is merely part of the fill that was placed atop the old house site. That the structure burned is clearly demonstrated by the vertical profiles of the excavation (see Figures 6.4 and 6.6). A layer of burned debris can be seen lying atop the old ground surface outside the house basin, and the edges of the basin itself are also fired. Yet it appears that when the superstructure collapsed, the house basin had already partly filled with silt. This evidence of filling before burning indicates that the struc-

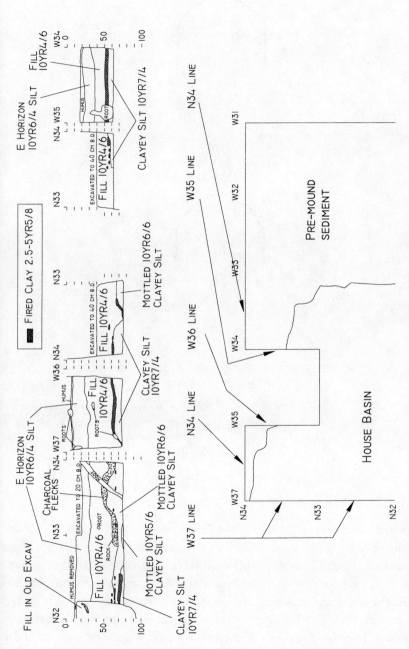

Figure 6.6. Vertical sections along north and west edges of Mound N excavation

HOUSE IS BUILT IN BASIN

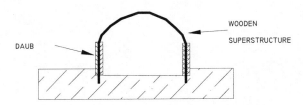

HOUSE IS ABANDONED,
DAUB WASHES INTO BASIN

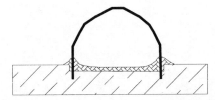

SUPERSTRUCTURE BURNS, TOP OF DAUB FIRES RED,
DEBRIS FILLS BASIN

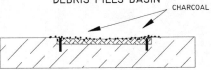

Figure 6.7. Model of the abandonment and burning of the sub–Mound N house

ture had stood empty for some time before burning, and during this abandonment some of the daub from the walls (and roof, which may also have
been daubed [see Chambers n.d.]) washed into the basin. This abandonment
period cannot have been more than a couple of years, for there was still
sufficient wood and other organic components of the superstructure to fuel
an intense fire. The burning of the walls rubified not only the remaining daub but also the edges of the house basin, where the walls extended
down below the surrounding ground surface. This scenario is illustrated in
Figure 6.7.

ARTIFACTS AND ACTIVITIES

For the purposes of analysis, the deposits in Mound N can be separated into three contexts: material inside the house at the time the walls collapsed/ burned; material deposited after the collapse and fire; and material in the backfill of the old excavation trench. In Table 6.1, all the artifacts from the excavation are tallied by these analytical groups. The chronological relationships between these contexts are not as straightforward as it may seem at first glance. Artifacts that were "inside," i.e., among or under the collapsed wall and roof material, may date to the use of the house. However, it is also possible that these may be items deposited in the house basin after the structure's abandonment, conceivably including items from the Late Woodland or even earlier components that eroded out of the surrounding matrix and were re-deposited in the house basin. So the artifacts "inside" the house may have little or nothing to do with activities of the house's occupants. Everything "above" the house comes from fill that was deposited after the house was burned, and because all this material is fill brought from somewhere else all the artifacts in this deposit are in secondary context. The artifacts that came as part of the fill may antedate the use of the house, be contemporary with it, or postdate it. Of course, after the fill was deposited, there may well have been items discarded on the surface which bioturbation has incorporated into the deposit, as is clearly the case with some glass bottle fragments and other recent items. The artifacts in the backfill of the old excavation trench presumably include items from both of these two previous contexts; these artifacts are thus in secondary or even tertiary context. To summarize this fairly complex situation, some of the artifacts from the excavation probably antedate the house, some from the "inside" context may relate to the use of the house itself, and artifacts from the "above" and "old trench fill" contexts may be a mixture of earlier and later periods.

The small numbers of artifacts from inside the house tell us little about activities inside the structure. The pottery is nearly all eroded, which suggests that these may be sherds that fell into, or were washed into, the open house basin after its abandonment. Several of the stone tools, e.g., the side-notched projectile point and the nutting stone, may also have been debris from previous occupations of the site. The projectile point, for example, is broken into multiple pieces as if it had been stepped on (they appear to be old breaks, not caused by my excavators). Presumably, some of the nondiagnostic items, such as flaking debris, also derive from earlier components.

The "inside" assemblage does have two notable aspects, however. First, several pieces of mica were found among the fired clay rubble of the house

Table 6.1 Prehistoric artifacts from Mound N

Description	Inside the house	Above the house	Old trench fill	Total	% of total
Pottery					
Sand-tempered (n=13)					
Baldwin Plain *var. Chalk Bluff*	1			1	*
var. Miller Slough			1	1	*
Furrs Cordmarked *var. unspecified*			1	1	*
Unclassified sand-tempered, eroded		3	7	10	0.5
Grit-tempered (n=1)					
Unclassified grit-tempered, eroded			1	1	*
Grog-tempered (n=571)					
Baytown Plain *var. McKelvey*	2	25	15	42	2.2
var. The Fork		3	2	5	0.3
Mulberry Creek Cordmarked *var. Mulberry Creek*	1	55	30	86	4.4
var. Coffee Landing			1	1	*
Unclassified grog-tempered, eroded	14	252	168	434	22.4
Unclassified grog-and-sand-tempered, eroded		1	2	3	0.2
Shell-tempered (n=1,354)					
Bell Plain *var. unspecified*		5	1	6	0.3
Mississippi Plain *var. Shiloh*		29	18	47	2.4
var. Shiloh discoidal		1		1	*
var. unspecified (shell and sand)		1		1	*
Moundville Incised *var. Moundville*		1		1	*

Unclassified shell-tempered, eroded	25	815	447	1,287	66.4
Unclassified shell-and-grog-tempered, eroded	1	1	1	3	0.2
Unclassified shell-and-sand-tempered, eroded	1	2	5	8	0.4
Total pottery	44	1,195	700	1,939	99.7
Chipped Stone					
Core	1	2	2	5	0.1
Shatter	76	1,545	1,305	2,926	84.4
Flake, cortical	5	43	19	67	1.9
Flake, noncortical	28	189	144	361	10.4
Flake, biface retouch		4	5	9	0.3
Flake, hoe resharpening		3	4	7	0.2
Flake tool (utilized flake)	1	36	17	54	1.6
Preform		2		2	0.1
Preform for a drill			1	1	*
Uniface		1		1	*
Biface		4	2	6	0.2
Awl		1		1	*
Drill		10	6	16	0.5
Scraper			4	4	0.1
Kirk Corner-notched projectile point	1			1	*
Unclassified side-notched projectile point		1		1	*
Hamilton projectile point		2		2	*
Madison projectile point		1	2	3	*
Total chipped stone	112	1,844	1,511	3,467	99.8

Continued on the next page

Table 6.1 Continued

Description	Inside the house	Above the house	Old trench fill	Total	% of total
Ground Stone					
Abrader		1		1	3.7
Grinding stone		5	2	7	25.9
Ground stone		6		6	22.2
Nutting stone	1			1	3.7
Red ocher	1	2	2	5	18.5
Yellow ocher			2	2	7.4
Saw		4	1	5	18.5
Total ground stone	2	18	7	27	99.9
Unworked Stone					
Chert, Tuscaloosa	235	6,370	4,939	11,544	42.5
Chert, unidentified		4	63	67	0.2
Metaquartzite	32	815	756	1,603	5.9
Unspecified metamorphic			2	2	*
Mica	5			5	*
Fossil coral	1	11	7	19	*
Fossil crinoid		6	3	9	*
Fossil, unidentified		1	1	2	*
Orthoquartzite	6	72	62	140	0.5
Sandstone		15	41	56	0.2
Sandstone, ferruginous		1	3	4	*
Limestone		22	10	32	0.1
Mudstone		5	3	8	*

Chalk	117		35	35	0.1
Conglomerate		3,993	2,986	7,096	26.1
Concretions	17	2,017	2,659	4,693	17.2
Small pebbles from Features 1, 2, 4, 5 (core holes)		1,874		1,874	6.9
Total unworked stone	413	15,206	11,570	27,189	99.7
Fired clay and daub	5	425	755	1,185	100.0
Carbonized plant material	27	527	2,777	3,331	100.0

*less than 0.1%

walls. The mica was noted at the time of the excavation, and it was clearly among the rubble, not in deposits that accumulated inside the house before it burned. The mica must have been inside, or perhaps on, the wall of the house at the time it burned. Mica being a nonlocal material that was generally highly valued in Mississippian cultures, its presence inside the house indicates that the house's occupants had better-than-average access to this status-display material. In the 1930s Roberts found mica fragments on two house floors flanking the plaza, west of Mound D. That location is analogous to the location of Mound N, which flanks the plaza and is west of Mound F. The other noteworthy aspect of the "inside" assemblage is what is absent: drills and saws such as those found in the overlying deposits. The significance of these tools is addressed below, but the important point here is that there is no evidence that the drills and saws derive from the house below Mound N.

The assemblage from above the debris of the burned walls is certainly a mixture of items from different periods. The Kirk corner-notched projectile point, for example, is an Early Archaic diagnostic, the grog-tempered and sand-tempered pottery are likely of Woodland date, and the shell-tempered pottery is of Mississippian date. Given that the majority of the pottery (71.5 percent) is shell-tempered, I suspect that the majority of the nondiagnostic artifacts are of Mississippian date, though of course it is impossible to specify which are and which are not. Thus, much of the flaking debris is likely of Mississippian date, along with some of the chipped and ground stone tools. It is unfortunate that the stone tools were found in a secondary, chronologically mixed deposit, because these tools do tell us something important about the Shiloh site.

Several of the kinds of stone tools in the fill above the house floor, e.g., small triangular arrowheads and utilized flakes, have been found at nearly all Mississippian sites in the region, but the drills and saws are not nearly so common. The drills (see Figure 3.21) are small tools, 1.5–4.0 cm long, made from flakes or blades of chert. Their lateral margins have steep, unifacial retouch from the ventral face that creates a narrow, nearly conical shaft protruding from a wide base. In cross-section the drill bits are rectangular or plano-convex. The tips and chipped edges on some specimens are visibly abraded, indicating that the tools were applied to a hard material, probably harder than wood. Where visible, the wear rarely if ever extends more than 1 cm from the tip, indicating that the material being drilled was not very thick (or at least that the holes were not very deep). Of the 10 drills found in fill above the burned house, 2 were made from Tuscaloosa chert, 1 from Ft. Payne chert, and the other 7 from unidentified cherts (in several instances these may simply be unusually colored Tuscaloosa chert). This high frequency of nonlocal chert is unusual, given that chert was available literally at the edge of the site.

Such small drills are not common at sites in the Southeast, but morphologically and functionally similar tools have been found in several locations. The Mound N drills closely resemble the "expanded base microdrills" from the Shell Bluff site north of Columbus, Mississippi (Futato 1987:172–173, see esp. Pl. 27 e–g). In manufacturing technique they are unlike the microdrills from American Bottom in Illinois (e.g., Ahler and DePuydt 1987:24–28; Mason and Perino 1961; Perino 1960; Yerkes 1987:Fig. B20h, i), which are bifacially worked from narrow prismatic spalls or splinters. They also differ from the cylindrical microdrills bifacially worked from blades found at a number of sites in the Tombigbee and Black Warrior valleys (Astin 1996:76; Ensor 1981:243–266; Pope 1989) and the bipolar-blade microdrills from the Zebree site (Morse and Morse 1983:222–224; Sierzchula 1980). Analysis of microwear on the American Bottom drills (Yerkes 1983, 1987) and the cylindrical microdrills from Black Warrior sites (Pope 1989) indicates that those tools were mostly used to drill holes in shell. Mussel shells from the Tennessee River are hard enough and thin enough to account for the visible wear on the Mound N drills, though confirmation of the source of the wear would require replication experiments and microscopic analysis. The Tennessee River, before disruption by dams and pollution, had "the most diverse and abundant mussel fauna of any river in North America" (Parmalee and Bogan 1998:30). It would not be surprising if people at Shiloh were making shell beads from this local resource.

Drills like these have not been found previously at Shiloh. In the case of the 1933–1934 excavation, the apparent absence of drills is a function of the lack of screening or of a lack of recognition of these small tools: the backfill in the old excavation trench contained 6 drills, in addition to the 10 we found in intact fill above the burned house. Gerald Smith (1977:12) did recover a "drill bit" from excavation in the plaza area south of Mound F, but he provided no description or illustration of the item. His excavations elsewhere on the site, the excavations on Mound A by Ehrenhard and Beditz, the Queens College excavations on Mound 7, and the SEAC excavations in several parts of the plaza did not encounter any drills even though all of these excavations were screened. While these other excavations are not extensive nor do they encompass all parts of the site, it appears that the distribution of drills on the site is spotty. Again, it needs to be stressed that the drills from Mound N were in fill that was brought from somewhere else at the site, so that the place where these drills were used is not known. However, it does seem possible at this point to conclude that drills were used, perhaps to drill shell, at only a few locations at the site rather than in every household in all parts of the community.

The date of the Mound N microdrills is not known. Elsewhere, micro-drills have been found in both Late Woodland (e.g., Tombigbee and Black Warrior valley sites) and Mississippian contexts (e.g., Cahokia, Zebree). The Shell Bluff microdrills—those morphologically most similar to the Mound N tools—are of Late Woodland date. While this may suggest that the Mound N drills are of Late Woodland date, the fact that over 70 percent of the pottery in this mound is of Mississippian date suggests a Mississippian date for these tools. The only safe conclusion is that we do not know for sure the age of these tools.

The saws may also have been used in the manufacture of shell ornaments, specifically to saw out the square blanks for making disc beads from mussel shells. Like the drills, these sandstone saws (Figure 3.23) have parallels at Cahokia (e.g., Pauketat 1993:Plate 5.3) and have been found in contexts where shell beads were produced (Ahler and DePuydt 1987:24–28). Also like the drills, the Mound N saws were used on a thin material (or at least to make only shallow cuts), for the wear extends less than 1 cm back from the edge on all examples. The raw material for these saws is a ferruginous sandstone, most likely tabular or sheet-like concretions in the Tuscaloosa sands that crop out in the ravines along the site margins. The same sort of ferruginous sandstone, also probably from the Tuscaloosa Formation, was used to make identical saws found at Moundville (Vernon J. Knight, Jr., personal communication; Markin 1997). Knight suspects that the Moundville saws were used to cut greenstone, and there is in fact a piece of greenstone with a saw groove from west of Mound D at Shiloh (lower left in Figure 3.23). However, without better contextual information from Shiloh or use-wear analysis (if that is possible on sandstone), it would be premature to conclude what the Mound N saws were used to cut.

Among the other tools in the fill above the burned house are an abrader, five grinding stones, and six pieces of ground stone. It may help to clarify the distinctions between these similar terms. The abrader is a small (2 cm diameter) metaquartzite pebble that has facets and striations indicating that it was used to abrade or polish some hard material. The grinding stones are fragments of sandstone that have one or more surfaces artificially smoothed by grinding, with the other surfaces left unmodified. Thus, the function of these items was to grind something else. In contrast, the ground stone artifacts appear to have been ground to a predetermined shape, such that the grinding was not the object's function but was instead the method of manufacture. Unfortunately, all of the ground stone items above the burned structure are fragments too small to reveal the shape or size of the finished item. None of

Table 6.2 Material type of the shatter from Mound N

Material	Inside the house		Above the house		Mixed		Total	
	N	%	N	%	N	%	N	%
Tuscaloosa chert	59	77.6	1,190	77.0	984	75.5	2,233	76.4
Metaquartzite	5	6.6	64	4.1	58	4.5	127	4.3
Orthoquartzite	3	3.9	20	1.3	14	1.1	37	1.3
Ft. Payne chert	1	1.3	13	0.8	39	3.0	53	1.8
Dover chert	0	0	45	2.9	30	2.3	75	2.6
Mill Creek chert	0	0	0	0	2	0.2	2	0.1
Unidentified chert	8	10.5	209	13.5	176	13.5	393	13.4
Metamorphic	0	0	4	0.3	0	0	4	0.1
Total	76	99.9	1,545	99.9	1,303	100.1	2,924	100.0

these items—abrader, grinding stones, ground stone—is grooved in a fashion that would suggest sharpening of wooden or bone points or rounding of shell beads. The ground surfaces are either planar or only gently curved. Other than the abrader, it is not clear how any of these items was used.

Unlike the ground/grinding stones, the function of chert hoe blades is well known. Three chips produced by resharpening chert hoe blades were found in the fill of Mound N. One of the hoe flakes is of Dover chert, the other two of Mill Creek chert. Wherever the fill of Mound N came from, at least two different hoes were resharpened there.

There is also an awl in the fill above the burned structure. This 3.5-cm-long tool has a sharp point flanked by a serrated edge. Although I have called it an awl based on its shape, the tool could also have been used as a scratcher, knife, or something else. The tool is made of a dark gray, nearly black, chert that may be Ft. Payne but lacks the bluish cast often seen in Ft. Payne.

Other tools (biface, unifaces, flake tools) found in the Mound N fill are less indicative of function. Apparently a variety of cutting tasks were performed, often with expedient tools.

Manufacture of chipped stone tools is indicated by the two cores, two preforms, four flakes of bifacial retouch, and the quantities of cortical and noncortical flakes and shatter. Most of the knapping debris is Tuscaloosa chert, as exemplified by the listing of shatter by material type shown in Table 6.2. As was the case with the knapping debris at House Mound 7 (see Chapter 5), the first step in working with the Tuscaloosa chert apparently was to heat it. To save time in sorting the artifacts, we did not attempt to distinguish between heat-altered and unaltered items, but impressionistically I did not see any difference between the Mound N and Mound 7 chert in frequencies of heat alteration. After the heat treatment, suitable materials were used as-is (flake tools) or modified for use.

As discussed in Chapter 5, at House Mound 7 it looked like most of the nonlocal chert arrived already worked to some degree. In the fill of Mound N, by contrast, at least some kinds of nonlocal raw materials arrived with cortex still attached. Both Dover and Mill Creek are represented by cortical flakes, and 37.2 percent of the cortical flakes were nonlocal or unidentified raw materials. This percentage is higher than the percentage of nonlocal plus unidentified material in the shatter. Given that the sample size of cortical flakes is only 43, it is risky to put too much interpretive weight on these numbers. But the data do appear to indicate that wherever the Mound N fill came from, knappers there at least occasionally used untrimmed blocks of nonlocal raw material, even distant raw material like Mill Creek chert.

The pottery from the fill of Mound N is mostly shell-tempered, with small numbers of grog-tempered types such as Baytown Plain and Mulberry Creek Cordmarked scattered among the predominant shell-tempered pottery. Given the chronological ambiguity of the Mound N contexts, I do not see any way that these deposits can help resolve the question of whether grog-tempered and shell-tempered pottery were in use simultaneously at Shiloh. Nor does the pottery from Mound N reveal much about the sorts of social differences between households that were to have been the focus of this excavation.

Elsewhere in the Mississippian world, researchers have compared vessel assemblages from different contexts, ratios of serving ware to cooking ware in different contexts, vessel size differences in different contexts, and so on. I am prevented from making such comparisons using material from Mound N by the high degree of erosion of the pottery, particularly the shell-tempered pottery. In the fill above the burned structure, nearly 96 percent of the shell-tempered sherds were too eroded to assess whether the original surface had been plain, burnished, or decorated. The remaining shell-tempered sherds yield a serving:cooking (i.e., burnished:plain) ratio of 5:32 (i.e., 13.5 percent of the 37 sherds are burnished). This is neither particularly high nor particularly low by Mississippian standards, but normally such ratios are calculated on samples of hundreds of sherds rather than a few dozen.

We are in no better shape when it comes to assessing what shapes of vessels were present. Only nine of the shell-tempered sherds are rims, along with one jar shoulder. Of the nine, only five are large enough to reveal what shape of vessel they came from. Two of the rims are from Mississippi Plain *var. Shiloh* jars. One rim is from a small, eroded, shell-tempered bottle which had an engraved or fine-line incised motif that was too poorly preserved to make out but which may be a 3-line running scroll. The other two rims are from Bell Plain bowls, both of which are either outslanting or shallow flaring-rim shapes. Thus, we know that there were burnished bowls, decorated bottles, and plain jars. All these vessel shapes are known to occur elsewhere in the region during the period A.D. 1050 to 1400 when Shiloh was occupied, so it is not at all surprising to find these vessels at Shiloh.

Only one of the shell-tempered rims from above the burned structure was sufficiently intact to permit an estimate of orifice size. This *Shiloh* jar rim had an orifice of 8–9 cm radius (16–18 cm diameter), which falls in the middle of the range known from the rims collected during the 1933–1934 excavations.

To put it bluntly, the pottery from the fill above the burned structure does not tell us much about the social status of the people who lived wherever that fill originally came from.

So far, I have discussed the prehistoric artifacts from inside the burned house, and those from the fill stratigraphically above the burned house. This leaves for examination the artifacts recovered from the backfill in the old excavation trench. Because this trench penetrated through the floor of the burned house, the backfill presumably contains a mixture of items from inside and from above the house. When the trench was excavated in the 1930s, the workers may have collected some of the artifacts, though none of the provenienced artifacts in the 1933–1934 collection comes from this mound. Clearly, however, most of the artifacts were not collected by those shovelers, for in 1999 we recovered more artifacts in the backfill of this one trench than Frank Roberts collected in his entire project. Of course, the sherds collected by the CWA workers are generally much bigger than ours.

The artifacts in the backfill of the old excavation trench almost precisely duplicate those in the fill above the burned house. The major point of this observation is that the most likely source of the backfill is the fill above the burned house. Though it might seem obvious that the trench would have been backfilled with its original contents, we do not actually know this to be the case. Photos of the 1933–1934 excavation show that, in some instances, excavation spoil was wheelbarrowed to spoil piles dozens of meters from the excavation. However, this appears to have been done only where there were broad horizontal excavations, and in most instances of trenching the trench spoil was simply piled up along the trench sides. Nevertheless, at Mound N the great similarity of the backfill and the original fill does make the job of interpretation easier; had there been notable differences there would always be a question about whether the backfill might have come from elsewhere on the site.

To avoid a great deal of repetition, I will describe what the backfill artifacts add to the picture already drawn from the artifacts found in the fill above the house. For pottery, the principal additions are several other sand- and grog-tempered sherds, and, among the shell-tempered pottery, three additional rim sherds. One of these rims is too eroded and small for certainty, but it is probably from a jar. Another is a Mississippi Plain *var. Shiloh* out-slanting or shallow flaring-rim bowl. The third has an eroded surface but is clearly the vertical cylindrical neck and lip of a bottle. The pottery, therefore, adds little to the picture developed from the artifacts in undisturbed fill.

The chipped stone tools in the old trench's backfill include only one kind of tool not present in the undisturbed fill, namely scrapers. Four tools in the backfill were classified as scrapers on the basis of steep retouch on one or more sides of the tool. None is particularly formal, that is, none has been retouched to achieve a predetermined shape but instead has a shape that de-pends on the shape of the original flake from which it was made. It is a bit surprising to find four scrapers in the backfill and none in the undisturbed fill, and on this basis we may wonder (but not conclude) whether they derive from the burned house rather than the overlying fill.

The unmodified stone in the backfill is almost identical to the unmodified stone in the undisturbed fill. The sole exception is material I have called chalk, 35 pieces of which were recorded in the backfill. Chalk crops out only a few miles to the north of Shiloh, at Chalk Bluff, which is the northernmost limit of the Selma Chalk formation. But a word of caution is appropriate here. Immediately to the north of Mound N, there used to be an interpretive trail that was graveled (see Chambers n.d.). The weathered white limestone gravel is very similar in texture to chalk, and like chalk it reacts with dilute hydrochloric acid. Thus, macroscopically it is very difficult to distinguish between the weathered gravel and chalk. Of the 35 items coded as chalk, 34 came from the surface level of one grid square. Given these circumstances, it is certainly possible that these "chalk" pieces are actually gravel scattered from the interpretive trail.

In short, the backfill in the old excavation trench adds little information to what we know about Mound N, though it does nearly double the size of the artifact sample.

In addition to the prehistoric artifacts, Mound N yielded items of Historic origins. Unlike House Mound 7, where the Historic materials appear to de-rive from the Civil War camps and battles, at Mound N the Historic artifacts all appear to be of twentieth-century origin (see Table 6.3). Items such as the machine-made beer and soft-drink bottles probably derive from careless park visitors, and the .22 caliber bullets clearly derive from violators of park regu-lations that bar the use of firearms. The enameled pin bears the design or logo of the Royal Ambassadors, a Baptist youth organization founded in 1908 (Southside Baptist Church 2001). Thus, all of the Historic artifacts appear to represent accidental loss and litter during the past century, a finding not sur-prising given the mound's location next to the road and parking area.

Table 6.3 Historic artifacts from House Mound N

Description	Above the house	Old trench fill	Total
Bullets .22 caliber long rifle, hollow point		1	1
.22 caliber	1		1
Commemorative pin, enameled	1		1
Nozzle, nonferrous metal		1	1
Pop-tab from beverage can		3	3
Beer bottle fragments	45	2	47
Soft drink bottle fragments	5		5
Indeterminate bottle fragments	3		3
Leather fragment		1	1
Concrete		2	2
Asphalt	8		8
Slag or clinker		1	1
Total historic artifacts	63	11	74

DATING ANALYSES

I have left to last a discussion of the radiocarbon dating analyses of charcoal from Mound N. Unfortunately, the burned debris of the house itself yielded only very small pieces of charcoal, many of which came from an area in or near a collapsed rodent burrow. The integrity of these samples is suspect, and they could be dated only by the relatively expensive accelerator dating technique. Instead, I submitted two samples of wood charcoal for conventional radiocarbon analysis, one from the fill of the old excavation trench and the other from a context that could have been either burned debris of the house or fill placed atop the burned debris. Based on the evidence from the excavation and from the artifacts, both samples were expected to provide dates that could be earlier than the house (if the charcoal derived from fill translocated from earlier deposits elsewhere) or that might date the house itself (if the charcoal derived from the house's wall posts). There was also a chance that the charcoal from the old trench fill might have been contemporary material introduced during the backfilling in 1934, in which case the charcoal should yield a nearly modern date. Thus, the expected dates were either before A.D. 1400 or, for the backfill sample only, after A.D. 1900. The estimated ages, however, did not conform to my expectations.

The radiocarbon sample from the old excavation trench was a single piece of wood charcoal weighing 35.9 g. Because this was a sizeable chunk of wood, it could already have been decades old at the time it burned. Thus, if this

Table 6.4 Radiocarbon assays of samples from 1999 excavations

Lab no.	SHIL catalog no.	Conventional ^{14}C age	Calibrated* date ranges	
Beta-143851	SHIL 07304	320 ± 60**	1σ :	AD 1490–1650
			2σ :	AD 1440–1670
Beta-143852	SHIL 09825	560 ± 60***	1σ :	AD 1300–1360
				AD 1380–1430
			2σ :	AD 1290–1440

*   Calibrations were obtained using OxCal v. 3.4 (Bronk Ramsey 2000)
**   Measured ^{14}C age of 360 ± 60 adjusted for –27.9 o/oo δ^{13}C
*** Measured ^{14}C age of 620 ± 60 adjusted for –28.6 o/oo δ^{13}C

were charcoal that was introduced into the backfill in the 1930s, the true age might be in the late 1800s or early 1900s. Alternatively, if the sample were prehistoric, it should date no later than the end of occupation at Shiloh, which on the basis of pottery cross-dating I estimate at A.D. 1400. Yet, the calibrated, one-sigma date estimate for this sample (Beta 143851; see Table 6.4 and Figure 6.8) is cal A.D. 1490–1650. Even at two standard deviations, the calibrated age estimate does not come within a century of either of the expected age ranges. There is no evidence that the charcoal came from later intrusion or a burned tree stump; the sample came from what appeared to be undisturbed fill. So, if the age assessment is correct, it suggests that there may have been occupation at Shiloh until at least the mid-1400s or early 1500s. Possible support for such a late occupation comes from a radiocarbon assessment on wood charcoal excavated from the penultimate surface of Mound A in 2001. The calibrated, one-sigma age estimate for this sample is cal A.D. 1410–1445 (David Anderson, personal communication). Ongoing excavations on Mound A have recovered other dateable samples from that mound surface as well as several earlier ones, so additional chronological information may be available soon. At the moment, however, a date in the 1500s for the fill of Mound N is anomalously late.

The radiocarbon assessment of the sample from the undisturbed fill of Mound N was not quite as aberrant as the previous date. This sample consisted of 33.3 g of wood charcoal, not one single piece but instead multiple small fragments. As was done for all samples, the stable carbon-isotope ratio was calculated and the date adjusted in accordance with the result, to preclude plants with C4 photosynthesis from skewing the estimated date. The ^{13}C/^{12}C ratio for this sample was fully consistent with the sample being all native species with C3 photosynthesis. Because the sample came from 25–35 cm below surface (30–40 cm b.d.) and there were no historic artifacts in this level, I believe the sample was part of the fill that was deposited atop the

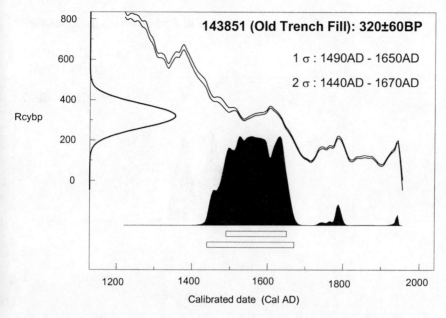

Figure 6.8. Calibration of radiocarbon assay from backfill in old excavation trench, Mound N

burned house. This excavation level in the N33 W36 square, where the sample was found, had an unusually high density of fired clay pieces and charcoal, so that it was also possible that some of the material in this unit was a relatively high-standing portion of the burned wall of the house. Because I do not believe the fill substantially postdates the burning of the house, and because the burning must have occurred not many months after the abandonment of the house, the true age of this sample of charcoal might be earlier than the house but not more than a few years after the date when the house burned. Based on other dating information from the site, I expected the date of the house to be earlier than A.D. 1400. The radiocarbon assessment (Beta 143852; see Table 6.4, Figure 6.9) indicates a one-sigma calibrated range from A.D. 1300 to 1360 or 1380 to 1430; at two standard deviations the calibrated age range is A.D. 1290–1440. This suggests that the Mound N house was built late in the sequence at Shiloh.

To be honest, I did not expect either date to be later than A.D. 1300, given Shiloh's lack of such characteristic later Mississippian vessel forms as deep flaring rim bowls, hemispherical bowls with beaded rims, and short-necked jars. Based on the absence of these pottery modes, in earlier reports (Welch 1998b, 2000, 2001) I estimated the end of occupation of Shiloh at A.D. 1300. The radiocarbon dates, however, suggest that I was off by a century or more.

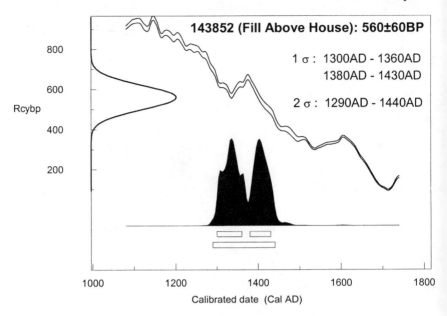

Figure 6.9. Calibration of radiocarbon assay from fill in Mound N

Dating analysis of samples from the 2001–2003 Mound A excavations should help clarify the chronology of the site.

EVALUATION OF THE INVESTIGATION

One result of my excavation in Mound N was inadvertent documentation that the 1933–1934 excavations were more extensive than even the field photographs, let alone the excavation notebooks, indicate. Until excavating in Mound N, I had questioned the accuracy of Roberts's (1935:65) statement that "trenches through the flats revealed the traces of 30 houses." As discussed in Chapter 4, the excavation documents do not confirm that nearly this many houses were encountered, but with the information that much of the excavation was not documented in any way, this number seems less implausible.

The house beneath Mound N differed from the one excavated the previous season in having its floor in an excavated basin. Floor basins do not appear to be common at Shiloh, inasmuch as Roberts (Stirling 1935:395) said that most floors lay "on or slightly below the ground level" and that the latter were "no doubt due to constant sweeping of the area" rather than to the intentional excavation of floor basins. Thus, the floor basin of Mound N's burned structure—clearly an intentionally excavated basin rather than an incidental "dishing" of the floor by repeated sweeping—adds a new variety of architecture to the repertoire known for the site.

Elsewhere in the Southeast, such "semi-subterranean" houses are common at Mississippian sites. To the northwest in the American Bottom in Illinois, for example, recessed house basins were constructed during both Emergent Mississippian and Mississippian periods, from roughly A.D. 700 to 1400 (Milner 1998:91–92). To the southeast in the Moundville area, this variety of architecture is restricted to late West Jefferson and early Moundville I times, roughly A.D. 1000 to 1200 (Knight et al. n.d.; Scarry 1995:238–239; Welch 1998c:144–146). Roughly the same time span is evident along the central Tombigbee River (Jenkins and Krause 1986:78). It is not clear whether the form is also chronologically restricted along the Tennessee River in northern Alabama and western Tennessee. No semi-subterranean houses are mentioned in the reports of excavations in the Wheeler (Webb 1939) or Pickwick (Webb and DeJarnette 1942) reservoirs, or for the Obion site in northwest Tennessee (Garland 1992:113–114). In eastern Tennessee, recessed house basins are found from around A.D. 900 (Martin Farm phase) right into the Historic era (Schroedl et al. 1985; Sullivan 1995b). Given the radiocarbon assays from Mound N, it looks like semi-subterranean floors at Shiloh do not have the consistently early date seen at Moundville and along the central Tombigbee River.

In the previous chapter I laid out reasons for concluding that parts of the site had experienced sheet erosion around occupied houses, leaving their floors pedestalled above the surrounding eroded surface. The floor beneath Mound N, however, was *not* pedestalled, a fact that deserves explanation. The explanation, I believe, lies in Mound N's location 23 m downslope from the base of Mound F. Wash from the 3-m-tall Mound F creates a shallow blanket expanding out from the mound base, visible on the surface today. This blanket extends to about the east side of Mound N. Indeed, some of the sediment inside the house basin may actually be wash from Mound F, although that would depend on where the door to the structure was. So sheet erosion around Mound N may have been offset by deposition of wash from Mound F. I have no data other than topography to substantiate this hypothesis, but I do not believe the lack of visible pedestaling at Mound N proves that my hypothesis of pedestaling at Mound 7 is incorrect. Whether, and by how much, house floors at Shiloh were pedestalled by sheet erosion outside the house will depend in each instance on local topography and on the duration and intensity of foot traffic around the house.

So little of the semi-subterranean floor of the building under Mound N was exposed that it is premature to conclude what kinds of activities transpired in the building. To generalize—perhaps unwarrantably—from the small excavated portion, it appears that the house was cleaned out at abandonment. On the other hand, the finding of mica flakes beneath collapsed fired wall debris does suggest that not everything was removed and that the users of the building had a fairly high status within the society. This tantalizing piece of information makes it even more frustrating that we did not find a full suite of materials lying on the floor to document the set of activities that took place in one such high-status household. Even so, this discovery does suggest that there were indeed social distinctions between the households at the margin of the site and higher-status households nearer the center. The excavation's original goal of investigating such social distinctions has thus been partially achieved.

The occurrence of more than a dozen drills and several saw blades in Mound N suggests that shell beads were manufactured somewhere on the site. Because the drills were found in mound fill (and in backfill in the 1933–1934 trench) rather than in the burned building itself, we cannot specify where on the site this craft activity took place. These small and fairly unprepossessing artifacts have not been found (or noticed) by previous excavators, but this may tell us less about the spatial restriction of the craft activity than it tells us about the usefulness of artifact collections from unscreened excavations.

The final important result of the Mound N excavation is that it indicates that occupation at Shiloh may have extended to ca. A.D. 1400, a century later than current thinking about the pottery chronology of the central Tennessee River valley suggests. It will be helpful to obtain dating assays from samples in better context than mound fill. Mound fill, by its nature, is not a very edifying context for dating.

7   SEAC Fieldwork in 1999

Paul D. Welch, David G. Anderson, and
John E. Cornelison, Jr.

In discussions with staff of the Southeast Archeological Center (SEAC) about the feasibility of preparing a comprehensive report on the archaeology of Shiloh Indian Mounds, it became clear that several mapping problems could most easily be addressed by the skills and technology available to SEAC personnel. Accordingly, a short field project was designed (see Anderson, Cornelison, Smith, and Welch 1999) to be carried out by SEAC staff specifically to provide information needed for a synthesis of Shiloh archaeology. The SEAC crew were in the field in July 1999, the same time as Welch's Queens College crew, so that Welch could observe and participate in the SEAC fieldwork.

While the needs of this report dictated the objectives of the SEAC fieldwork, the means to achieve these objectives were left up to the SEAC archaeologists. The project was headed jointly by David Anderson and John Cornelison, and Welch attributes the successful achievement of the project goals to Anderson and Cornelison's carefully designed and skillfully executed fieldwork. The objectives of their work were as follows:

1. Tie the Welch 1998 grid system to the UTM coordinate system.
2. Map the full extent of the palisade, including locations of bastions.
3. Relocate several backfilled excavation units from 1933–1934 to provide on-the-ground points that have known coordinates in the 1933–1934 grid system and the 1998 grid system.
4. Excavate a test unit in the "Dike," a linear ridge feature of unknown age and function.

The first two objectives were met by use of a global-positioning satellite (GPS) receiver, with decimeter-scale accuracy. The GPS survey of the palisade, conducted simply by walking along the visible embankment, reveals that it extends farther north and farther south than Roberts's map shows and that it forms a C-shape with bastions at fairly regular intervals averaging 53 m. In calculating this average we assumed that the apparently uninterrupted stretches of 109 m and 115 m had each originally been interrupted by one no-longer-visible bastion, and we excluded the stretch of 78 m at the southern end of the palisade where the adjacent bastions face each other across a wide, deep ravine in which it would have made no military sense to erect a bastion. This 53-m spacing is greater than the 30-m average reported for 22 Mississippian palisades by Milner (1999:120), though still far short of the strangely large 73-m spacing for the nearby Savannah site (Stelle 1871:408–409; Welch 1998a:82). The total length of the portion of the palisade that we could map with confidence is 690 m, and if the northeastern end extends to where Gerald Smith (1977:4–5) believed he detected it north of Mound H, the total length would be 900 m. It is also possible that the palisade extends farther to the southeast, but we were unable to track it across a large ravine there.

The third and fourth goals of the SEAC fieldwork were tackled with a combination of remote sensing and test excavation. There were several reasons for employing remote sensing. First, if it proved successful at relocating units, it would reduce the amount of excavation needed to find on-the-ground points with known 1933–1934 grid coordinates. Second, if successful, remote sensing would allow mapping of the entirety of the 1933–1934 excavations, something not possible from the extant records alone. There was extensive discussion of which remote sensing technique might work best.

Each remote sensing technique has advantages and limitations, and the best choice of technique always depends in part on the field conditions. Given the abundance of historic metal items on the site, both of Civil War origin and more recent tourist litter, magnetometry and gradiometry were identified as potentially yielding results too "noisy" to be useful. The presence of depressions with standing water at the site suggested that large differences in soil moisture content might make resistivity and conductivity difficult to interpret. This would also have some effect on ground-penetrating radar (GPR), but radar was the technique selected because it seemed less problematic than the other techniques. Radar, however, is a more complex technology than the others, and the usefulness of the results depends greatly on the skill of the operator in tuning the equipment to the field conditions, as well as on the skill of the person evaluating the receiver's output. We were able to enlist the services of an expert GPR technician, David Bean. He had been employed full-time for seven years conducting GPR surveys on the Department of Energy's Savannah River Plant and had also performed GPR surveys on archaeological sites. He thus brought considerable skills in employing the technology and interpreting the output.

The immediate goal of using GPR was to locate radar anomalies that might be backfilled excavation units. Test excavations would then check on the validity of these potential identifications. If the remote sensing results were accurate, then relocating backfilled units would require minimal (or no) invasive excavations. If unsuccessful, finding backfilled units might require

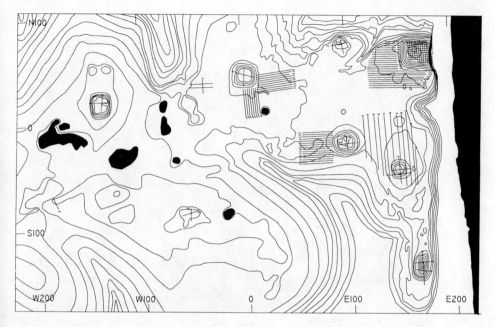

Figure 7.1. Locations of ground-penetrating radar transects

more extensive excavations and result in greater disturbance to intact archaeological deposits than was desirable. At Shiloh, the GPR yielded results
that were mixed but nevertheless useful. Before describing the test excavations that verified the locations of backfilled units, the results of what turned
out to be a very extensive GPR survey of the site are given.

GROUND-PENETRATING RADAR SURVEY

In the hands of an operator with the skills to tune the equipment expedi-
tiously, GPR surveying proceeds rapidly. Because the radar receiver is pulled
along the ground at a normal walking pace, the most time-consuming part
of the fieldwork is laying out the transects along which the radar receiver is
pulled. The SEAC crew used tapes to lay out sets of parallel transects in
several areas of the site. Along each transect, marks were spray-painted on
the ground at 2-m intervals. The start and end points of each transect were
then tied to the 1998 grid system using a laser total station. In five days, the
GPR operator surveyed 134 transects (see Figure 7.1) totaling 3,532 m.

As the operator pulled the GPR receiver along a transect, he pushed a
button at each 2-m interval. The button-push created a mark on the GPR
output, which permits distance interpolations on the output. For example, an
anomaly that lies halfway between the mark for 2 m and the mark for 4 m

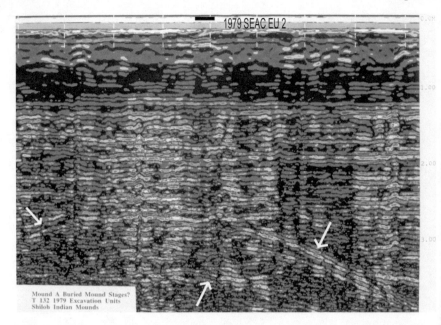

Figure 7.2. Ground-penetrating radar output showing possible stratification in Mound A

would be approximately 3 m along the transect. In the parts of the site where test excavation was planned, the operator interpreted the output in the field and spray-painted marks on the ground at locations that on the GPR output looked like edges of backfilled excavations. A sample of the GPR output is shown in Figure 7.2. The transect runs from left to right, and depth is shown by the vertical axis. The gray shades show the strength of radar reflection by location and depth. A backfilled excavation might show up as a vertical band or rectangle in which the reflections were of different strength than in the surrounding matrix.

It takes skill and experience to interpret the GPR output, and because the authors had neither we were fortunate that David Bean provided these interpretations orally in the field and later in written form directly on paper copies of the output. We merely entered the features he identified onto the site map. The excavation photographs from the 1930s show generally linear excavations, usually running east-west. Thus, if the GPR successfully identified backfilled excavation units, we ought to see features on adjacent transects forming east-west alignments. We would also expect to see indications of excavation in those locations where photographs and field notes clearly identify excavation units. The success of the GPR survey, however, was mixed.

The GPR survey suggests that there are far more, far larger, and far more irregularly placed excavations than the 1933–1934 records indicate. That there were more excavation units than the records reveal was later confirmed by test excavations, so in a general sense the GPR results are not wholly misleading. The GPR operator also in several instances identified the edges of old excavation units with an accuracy of about ± 10 cm, as confirmed by test excavation. But there was also a problem with "false negative" results.

A "false negative" result would be a failure to indicate that an old excavation unit was present even though in reality there was one. By comparing the annotated paper GPR output with the results of subsequent test excavations, we found that the GPR failed to detect about 70 percent of the old excavation edges (see Welch 2001:259–262 for full documentation of this issue). Clearly, while the GPR did detect some of the excavation edges, and with impressive accuracy, the absence of any detected excavation cannot be taken as proof of undisturbed deposits.

Part of the reason the GPR was not more successful is that there may have been too much excavation in this area. To some degree, detecting excavation edges requires distinguishing disturbed areas from undisturbed ones, and if most of the area is disturbed it would be difficult to detect the excavation edges. Another possible problem is that the test excavations, both those in 1999 and an excavation by Gerald Smith (1977:7–8), confirm that some parts of the plaza area have prehistoric midden and fill deposits. The radar-reflecting characteristics of such deposits may be quite similar to the same material when redeposited as backfill.

In short, GPR appears to be a useful tool for relocating the old excavation units, though not a panacea. It sometimes worked spectacularly well, but when the GPR failed to indicate a subsurface feature, that failure was not a reliable indication of what was really below the surface at Shiloh. In the future, additional remote sensing technologies should be tried, but ultimately all remote sensing results may have to be confirmed by test excavation. Even though we were not able to use the GPR survey to construct a map of the old excavation units, it did enable us to locate several old excavations, including one for which we know the 1933–1934 grid coordinates.

In addition to using the GPR in the areas where there were excavations in 1933–1934, we also surveyed a grid of transects atop Mound A. The goal here was not to relocate old excavations but to see whether radar would reveal any stratigraphy in the mound. On six of the transects, the GPR indicated deeply buried radar-reflecting surfaces. Typically these surfaces describe arcs (see Figure 7.2), suggesting that in its early stages the mound summit might have been rounded rather than flat. Exactly what these radar-reflecting surfaces represent, however, cannot be discerned from the radar alone. They may be mound stages, features, episodes of filling, or the percolation fronts of water seeping into the mound after rainfall events. Even though it is not clear what the radar reflections represent, the GPR results on Mound A were invaluable in planning for the mitigation excavation of Mound A. Based on the results of the 1-×-1-m sounding excavated in Mound A in 1979 (Beditz 1980b), reviewed in Chapter 2, Mound A was thought to have been built as a single fill episode which would not be particularly complex to excavate. Largely because of the GPR results, however, the planning for the 2001–2003 excavation assumed that the mound might have considerable internal complexity. This has turned out to be the case, with multiple floor surfaces present even in the upper meter of deposits.

TEST EXCAVATIONS

For the purposes of analysis and reporting, the 1999 SEAC test excavations can be grouped into three separate areas. One area is south of Mound F, where 19 1-×-1-m units were excavated in an effort to relocate backfilled 1933–1934 excavations. The second area of test excavation was on the apron immediately west of Mound A, where 12 1-×-1-m units were excavated to relocate the north-south trench along Roberts's W372 grid line. The third focus of test excavation in 1999 was the "Dike," into the south side of which we excavated a 1-m-wide cut to obtain a vertical cross-section of this enigmatic feature.

Because the reason for the test units south of Mound F was to relocate old excavations, the 1999 test units were excavated only deeply enough to show whether the edge of an old unit was present. In most instances, excavation stopped at 10 cm below surface, though in a few instances it went as deep as 20 cm in order to provide a level surface across a number of contiguous units. Many of the units excavated were partly in old backfilled areas and partly in undisturbed deposits. Other units were wholly within old backfill or wholly within undisturbed areas, and it was sometimes difficult to tell which was which. Furthermore, in units outside the old excavations there may be redeposited artifacts from backdirt that was left on the surface. Because of these issues, and because the 1999 excavations rarely went deeper than the point at which disturbed could be distinguished from undisturbed, no effort was made in the field or in the analysis to keep the artifacts from backfill separate from those in undisturbed deposits. The area encompassed is not large, covering only 17 m east to west and 10 m north to south.

The westernmost units appear to have been outside the 1933–1934 excavations, and they have pale, silty sediments with abundant soil concretions. The Munsell color values (the number before the slash, e.g., the 7 in 10YR7/4) are 6 or 7. This appears to be a good diagnostic of undisturbed near-surface soil

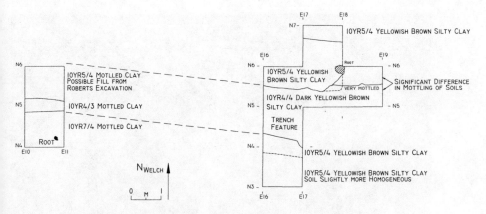

Figure 7.3. Plan of units showing old excavation trenches south of Mound F

in this part of the site and matches the leached E horizon found on the not-previously-excavated portion of Mound N not far away (see Chapter 6).

In the other excavation units, sediments with higher clay content and color values of 4 or 5 appear to be backfill in old excavation units. In one instance, both sides of the old excavation trench were exposed (see Figures 7.3 and 7.4). Several meters to the north, inside the area which the 1933–1934 records suggest might be a block excavation (see Figure 7.5), it is less clear what the deposits are.

Several test units were placed near the southeastern corner of the block designated as N50–60 / W780–820 in Roberts's grid. Because of the unusual, 10-X-40-ft dimension of this block, we expected to find that these coordinates defined a large excavation. That may be the case, but we did encounter a patch of what appears to be undisturbed deposit (with a color value of 7) in unit N12 E10, in the center of the block (see Figure 7.5). This patch of apparently undisturbed deposit does not have clean east-west or north-south edges, nor does another apparently undisturbed patch in unit N11 E14. Most of what was excavated appears to be backfill, but we could delineate neither the southern nor the eastern margin of the excavated area.

Compared to the nearby Mound N excavation (see Chapter 6), there are relatively few kinds of artifacts present (see Table 7.1). Like the pottery from Roberts's excavations in the plaza area (see Chapter 4), the pottery is predominantly (59.5 percent) grog-tempered. Unlike the obviously selective collection from the 1930s, the vast majority of 1999 sherds are eroded. This is not surprising, given that all the excavated material came from very near the modern surface. There is little indication of flaking activity, and the only chipped stone tools found include five miscellaneous biface fragments, two

Figure 7.4. Old excavation trench south of Mound F, looking south

Hamilton points, and one Madison point. The Madison and one of the Hamiltons are made of Tuscaloosa chert, and the other Hamilton is made of Dover chert. There is no chert from farther afield than that, and in particular there is no Mill Creek chert. There are two items of ground stone, one a fragmentary polished greenstone axe head, the other a small (ca. 1 cm diame-

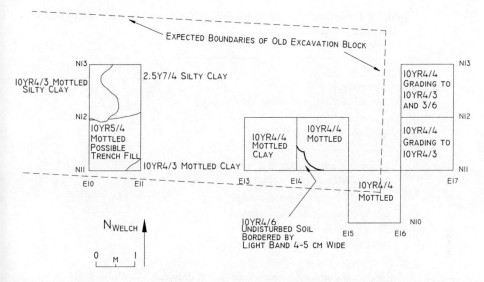

Figure 7.5. Plan of units in area of old block excavation south of Mound F

ter by 0.6 cm thick) pentagon of mudstone. The latter is not particularly smoothly finished, but the shape does appear to be artificial. During the excavation, considerable interest arose about what appeared to be a ground stone bead, but this turns out to have been merely a hollow crinoid-stem fossil that bears no evidence of working or wear. Had the fossil ever been strung on a necklace, delicate wings of stone inside the central hollow of the fossil would surely have broken off or worn away, so it is clear that this and all the other crinoid stem sections found at the site are merely natural components of the Tuscaloosa gravels rather than beads. This collection of artifacts tells us very little about activities that transpired in the area south of Mound F, except perhaps that the area was not used in a way that resulted in large numbers of artifacts being left lying on the ground here. It could, for example, have been a plaza area.

The five historic artifacts (see Table 7.2) from these excavations are even less exciting. Except possibly for the brick, these are all of twentieth-century rather than Civil War vintage.

The second area of test excavations in 1999 was the apron west of Mound A, where we excavated twelve 1-×-1-m units in four blocks (see Figure 7.6). All of these blocks lay along the line of Roberts's north-south trench, and finding the edges of that trench allows the 1933–1934 grid system to be tied to the current grid system. In some places the edges of the old trench were very clearly distinct from the undisturbed deposit around it (see Figure 7.7). In the northernmost of the excavation blocks west of Mound A, however,

Table 7.1 Prehistoric artifacts from 1999 SEAC excavations south of Mound F

Description	Total	% of total
Pottery		
Bone-tempered (n=1)		
Turkey Paw Cordmarked *var. Moon Lake*	1	.2
Grog-tempered (n=307)		
Baytown Plain *var. McKelvey*	41	8.0
var. unspecified	1	.2
Mulberry Creek Cordmarked *var. Mulberry Creek*	78	15.2
var. Coffee Landing	2	.4
Unclassified grog-tempered, eroded	184	35.8
Unclassified grog-and-sand-tempered, eroded	1	.2
Shell-tempered (n=207)		
Bell Plain *var. unspecified*	1	.2
Mississippi Plain *var. Shiloh*	6	1.2
Unclassified shell-tempered, eroded (incl. 1 discoidal)	198	38.5
Unclassified shell-and-sand-tempered, eroded	2	.4
Total pottery	515	100.3
Chipped Stone		
Core	1	.1
Shatter	575	85.7
Flake, cortical	16	2.3
Flake, noncortical	61	9.1
Flake, biface retouch	3	.4
Flake tool (utilized flake)	7	1.0
Biface	5	.7
Hamilton projectile point	2	.3
Madison projectile point	1	.1
Total chipped stone	671	99.7
Ground Stone		
Greenstone axe head fragment	1	50
Ground stone pentagon	1	50
Total ground stone	2	100
Unworked Stone		
Chert, Tuscaloosa	4,382	64.6
Metaquartzite	418	6.2
Unspecified metamorphic	4	.1
Fossil, bivalve	1	<.1

Continued on the next page

Table 7.1 *Continued*

Description	Total	% of total
Fossil coral	10	.1
Fossil crinoid	6	.1
Orthoquartzite	23	.3
Sandstone	5	.1
Sandstone, ferruginous	4	.1
Sandstone, micaceous	1	<.1
Limestone	5	.1
Shale, micaceous	1	<.1
Conglomerate	1,288	19.0
Concretions	638	9.4
Total unworked stone	6,786	100.1
Fired clay and daub	149	100
Carbonized plant material	69	100

Table 7.2 Historic artifacts from 1999 excavations south of Mound F

Description	Total
Pop-tab from beverage can	1
Beer bottle fragment	1
Brick fragment	1
Asphalt	2
Total historic artifacts	5

there were no readily apparent edges. This excavation is located at the juncture of the 1933–1934 north-south trench with a trench running to the west. The 1999 excavation here consists of four 1-×-1-m units forming a T with the stem pointing south. Based on careful comparison with the field photographs from the 1930s, as well as the projected line of the old trench as seen a few meters to the south, it is all but certain that the eastern part of the T's crossbar must overlap the edge of the old north-south trench. Yet, only a gradual color change was visible across this unit.

There is a simple reason why the 1933–1934 trench on the apron west of Mound A was easily visible in some places but not others. It has to do with the way the old trench was backfilled. The apron through which the trench was excavated consisted of two distinct fill episodes composed of strikingly different sediments. The upper fill episode consisted of "darker earth filled

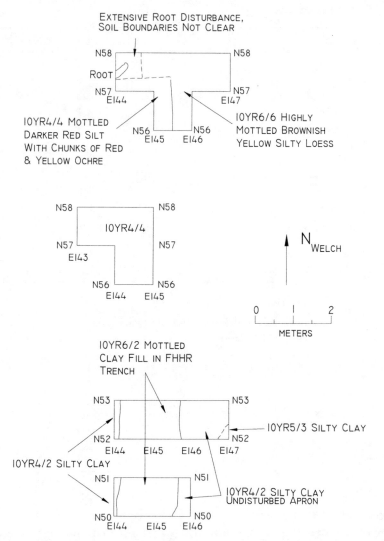

Figure 7.6. Plan of excavation blocks on the apron west of Mound A

with charcoal, red & yellow ochre, bits of red earth (burned clay), shell fragments, occasional bone fragments, burned rocks," while the lower fill episode was composed of a gray clay (Roberts 1933–1934:28–29). Where the
near-surface part of the old trenches was backfilled with the gray clay, it
stands out dramatically from the "darker earth" of the upper fill (as in Figure
7.7), but where the near-surface part of the old trench was backfilled with the
"darker earth" of the upper fill, it does not stand out from the surrounding,
intact, upper fill deposit.

As was the case south of Mound F, the artifacts from the 1999 excavations

Figure 7.7. Backfilled 1933–1934 trench west of Mound A between N52 and N53

west of Mound A come from a combination of backfill and undisturbed apron fill. No effort was made to separate these two contexts, so the artifacts from all four excavation blocks will be grouped for analysis. The prehistoric artifacts are listed in Table 7.3, the historic items in Table 7.4.

The prehistoric assemblage from west of Mound A (see Table 7.3) is more

Table 7.3 Prehistoric artifacts from 1999 excavations west of Mound A

Description	Total	% of total
Pottery		
Sand-tempered (n=4)		
Baldwin Plain *var. Miller Slough*	1	.1
Unclassified sand-tempered, eroded	4	.4
Limestone-tempered (n=3)		
Unclassified limestone-tempered, eroded	3	.3
Bone-tempered (n=1)		
Turkey Paw Plain *var. Turkey Paw*	1	.1
Grit-tempered (n=1)		
Unclassified cordmarked	1	.1
Grog-tempered (n=293)		
Baytown Plain *var. McKelvey* (incl. 1 ground triangle)	45	4.7
var. The Fork	2	.2
Mulberry Creek Cordmarked *var. Mulberry Creek*	64	6.7
Unclassified incised or stamped	1	.1
Unclassified grog-tempered, eroded	180	18.9
Unclassified grog-and-sand-tempered, eroded	1	.1
Shell-tempered (n=651)		
Bell Plain *var. unspecified*	13	1.4
Mississippi Plain *var. Shiloh*	50	5.2
var. unspecified (shell- and grog-tempered)	2	.2
Barton Incised *var. unspecified* (shell tempering only)	2	.2
var. unspecified (shell-and-sand-tempering)	1	.1
Moundville Engraved *var. unspecified*	1	.1
Unclassified cordmarked	1	.1
Unclassified incised	3	.3
Unclassified shell-tempered, eroded	577	60.5
Unclassified shell-and-grog-tempered, eroded	1	.1
Total pottery	954	99.9
Chipped Stone		
Core	1	<.1
Shatter	1,953	93.5
Flake, cortical	37	1.8
Flake, noncortical	83	4.0
Flake, biface retouch	5	0.2
Flake tool (utilized flake)	1	<.1
Hoe flake	1	<.1
Preform	1	<.1
Biface	3	0.1
Copena point	1	<.1

Continued on the next page

Table 7.3 *Continued*

Description	Total	% of total
Bradley Spike	1	<.1
Madison point	2	0.1
Untyped stemless points	1	<.1
Total chipped stone	2,090	99.7
Ground Stone		
Galena	1	3.2
Red ocher	27	87.1
Ground sandstone	3	9.7
Total ground stone	31	100.0
Unworked Stone		
Chert, Tuscaloosa	9,684	71.2
Chert, Ft. Payne	1	0.0
Metaquartzite	779	5.7
Fossil, bivalve	1	0.0
Fossil coral	18	0.1
Fossil crinoid	4	0.0
Orthoquartzite	23	0.2
Sandstone	29	0.2
Sandstone, ferruginous	12	0.1
Sandstone, micaceous	1	0.0
Mudstone	1	0.0
Limestone	113	0.8
Shale	2	0.0
Conglomerate	2,456	18.1
Concretions	479	3.5
Total unworked stone	13,603	99.9
Fired clay and daub	854	100.0
Carbonized plant material	21	100.0
Fauna		
Bone	5	26.3
Mussel shell	14	73.7
Total fauna	19	100.0

diverse than that from south of Mound F. This is no doubt due in part to the larger sample size but is probably due mostly to a difference in the nature of the deposits excavated. The fill composing the upper layer of the apron around the mound appears to be redeposited midden, a conclusion supported both by its dark color and the wide variety of time periods represented. The pottery includes small numbers of Woodland sand-tempered,

Table 7.4 Historic artifacts from 1999
excavations west of Mound A

Description	Total
Glass bottle fragments	26
Beer bottle fragment	1
Whiteware	4
Redware	1
Plastic fragments	2
Plastic labeling tape	1
Fragments of wooden grid stakes	3
Lead shot, #00	1
Iron nails, wire	2
Iron fragments	6
Brick fragments	29
Asphalt	21
Total historic artifacts	97

limestone-tempered, and bone-tempered sherds and a larger number of Late Woodland plain and cordmarked grog-tempered sherds. Among the chipped stone tools, the Bradley Spike is of Late Archaic/Gulf Formational age (Cambron and Hulse 1975:19), and the Copena point is of Middle Woodland date (Justice 1987:207). The presence of mussel shells, deer bones, and fragments of fired clay are also consistent with a midden origin for this deposit.

Having both Roberts's collection (see Table 4.3) and the screened collection from the 1999 excavation of the same area allows us to examine the collection biases of the 1930s excavators. Grog-tempered pottery is distinctly more abundant in the 1999 collection (30.7 percent) than it is in the 1933–1934 collection (15.9 percent), but the reason for this is not clear. The only reasons we can suggest for why there might have been a bias against collecting grog-tempered pottery is that it may have been perceived as less attractive or that the pieces may have been smaller on average than the shell-tempered pottery. The 1933–1934 excavators clearly had a bias toward collecting larger pieces of pottery, decorated sherds, and especially rims. Another possible explanation of the greater abundance of Woodland pottery in the 1999 collection is that the 1933–1934 collection contains disproportionate numbers of sherds from the occupied surface of the first apron stage, which would have yielded principally (or exclusively) shell-tempered pottery. By contrast, the 1999 excavation sampled only the redeposited fill, which would yield a more chronologically mixed collection. This is speculation, however, and it is also possible that the difference in the sherd ratios of Woodland to Mississippian is merely sampling error. The 1930s excavators most certainly had a bias against non-diagnostic chipped stone, as shown by the 13:1 ratio of stone to sherds in the 1999 collection compared with a ratio of 0.01:1 in the 1933–1934 collection. Even tools were sometimes missed in the 1930s if they were small.

The 1999 collection from the apron west of Mound A also contains historic items. None of these are diagnostically of Civil War origin. Some, such as the redware and whiteware sherds, and possibly the brick fragments, are likely to originate from the summer cottage used by Park Superintendent Delong Rice from 1914 to 1929 (Beditz 1980a:30; Smith 2004:125). Others no doubt come from foot traffic along the gravel path (once asphalt) leading to the stairs up the mound; this is clearly the origin of the asphalt listed in Table 7.4 and the limestone pebbles listed in Table 7.3. Several of the items listed in Table 7.4 are, ironically, of archaeological origin. The wood fragments are pieces of sawn and milled lumber, similar to the wooden grid stakes used by Roberts. Some of these pieces of wood were recovered from within the backfilled trench, which establishes their origin securely. The plastic labeling tape bears embossed letters spelling "JERRY" and may have come off of one of Gerald Smith's tools when he was installing a grid monument on the apron in 1976. Of course, the label could have fallen off a tourist's possession, but that makes a less interesting story.

The principal reason for excavating test units on the apron west of Mound A was to relocate the 1933–1934 trenches and thus be able to match their grid coordinates to the 1998 Welch grid. In this, the excavations were a qualified success. The edges of the north-south trench were found, permitting the east-west coordinates of the two grid systems to be matched within a few centimeters. However, the failure to delineate the intersection of the north-south trench with the east-west trench leaves room for a grid mismatch of 20 to 30 cm. The research design also mentioned the possibility of reexcavating a portion of the deep trench to expose the apron's stratigraphic profile. Pressures of time and questions about the advisability of using a backhoe to accomplish the reexcavation left this goal unfulfilled.

The third locus of excavations by the SEAC archaeologists in 1999 was the "Dike." This name appears on the 1933–1934 site map, attached to a linear ridge that is visible for 180 m or more (see Figure 7.8). There is no indication that Roberts excavated any part of this feature (his field notes contain several mentions of excavations on a dike, but those are references to the much broader, built-up ridge running west from Mound D). With the other earthworks at the site pretty well accounted for, this unusual feature has elicited puzzlement from every archaeologist who has seen it. The ridge is sufficiently close to the historic Browns Landing Road that a historic origin cannot be ruled out, but there is no evident reason for such a feature to have been

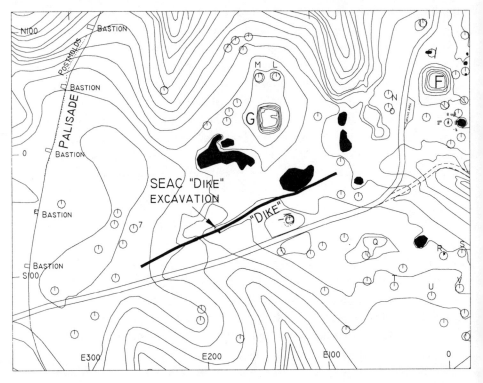

Figure 7.8. Detail of site map showing the Dike

constructed in Historic times. The orientation and location of the ridge would not have made it useful at any point during the Civil War battle, so a Civil War origin seems unlikely. By default we are left with a prehistoric origin.

To gain additional information about the feature, a 1-m-wide trench was excavated from the southern edge to the center, orthogonal to the ridge, at a point where the ridge is 50–60 cm high and particularly well defined. A GPR transect across the ridge at this point showed a radar reflection about 60 cm deep, presumably the surface under the ridge. This in itself is a significant observation, indicating that the ridge is a built-up feature rather than a ridge left high by the removal of soil to either side (as by the erosion documented in Chapter 5). On excavation, however, the ridge proved to be just as puzzling inside as it is on the outside.

The ridge is composed of compact silt with astonishing quantities of sesquioxide (iron-manganese) concretions. In the upper 40 cm of the ridge fill, the concretions ranged from pea-sized to marble-sized, but in the lower 20 cm they were as large as golf balls. Excavation of this deposit required a pickaxe. At about 60 cm below the top of the ridge (see Figure 7.9) the

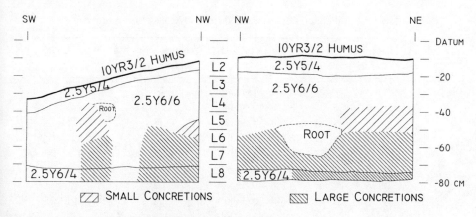

Figure 7.9. Vertical profiles of Dike Excavation Unit 4

sediments became grayer and less indurated, though concretions were still numerous. Excavations were halted at 70 cm below the top of the ridge. The basal grayer layer is probably the original ground surface (buried A horizon) beneath the ridge. Where the sediment of the ridge came from is not known, insofar as such abundance of concretions has been seen nowhere else on the site. One 10-cm-thick level in a 1-×-1-m unit produced about 17 kg of concretions. The weight (81 kg, total) and volume of this material was so great, and its interpretive value so low, that after being washed and dried it was weighed in the field and discarded. The weights of discarded concretion are presented in Table 7.5 (note that the excavation levels in the table are measured below a datum approximately 10 cm above the highest point of the ridge). Setting aside the unusual nature of the sediments, the important result of the excavation was confirmation that the ridge is a built feature.

The artifactual content of the Dike is singularly unenlightening. One iron chain link was found in the uppermost level of the Excavation Unit 6, at the edge of the ridge. One piece of fired clay was found in the uppermost level of Excavation Unit 4, at the center of the ridge. All the other items recovered were nondiagnostic pieces of stone, including 5 noncortical flakes, 134 pieces of shatter, and 1,285 unmodified pebbles. None of these items clarifies when the ridge was built.

Because there was no charcoal for radiocarbon dating and no pottery for cross-dating was found in the Dike excavation, we turned to oxidizable carbon ratio (OCR) dating. This procedure is widely regarded by archaeologists as an experimental technique, the validity of which has not yet been established. The technique assays sediment samples and is claimed to estimate the age at which fresh organic matter was last incorporated into the sediments. Three samples were submitted for assay: one from 8–22 cm below surface,

Table 7.5 Soil concretions discarded from Dike excavation units

Excavation Unit	FS #	Level	Weight as measured in field, in lbs	Weight in kg
4	38	3 (20–30 cm bd)	10	4.5
4	39	4 (30–40 cm bd)	25	11.3
4	51	5 (40–50 cm bd)	38	17.2
4	52	6 (50–60 cm bd)	28	12.7
4	53	7 (60–70 cm bd)	37	16.8
4	54	8 (70–80 cm bd)	35	15.9
5	40	4 (30–40 cm bd)	2	0.9
5	42	5 (40–50 cm bd)	4	1.8
6	41	4 (30–40 cm bd)	*	*

*sample accidentally discarded before weighing

one from 24–35 cm below surface, and the third from 52–64 cm below surface. These correspond roughly to L. 3–4, L. 5, and L. 8, respectively, in Figure 7.9. Inasmuch as the lowest sample came from what is interpreted as the A horizon beneath the Dike and the upper two samples from the Dike fill, it was expected that the lowest sample would have a different date from the upper two. Because the upper two samples come from redeposited B-horizon loess which presumably was last receiving fresh organic matter at the time it was deposited on what was the ground surface during the Pleistocene, the date of the upper two samples was expected to be thousands of years earlier than the date of the lowest sample. The OCR assays did not conform to expectation, however. In order from top to bottom, the samples yielded estimates of A.D. 1780 ± 5, A.D. 1320 ± 20, and A.D. 960 ± 30. Given their lack of agreement with the inferred depositional processes and the unvalidated status of the dating technique, it is not clear what, if anything, these assays tell us.

The question of why the Dike was built is no easier to answer than the question of when it was built. If one projects the line of the Dike eastward, it leads more or less to Mound A. Possibly, therefore, the ridge is a causeway of sorts built to provide a straight, dry path from the landward side of the site to the ceremonial center of the community. But this is speculation founded on extrapolation rather than a conclusion built solidly on facts.

EVALUATION OF THE INVESTIGATION

The fieldwork carried out by SEAC personnel in 1999 accomplished the most important of the stated goals and did so in a remarkably brief ten days of work with a crew of seven. The 1998 Welch site grid is now tied to UTM coordinates, the 1933–1934 grid is tied to the 1998 grid, the full visible extent of the palisade and its bastions have been mapped, and the Dike has been shown to be a built feature. Ground-penetrating radar helped relocate some of the old excavation units but proved to have an erratic record in this regard. The radar also provided dramatic evidence of buried surfaces inside Mound A, though precisely what these surfaces are cannot be ascertained from the radar alone. While some of these achievements are not intrinsically of great interest, they were of enormous importance for future work at the site. Without the work directed by Cornelison and Anderson, the matching of the 1993–1934 grid and the 1998 grid would have been off by about 3 m, the 1998 grid would not be connected to any larger coordinate system, and we would still be wondering whether the Dike is a built feature.

As important as the results of the 1999 fieldwork were for the preparation of this report, the SEAC fieldwork's most significant impact has been on the planning for mitigation excavation of Mound A. Based on the only other reported archaeological investigation of Mound A, it had been thought that the mound fill could be removed as a single unit with no significant loss of information. After the radar survey atop Mound A, that was no longer a viable conclusion. Fortunately, this revision in our understanding of the mound's internal complexity came in time to assist in the process of planning the excavation of that portion of the mound threatened by the expected collapse of the river bluff.

8 Shiloh in Context

An understanding of the community that built and lived at the Shiloh site requires a consideration of the neighborhood and region within which that community lived. The research at Shiloh, in particular the revised understanding of the chronology of the site, allows us to add detail to the picture presented by Gerald Smith (1977:15–24) as well as to correct several facets of his discussion. Essentially, the picture Smith painted was one of two occupations at Shiloh. The first was a Late Woodland community that built Mound C and used it for burials. The second was a Late Mississippian community contemporary with the Kogers Island phase sites immediately upriver. This Late Mississippian community, Smith argued, differed from the Kogers Island–phase communities in that it was culturally related to communities in the Cairo Lowland region instead of to those near Moundville, Alabama. Smith also called attention to several nearby Mississippian sites within 30 km of Shiloh and a striking absence of Mississippian mound sites downriver from this cluster. With the improved understanding of Shiloh's chronology, several parts of this picture can now be readjusted.

THE SHILOH PHASE

Within 44 km upriver and 24 km downriver of Shiloh, there are at least five and possibly as many as nine other Mississippian mound sites. Much of what is known about these sites comes, as is so often the case with mounds in the Southeast, from a report by C. B. Moore (1915:208–233). The mound sites Moore described are listed in Table 8.1, with an assessment of their probable age. The sites of definite or possible Mississippian age are shown in Figure 8.1. Information from Moore and subsequent researchers shows no Mississippian mounds for more than 50 km straight-line distance downriver from the Swallow Bluff Island site (see Autry and Hinshaw 1981:69) and a similar straight-line distance upriver from the Swan Pond/McKelvey site (Meyer 1995; Walthall 1980; Webb and DeJarnette:1942). There is a similar gap to the west (Mainfort 1992; Prentice 2000:Figs. 40, 41) and the east (Suzanne Hoyal, personal communication). Thus, the Mississippian mound sites from Swallow Bluff Island to Swan Pond/McKelvey constitute a clearly bounded cluster

Table 8.1 Mound sites near Shiloh

Name	Moore's Description	Diagnostic artifacts found by Moore [and/or others]	Chronological assessment
Old Furnace Landing	Mound 2 ft. high, 95 ft. diameter, badly disturbed, no excavation by Moore	None found	unknown
Swallow Bluff Island	Larger mound: rectangular, 18 ft. high, 130x130 ft. base, flat summit 50 ft across. Smaller mound: 9½ ft. high, 90 ft. diameter, summit 30 ft. across.	Stone box graves in both mounds, containing: shell-temp. bottles; 2-handled jars; 2-handled incised jar; jar with handles and row of knobs around body	Shiloh Phase
Old Callens Landing	Mound rectangular, 8½ ft high, 106x56 ft base, flat summit	None found	possibly Mississippian
Dickeys Landing	Mound 11 ft. high, 95–145 ft. across, much plowed over	None found by Moore (Welch found shell-tempered pottery on surface in 1996)	probably Mississippian
Williams Farm	Several low mounds, no excavation by Moore [see Stelle 1871]	None found	probably pre-Mississippian
Savannah	17 mounds, 2 bastioned palisade lines; no excavation by Moore [see Stelle 1871; Welch 1998a]	(Welch: chunkey stones, chert hoes, shell-tempered pottery)	Shiloh Phase
Wolf Island	Larger mound: rectangular, 12 ft. high, 115x165 ft. across, flat summit. Smaller mound: circular, 5 ft. high, 50 ft. diameter	Burials in small mound had: 2-handled jar; hemispherical bowl with bird-effigy rim adorno and "tail" lug	Shiloh Phase
Perkins Bluff	A number of small mounds a few inches to 4 ft. high and 15 to 35 ft diameter	None found by Moore; a second-hand report of a shell with "letters" lying near a skull	probably pre-Mississippian

Continued on the next page

Table 8.1 *Continued*

Name	Moore's Description	Diagnostic artifacts found by Moore [and/or others]	Chronological assessment
Pittsburg Ferry	Mound circular, 4½ ft. high, 80 ft. diameter; plowed over	Bowl with animal head on one side and "tail" lug; globular bottle with angular base; 2-handled jar; asymmetrical yellow bottle with conical neck	Shiloh Phase
Shiloh (Pittsburg Landing)	No excavation by Moore	(see Chapter 4)	Shiloh Phase
Nash Landing	Mound 10 ft. high, badly dug away; no excavation	None found	unknown
below North Carolina Landing	Larger mound: rectangular, 7 ft. high, 100x150 across, flat summit, plowed over and partly cut away. Smaller mound: 3 ft. high, 50 ft. diameter, irregular shape, partly cut away.	None found, but the layout is similar to the Wolf Island and Swallow Bluff Island sites	probably Shiloh Phase
near North Carolina Landing	Mound 7 ft. high, 90x55 ft. across, much plowed over	Post holes and fire basins in mound; red-filmed narrow-neck bottle; wide-neck bottle	Shiloh Phase
Boyds Landing	Mound 7 ft. high, 70 ft. diameter, partly washed or dug away [see Webb and DeJarnette 1942: 39–41]	Several masses of galena; no fireplaces or other evidence of occupancy [Webb and DeJarnette add: small copper celt similar to one from a Middle Woodland mound at Savannah site]	Copena
Swan Pond [McKelvey]	Mound rectangular, 7 ft. high, 70x70 ft base; no excavation by Moore [see Webb and DeJarnette	[Webb and DeJarnette: kneeling human sandstone effigy; 2-handled and 4-handled jars;	Shiloh Phase

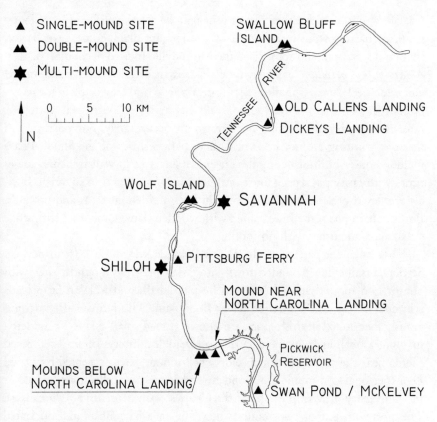

▲ SINGLE-MOUND SITE
▲▲ DOUBLE-MOUND SITE
★ MULTI-MOUND SITE

0   5   10 KM

N

SWALLOW BLUFF
ISLAND

TENNESSEE RIVER

▲ OLD CALLENS LANDING
DICKEYS LANDING

WOLF ISLAND
★ SAVANNAH

SHILOH ★ ▲ PITTSBURG FERRY

MOUND NEAR
NORTH CAROLINA LANDING

MOUNDS BELOW
NORTH CAROLINA LANDING

PICKWICK
RESERVOIR

▲ SWAN POND / MCKELVEY

Figure 8.1. Mound sites of the Shiloh Phase

focused around the Shiloh and Savannah multiple-mound, palisaded towns.
Five of the sites have pottery shapes and styles duplicated at Shiloh, and none
has artifacts suggesting a date later than the ca. A.D. 1400 abandonment of
Shiloh. Thus, all of the available evidence indicates that these sites were occupied during the same time span as Shiloh, though they were not necessarily
occupied continuously through the entire span. This spatially and chronologically discrete cluster of communities probably corresponds to our notion
of a distinct society.

If, as seems likely, the Mississippian communities that built the mound
sites near Shiloh and Savannah constituted a distinct society, then it is appropriate to apply the notion of an archaeological phase to these settlements. The
Shiloh Phase, then, consists of archaeological components in the district lying
roughly between the McKelvey site and the Swallow Bluff Island site, dating
between A.D. 1050 and 1400 and having shell-tempered pottery similar to that
at Shiloh. Diagnostic elements of this pottery include jars of Mississippi Plain

var. Shiloh paste, with either two or four parallel-sided handles of loop, loopy strap, or narrow strap form. Some of the jars are plain, some have Barton Incised decoration, and some have the Moundville Incised decoration of *vars. Moundville, Carrollton,* or *Snows Bend.* Narrow-neck (also called carafe-neck) and wide-neck bottles, shallow flaring-rim bowls, and tray or plate forms are present in Bell Plain ware. Incision and engraving on burnished pottery is rare. Red- and white-filming are known to occur rarely, but positive and negative painting are not known. Other characteristics of the Shiloh Phase include houses built of bent poles set either singly or in wall-trenches, sometimes with entry passages. House outlines vary from round to squarish. Burials are flexed or semiflexed and occur in both residential areas and mounds. Burials are in pits sometimes roofed with wooden slabs, sometimes with stone slabs, and sometimes with no roofing.

The settlement pattern of the Shiloh Phase is known, at least in outline. Settlements include palisaded town sites with multiple mounds, sites with one or two mounds (not known to be palisaded), and isolated farmsteads scattered across the Tennessee River floodplain. The farmsteads, not previously mentioned in this report, are known from a small survey I conducted in 1996, as well as from the occurrence of small numbers of shell-tempered sherds near the surface of much older shell-mound sites excavated by David Dye (personal communication, and my inspection of collections housed at the University of Memphis and at the Charles Nash Museum at Chucalissa). The sites with one or two mounds may not have had substantial nucleated populations, inasmuch as Moore and more recent archaeological visitors have not observed extensive shell-tempered occupations beside the mounds. Instead, the mounds may have served as foci for neighborhoods of scattered farmsteads. The mound site at Swallow Bluff Island, however, may have had a nucleated residential zone, for an extensive buried midden zone with shell-tempered pottery is visible in the eroding river edge (Welch 2003, 2004). Unfortunately, this site is being eaten away by riverbank erosion exacerbated by unlawful construction activities of developers who owned the site in 1999 (Hays 2000). As of 2003, riverbank erosion has removed almost all of the large mound, and the small burial mound had been thoroughly cratered by pothunting. Other than the damage to the mounds and the erosion of the riverbank, the Swallow Bluff Island site is well preserved. At least, it is in better shape than Wolf Island (Smith 1977:15), Savannah (Moore 1915:221), and Swan Pond/McKelvey (Webb and DeJarnette 1942:9–25), which are largely obliterated.

The chronology of settlements within the Shiloh Phase is currently unknown, so it is not clear whether all of the mound sites were occupied for the whole duration of the phase or whether settlements shifted during the several centuries of the phase. Also not known is whether both of the multiple-mound, palisaded towns were occupied at the same time or sequentially. If they were occupied at the same time, it is interesting to speculate what the relations were between these two towns.

Taking note of the frequent occurrence of white clay with burials in Shiloh's Mound C, the capping of the initial mound with a deposit of white clay, and the deposition of an obviously important pipe in the central tomb of the mound, I previously suggested (Welch 2001:290–291) that Shiloh might have been a White town. As Hudson (1976:235) put it—describing the Creeks but to some degree applicable to other southeastern groups as well—white is "the color of that which is old, established, pure, peaceable, holy, united, and so forth." In contrast, red was "the color associated with conflict, war, fear, disunity, and danger." Red, the opposite of old and established, was also connected to recent arrivals, and immigrant groups were conceptualized as "Red towns" in contrast with the older established "White towns." Within towns, individual clans were also conceived of as white or red, depending on their respective ages, their orientation toward neighbors, and their ritual functions. The details of such belief systems varied from group to group, they were likely more complex than this simple sketch, and they may not have been the same in the A.D. 1050–1400 period as in the Historic era. Nevertheless, Shiloh's most important burials do not have any of the warfare-related symbolism seen at some other Mississippian sites and are associated with the color white and with a pipe, the quintessential eastern Indian symbol of peace.

Since the time that I suggested that Shiloh was a White town, excavation on Mound A has revealed a more complex color symbolism. At least three of the later stages of Mound A were surmounted by red clay summits, similar to those Roberts saw on Mounds E and F (see Chapter 5). The summits were not the only portions of Mound A that were colored. The most recent intact mound slope (which goes with the third surface from the modern summit) had horizontal bands of yellow, light gray, and red (Anderson and Cornelison 2002; Welch et al. 2003). Thus, white is associated with burials in Mound C on the south side of the site, there were red summits on mounds A, E, and F on the north side of the site, and at least one of the mounds had bands of additional colors on its flanks. Despite this blossoming of colors, my original suggestion that Shiloh may have been a White town could nevertheless be correct, inasmuch as the burials in Mound C—the only known high-status burials—have white symbolism.

To pursue this line of speculation a little further, if Shiloh was a White town perhaps Savannah was Red. If the Savannah residents were Mississippian *arrivistes,* what better way to lay claim to status than to settle on top of the ancient, hallowed, symbolically potent landscape of a Middle Woodland mound complex? Alas, so little of the Savannah site is left in the backyards and under the driveways of modern Savannah's oldest neighborhood that we may never be able to test this speculation. Admittedly this line of speculation about color symbolism of Shiloh and Savannah is highly uncertain, but it is worth thinking about because the distinction between Red and White towns was widespread among Historic Indian societies of the Southeast.

Turning back to matters chronological, it is also possible that Shiloh and Savannah were not contemporary but rather were sequential occupations. If they were sequential, then Savannah was most likely the later occupation, given the known early Mississippian date of Shiloh. It is worth noting, however, that there is no hint of occupation anywhere in the area shown in Figure 8.1 after A.D. 1450, so a post-Shiloh occupation at Savannah seems unlikely. Indeed, the Shiloh Phase as a whole seems to end at roughly the same time (as gauged by pottery styles) as the Kogers Island Phase begins upriver. Where people went from the Shiloh phase communities, and who their descendants might be, is addressed later in this chapter.

WHO WERE THEIR ANCESTORS?

Whether the people responsible for building the mounds were descendants of local Late Woodland communities, or whether there was immigration of at least some people from elsewhere, is a question that has been raised for virtually every large early Mississippian site (Blitz and Lorenz 2003; Smith 1984). In many locales the answers are still not known, and Shiloh is one of those. There is ample evidence of Late Woodland population in this stretch of the Tennessee River valley, so it is certainly possible that these people were the ancestors of the Shiloh inhabitants. In fact, there is ample evidence for Late Woodland occupation at Shiloh itself, but whether that Late Woodland community was the immediate ancestor of the Shiloh Mississippians depends partly on whether there is a chronological gap between the Late Woodland occupation and the Mississippian one.

The date of the Late Woodland—or at least the grog-tempered pottery-using—occupation at Shiloh remains a vexing issue. I am not able to assign a date to this occupation on the basis of pottery cross-dating, and none of the available radiocarbon assessments are relevant to the age of the grog-tempered pottery. But we can at least reject Smith's conclusion that Mound C is a Late Woodland construction. From the reasonably secure Stirling-phase origin of the Shiloh pipe and the presence of a shell ear spool, both of which were in a tomb built before most of Mound C and the other burials were deposited, Mound C is clearly of Mississippian date. Mounds A, E, F, and Q also are Mississippian in date, based on the presence of shell-tempered pottery in their fills. While Mounds B, D, G, and H are not yet dated, at this point there is little reason to think that they differ in age from A, C, E, F, and Q. We also know that the grog-tempered occupation at Shiloh was primarily located east of the modern park road across the site, much less than half the area enclosed by the Mississippian palisade. Though not definitive, this evidence suggests that the people who made the grog-tempered pottery were separate, earlier occupants of this location. Direct dating of pottery may clarify this issue in the not too distant future.

In addition to better chronological information, it will also be important to study the details of the shapes of Late Woodland and Mississippian pottery vessels. This approach has been fruitful along the lower Chattahoochee and Apalachicola (Blitz and Lorenz 2003; Scarry 1984). Detailed comparison of Late Woodland and Mississippian vessel shapes there showed local continuities despite changes in tempering agents and surface decoration, indicating that the Late Woodland potters remained in place while adopting new manufacturing and decorative techniques. That sort of detailed study is beyond the scope of this volume, so the issue of whether the Mississippians at Shiloh were all descended from local Late Woodland people has to be left unanswered at present.

WHO WERE THEIR NEIGHBORS, ALLIES, AND ENEMIES?

The people of the Shiloh Phase communities had neighbors, some of whom were allies or were neutral while others were hostile. At least, the effort it took to build the palisade around the site suggests that at one point the Shiloh community felt threatened. On the other hand, the fact that there is only one set of palisade posts, with no evidence of repair or rebuilding after those posts inevitably rotted, suggests that the perceived threat lasted no longer than the life of a wooden post in humid soils, perhaps five to ten years. But who were the allies and who were the enemies, and where exactly were the neighbors?

There were neighbors in every direction, albeit none very close. The locations of isolated sites as well as more substantial Mississippian populations between roughly A.D. 1100 to 1300 are shown in Figure 8.2. This interval was chosen for the map, despite being somewhat shorter than the A.D. 1050–1400 span of the Shiloh Phase because it greatly simplified the task of representing a dynamic social landscape on a static map. The map shows several isolated mound sites within 50–150 km of the Shiloh Phase sites (Bohannon 1972; Dye 2002; Garland 1992; Hoyal, personal communication; Mainfort 1992; Nash 1968; Rafferty 1995). Beyond that lies a ring of more substantial agglom-

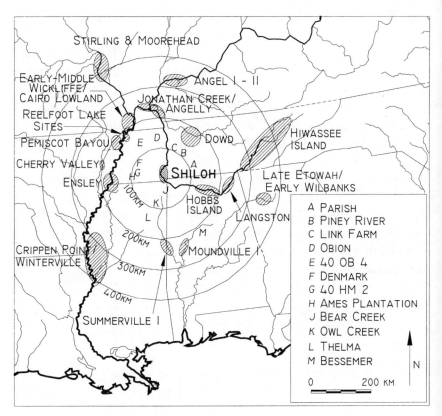

Figure 8.2. Sites and phases in the region around Shiloh

erations of communities, most of which lie more than 150 km distant (Barreis and Porter 1984; Blitz 1993; Brain 1989; Butler 1991; Clay 1997; Jenkins and Krause 1986; Johnson and Atkinson 1987; King 2003; Knight and Steponaitis 1998; Lafferty and Price 1996; Lawrence and Mainfort 1993, 1996; Lorenz 1996; Lowthert et al. 1998; Lumb and McNutt 1988; Milner 1998; Morse and Morse 1983; O'Brien 1977; Phillips 1970; Schroeder 2003; Schroedl et al. 1990; Smith 1992; Smith 1996; Smith 2000; Smith and Trubbitt 1998; Sullivan 1995a; Walthall 1980; Welch 1994; Wesler 2001). Even with its restricted time range the map is unrealistically static, for these communities were not all occupied at precisely the same time. In general, the isolated mound sites within 150 km of Shiloh tend to be very early and were abandoned by A.D. 1200 or so. Thus, Shiloh's earliest neighbors disappeared after a century or so, leaving the Shiloh Phase communities with a wider zone of uninhabited land around them.

It is not yet possible to say what relations Shiloh had with most of the sites and phases shown on the map. The presence of Ramey Incised vessels and the carved stone pipe, imported from the American Bottom, indicate that Shiloh's residents were on good political terms with the Cahokia polity. From the quantity of Dover chert in the chipped stone tool industry, it is also clear that Shiloh residents had connections to Link Farm, the site near the Dover chert quarries in west Tennessee. Further, the presence of Mill Creek chert at Shiloh suggests that the lower Tennessee and Ohio rivers were open to travelers to or from Shiloh. Given these artifactually demonstrable ties, it would be surprising if there were not also good relations with the other polities between Shiloh and Cahokia: Jonathan Creek, Kincaid, and Wickliffe. However, no direct connection between Shiloh and these three downriver sites has yet been documented.

What about connections up the Tennessee River? The river prehistorically, as in the Historic era, was a major artery of transportation. People and goods moving between the Etowah polity and Cahokia, for example, would most likely have passed through the Shiloh area. To illustrate his discussion of the external relations of the Etowah chiefdom, King (2003:Fig. 18) drew a map of Southeastern Ceremonial Complex goods moving from the Florida panhandle up the Chattahoochee River, through Etowah, over to the Tennessee River near Chattanooga, and thence westward. His west-pointing arrow ends in the Shiloh polity. Two copper-covered ear spools were found with a burial in Mound C in 1899 (Cadle 1902), and it is possible that the copper came from the deposits near the Tennessee–North Carolina border. More clearcut indication of connections between Shiloh and the Etowah region comes from the recent discovery of Etowah Complicated Stamped pottery in the fill of Mound A. Thus, it is certainly plausible that Southeastern Ceremonial Complex goods moved through the Shiloh area on their way between Etowah and Cahokia.

In addition to bestriding the river route, Shiloh is also near the apparently ancient trail now known as the Natchez Trace, which connects the Nashville basin, the lower Tennessee River, and the lower Mississippi River (see Tanner 1989:11). Once again, however, the artifactual record at Shiloh holds no definite evidence of ties either to the Nashville area or to the lower Mississippi valley. The sherds of several vessels with an incised running scroll motif (Figure 3.11) may indicate communication with the lower Mississippi valley, but as explained in Chapter 3 it is also possible that these sherds are from local imitations of foreign vessels rather than from actual imports.

Another neighbor of Shiloh was Moundville, in Alabama. While Moundville is known to have exchanged goods with communities along the Tennessee River in north Alabama (Welch 1991:183–190), a tie to the Shiloh polity is not definitely established. On display in the Tennessee River Museum in Savannah there is a burnished incised water bottle that, on the basis of shape and finish, could well be an import from Moundville. It came from the river-bank opposite Savannah, but whether it is truly a Moundville import is not clear.

Despite the location of Shiloh along several potentially important trans-portation corridors, there are not many exotics known from Shiloh. This may in part be due to the small size of the artifact collection from the 1930s exca-vation, but it should be remembered that the excavators had a predilection for recovering unusual and exotic goods. Of course, if goods were being moved *through* the Shiloh area, they would not necessarily wind up being deposited *at* Shiloh. Nevertheless, the low number and limited source-areas of the imports found at Shiloh are hardly persuasive evidence of an impor-tant involvement in the regional movement of display goods. Things coming into Shiloh, however, are only half the picture; the other half would be things made at Shiloh that went elsewhere.

So far, there is only one possible candidate for a kind of Shiloh-made good that may have been sent to neighboring communities: shell beads. The con-centration of drills and saws in the Mound N fill suggests that somewhere at Shiloh—wherever the fill originally came from—people were producing shell beads or possibly other display items of shell. The Tennessee River is well known for the abundance of its freshwater mussels (at least, before impound-ment, pollution, and overharvesting depleted the stocks). However, even though some of the Shiloh residents spent time producing beads, the absence of drills and saws in House Mound 7, in the areas excavated by SEAC in 1999, and in the areas excavated by Smith in 1976 suggests that most of the population was not involved in such production. If Shiloh did export shell beads, the site does not seem to have been a large-scale producer.

There is also a chance that amber beads may have come from the Shiloh area. So far, only one amber bead is known from a Mississippian site, a barrel-shaped specimen found at Moundville (Moore 1905:173). The Coffee phase of the Eutaw Sand formation that erodes into the river and stream banks in the north half of the Shiloh polity is known to produce amber (Jewell 1931:47). However, there are amber deposits elsewhere in the Southeast (Dahl-strom and Brost 1996:57; Ross 1998:28), and the amber in the Coffee sand is described as occurring in "small pellets" rather than the 4.5-cm-long mass of the Moundville bead. Thus it is only a possibility, perhaps an improbability, that the Moundville amber bead came from Shiloh.

While friendly relations between polities are manifest by the exchange of goods between them, hostile relations impede the flow of goods. Thus, one could potentially assess which of Shiloh's neighbors were hostile by examin-ing which of them were not exchanging goods with Shiloh. This is difficult to do at the moment, because there are so few known imports at Shiloh and no known exports. With such scarcity, it is difficult to know whether an absence of visible exchange signals hostility or merely insufficient excavation. Thus, it is premature to consider the absence of known exchange between Shiloh and the Dowd Phase communities near Nashville, or the communities near Memphis or in the upper Tennessee valley, as an indication of hostility.

In short, the residents of Shiloh appear to have participated for the most part in a domestic economy rather than having direct involvement with interpolity movement of display items. Despite the potentially strategic position of the Shiloh Phase sites, there is little evidence that the residents derived significant benefit from their politically strategic position. It looks like the Shiloh residents were, for the most part, farmers concerned primarily about their crops and their families. Whether this lack of visible involvement in regional political relations is directly related to the longevity of this usually unfortified community is a matter for future research.

WHERE DID THEY GO AND WHO ARE THEIR DESCENDANTS?

The Mississippian occupation and the building of the mounds at Shiloh took place between A.D. 1050 and 1400. We do not know the order in which the mounds were constructed or how the community size may have changed during the several centuries of occupation. We also do not know where the Shiloh residents went when they left the site. That they left the site alive is a conclusion not directly proven by any evidence but is instead an assumption made in the absence of evidence otherwise. There is, first, the absence of any obvious desecration of the site's important structures, which might be expected if an enemy had conquered these people. Second, the frequent occurrence of burned buildings at the site does not support the notion that the site was torched by victorious enemies, for the burned houses appear to have been intentionally abandoned and emptied of contents before burning. Third, the presence of human bodies on the floor of one of the burned houses is not an instance of people being trapped inside a burning building. Instead, the field observations prove that these were intentional burials added after the building had burned. Thus, there is nothing in the archaeological record to indicate that the departure from Shiloh was anything but peaceful. The same can be said about the other sites of the Shiloh Phase, though that may simply be the result of the very small extent of excavation on those sites. Where did the people go?

The Shiloh Phase ends about the same time that the Kogers Island Phase appears upriver in the Pickwick Basin. Given the nearly complementary ages of the Shiloh Phase and the Kogers Island Phase, and the apparent scarcity of early Mississippian occupation in the upper Pickwick Basin (Futato 1998:226; Meyer 1995:40–42; Walthall 1980:196–211), it is natural to wonder whether Kogers Island might represent a short-distance movement of people out of the Shiloh-Savannah area. This is entirely possible, for there are no clear indications otherwise. Like the Shiloh Phase pottery, Kogers Island pottery is stylistically more closely related to pottery at Moundville than to pottery of the lower Tennessee and Cumberland rivers (let alone the Mississippi valley). Indeed, Kogers Island people engaged in exchanges with people at Moundville, resulting in what appear to be Moundville-made pots, red shale pendants, and sandstone paint palettes being put in graves along the Tennessee River (Welch 1991:183–190). Deciding whether this attractively simple idea—that the Shiloh Phase people became the Kogers Island Phase people— is true will take more careful examination of the chronological and stylistic relations between Shiloh and Kogers Island than can be accomplished in this report. It is perhaps well to keep in mind that attractively simple ideas are often simply wrong, and also to recall that archaeologists do not have a foolproof way to decipher ethnic or societal identification from the archaeological record.

Regardless of where the Shiloh Phase inhabitants moved, the question of why they moved is an important one. Unfortunately, there is no clear answer. Since there is no evidence that the residents were driven away by external forces, the cause could have been that another location offered greater advantages than the location that had been occupied for centuries. Baden (1995) has argued that declining soil nitrogen, which is not significantly replenished by flood deposits or short fallow periods, would have imposed a time limit on how long a population could grow maize in a river floodplain. After all the available farmland had been used and depleted of nitrogen, the farmers would have been forced either to use alternative food sources or to move elsewhere. Under reasonable population density scenarios, Baden's figures suggest that two centuries is about the upper limit of sustainable maize agriculture in southeastern river floodplains. Under such circumstances, the Shiloh Phase population may well have perceived an advantage to moving upriver to a district that had not been farmed for several hundred years.

Another possibility is that the motivation for moving was political rather than economic. The Shiloh pipe and Ramey Incised pottery suggest some kind of political tie between the Shiloh polity and Cahokia. Cahokia collapsed or at least decentralized in the mid-1200s, which undoubtedly had profound effects on regional political networks. As alliances changed and power rebalanced, population movements would be expected. Yet the lag between Cahokia's collapse and the abandonment of Shiloh appears to be sufficiently long to raise a question about whether the two phenomena are related. The Shiloh abandonment also appears to occur long after Moundville's rise to political prominence, so it is also hard to see a connection between these two phenomena. Perhaps events elsewhere, in the lower Mississippi valley or in the upper Tennessee drainage, may have had some bearing. Overall, however, based on our current understanding of regional politics, there is no obvious candidate for an external cause of the abandonment of the Shiloh Phase communities.

One of the questions most commonly asked by visitors to the Shiloh Indian Mounds site is which group of Indians lived here. Archaeology does not yet have an entirely satisfactory answer. At a surficial level the answer is clear: we do not know the name that people of the Shiloh Phase communities used when referring to themselves. Furthermore, the group of communities that occupied this stretch of the valley moved elsewhere—perhaps multiple different elsewheres—hundreds of years before the era when tribal names began to be recorded in writing, and thus there is no guarantee that this set of communities corresponds in any direct way with historically known tribal groups such as the Chickasaw, Creek, Choctaw, and so on. But the people who lived in the Shiloh Phase communities most likely had descendants in one or more of the historically known Indian groups, and who those historic descendants were is a good question.

A case can be made for the Shiloh phase occupants being culturally similar to the historic Muskogean groups: the Chickasaw, Choctaw, and the various Creek towns. There are two lines of archaeological evidence consistent with a Muskogean identity. The first is pottery styles. Jenkins (2001; Jenkins and Krause 1986) sees the Mississippian assemblages of the middle and upper Tombigbee drainage, along with those of the Black Warrior drainage and the Tennessee River in north Alabama, sharing sufficient similarities that all of these local sequences deserve to be recognized as constituents of the "Moundville Variant." The concept of a variant (Jenkins and Krause 1986:1–17) is essentially that of a set of diachronic local sequences linked by internal similarities and distinct from other similarly constituted linked sequences. If an archaeological phase is comparable to an ethnographic culture, then a variant would consist of a set of related cultures. In fact, Jenkins (personal communication, 2001) argues that the Shiloh Phase people, along with the contemporary communities at Hobbs Island, Bessemer, Moundville, and Lubbub in Alabama, were culturally Muskogean, specifically western Muskogean (the branch of the Muskogean family that today is represented by Choctaw and Chickasaw). Most archaeologists are very cautious in equating groups of prehistoric pottery assemblages with subsequent historical cultural groups. The potential dangers in making such simple equations are demonstrated by the fact that the some of the historic Cherokee as well as some of the historic

Creeks descended from people who made Lamar pottery. Because extrapolating cultural similarity from similarity of pottery is so apt to be misleading, this line of evidence alone would not be particularly persuasive in arguing that Shiloh residents were Muskogean speakers.

The second line of evidence for connecting Shiloh with Muskogeans is the layout of the ceremonial precinct. Unfortunately, this argument is at least as tenuous as the one dealing with pottery styles. Classically, the Muskogean towns that were locales for important ceremonies were conceived as having an open plaza or square with council houses or other public buildings arrayed around it, the whole surrounded by the residences of local lineages. This is visible in the record Speck (1907) obtained from a Chickasaw informant, as well as the layouts of historic Creek towns summarized by Hudson (1976:218–222). In prehistoric and early historic times the public buildings were often atop mounds, so that the open central square or plaza was framed by mounds. This is the stereotypical Mississippian site layout, and it helps make archaeological sense of sites like Moundville (Knight 1998). However, many Mississippian sites do not conform to this specifically Muskogean model. Cahokia (Fowler 1997), for example, has multiple plazas framed by mounds, and at the Angel site (Black 1967) there is a plaza but many of the mounds are not near it. Other examples that do not fit the Muskogean stereotype include the Bottle Creek site (Stowe and Fuller 1993) in southern Alabama and the Winterville site (Brain 1989) in Mississippi. Shiloh's mounds (A, B, D, E, F, G, Q) do form a rectangle, with only the burial mound C and the small, irregularly shaped mound H—of indeterminate function—departing from the frame around the plaza. Thus, the layout of Shiloh conforms to the Muskogean stereotype. But this line of evidence, too, is not foolproof, as witness the nonstereotypical layout of mounds at Etowah, a site likely built and occupied by Muskogean speakers (King 2003).

In summary, two lines of archaeological evidence are consistent with the Shiloh inhabitants having a Muskogean culture. Precisely which group of Muskogeans is not clear, for archaeologists and historians have not yet knitted together the multiple strands of population movements, polity disintegrations, and ethnogeneses that occurred in the region during the period from 1400 to 1700 (but see Galloway [1995] for a good start).

The earliest written records for the region are the accounts of the de Soto expedition, which place the Chicaza (Chicksaw), Alimamus (Alabamas), and Sacchumas (Chakchiumas) in what is now northeast Mississippi in A.D. 1540. All of these groups spoke Muskogean languages, the Alabama language being somewhat less closely related to Chickasaw than is Choctaw (Haas 1978:Table 12; Munro 1987; Chakchiuma is not classified for lack of sufficient data). By the mid-1600s the Chickasaw lived near Tupelo, Mississippi, and were firmly

in control of the Shiloh area, but in 1542 they appear to have been farther
south. Galloway (2002) and Johnson (2000) argue that in the 1400s the proto-
Chickasaw were near Columbus, Mississippi, moving to the Tupelo area only
in the 1500s and 1600s. In the winter of 1540–1541, the Chicaza chief was seen
by the de Soto expedition as the dominant leader in the upper Tombigbee
drainage, having the chief of the Alimamus (Alabamas) and that of the Sacchumas (Chakchiumas) as tributaries (Hudson 1997:259–261). The location
of the Sacchuma village is not specified in the documents, but the Alimamus
were located northwest of the main Chicaza town. This places the Alimamus
nearer to the Shiloh area than the Chicaza were in 1540, even though the
Alabamas later moved to the central part of the state that bears their name.
Depending on the location of the Sacchuma village, the Chakchiumas might
also have a claim to the area, despite their location in the Yazoo basin in the
1700s. Swanton (1946:106) tells of a tradition that the Lyons Bluff site near
Starkville, Mississippi, was a Chakchiuma stronghold, and this is certainly in
the vicinity of the Chicaza town of 1540. Based on the written record, any of
these three historically known groups may have had ancestors at Shiloh.

Whatever the source or sources of the people who called themselves
Chickasaw, it was the Chickasaw who controlled west Tennessee from the
1600s through the 1830s (see Gibson [1971] and Atkinson [2004] for histories
of the Chickasaw). Because the United States obtained this portion of Tennessee from the Chickasaw, for the purposes of the Native American Graves
Protection and Repatriation Act (NAGPRA) the Chickasaw are the federally
recognized tribe that has precedence in consultations about proposed archaeological work at Shiloh. In planning the mitigation excavation on Mound A,
for example, planning meetings and consultations included a representative
of the Chickasaw Nation government. However, the fact that federal legisla-
tion requires consultation with the Chickasaw does not mean that archaeologists or Indians necessarily believe that the Chickasaw are the only federally
recognized tribe that had ancestors at Shiloh.

In short, there is as yet no simple answer to the question "where did the
Shiloh people go, and who are their descendants?" This unsatisfying result
is hardly rare. In many parts of the eastern United States, it has been difficult to connect the prehistoric archaeological record with the documentary
evidence of group identities and locations recorded by Euro-American ob-
servers. That does not mean the question will never be answered. It only
means we will have to do additional work to arrive at answers that will help
us understand the past societies that built and inhabited sites like Shiloh Indian Mounds.

References Cited

Ahler, Steven R., and Peter J. DePuydt
    1987   *A Report on the 1931 Powell Mound Excavations, Madison County, Illinois.* Reports of Investigations No. 43, Illinois State Museum, Springfield.

Allan, Aljean W.
    1984   Mound State Monument Palisade Excavations, 1978–1982. Paper presented at the 38th Annual Meeting of the Southeastern Archaeological Conference, Memphis, Tennessee.

Allen, Stacy D.
    1997a   Shiloh! The Campaign and the First Day's Battle. *Blue and Gray Magazine* 14(3):6–27, 46–64.
    1997b   Shiloh! The Second Day's Battle and Aftermath. *Blue and Gray Magazine* 14(4):6–27, 45–55.

Allsbrook, R. C.
    1995   Limestone, Grog, and Shell: An Intemperate View of Pottery Temper in the Tennessee Valley. Paper presented at the 60th Annual Meeting of the Society for American Archaeology, Minneapolis, Minnesota.

Anderson, David G., and John E. Cornelison, Jr.
    2001   Shiloh 2001 Trip Report. Memorandum on file at the Southeast Archeological Center, National Park Service, Tallahassee, Florida.
    2002   Excavations at Mound A, Shiloh: The 2002 Season. Paper presented at the 59th Annual Meeting of the Southeastern Archaeological Conference, Biloxi, Mississippi.

Anderson, David G., John E. Cornelison, Jr., David Bean, and Paul Welch
    1999   Illuminating the Past: Remote Sensing at Shiloh National Military Park. Paper presented at the 56th Annual Meeting of the Southeastern Archaeological Conference, Pensacola, Florida.

Anderson, David G., John E. Cornelison, Jr., George S. Smith, and Paul D. Welch
    1999   Research Design: Archaeological Fieldwork at Shiloh Mounds, Shiloh National Military Park, Tennessee, July 1999. Paper on file at Southeast Archeological Center, National Park Service, Tallahassee, Florida.

Anonymous
    1914   Manuscript copy of unsigned letter. Shiloh National Military Park archives Series 5, Box 2, Folder 129.

Astin, Robin L.
   1996   Mound M: Chronology and Function at Moundville. Unpublished Mas-
             ter's thesis, Department of Anthropology, University of Alabama, Tus-
             caloosa.
Atkinson, James R.
   2004   *Splendid Land, Splendid People: The Chickasaw Indians to Removal.* Uni-
             versity of Alabama Press, Tuscaloosa.
Autry, William O., Jr., and Jane S. Hinshaw
   1981   *A Cultural Resource Reconnaissance of the Tennessee National Wildlife Ref-*
             uge with Archaeological Survey of Selected Areas: Benton, Decatur, Henry,
             and Humphreys Counties, Tennessee. Volume 1. Report of Contract A-
             5608(78), U.S. Fish and Wildlife Service, submitted to Division of Ar-
             cheological Services, National Park Service, Atlanta, Georgia.
Baden, William W.
   1995   The Impact of Fluctuating Agricultural Potential on Coosa's Sociopolitical
             and Settlement Systems. Paper presented at the 52nd Annual Meeting of
             the Southeastern Archaeological Conference, Knoxville, Tennessee.
Bareis, Charles J., and James W. Porter
   1984   Research Design. In *American Bottom Archaeology: A Summary of the*
             FAI-270 Project Contribution to the Culture History of the Mississippi River
             Valley, edited by Charles J. Bareis and James W. Porter, pp. 1–14. Univer-
             sity of Illinois Press, Urbana.
Beditz, Lindsay C.
   1980a   Development of a Research Design to Assess "Significance" at Shiloh
             Indian Mounds, Shiloh National Military Park, Tennessee. Unpublished
             Master's thesis, Department of Anthropology, Florida State University,
             Tallahassee.
   1980b   Shiloh National Military Park, Tennessee, Excavations at Mound A. Re-
             port on file at Southeast Archeological Center, National Park Service,
             Tallahassee, Florida.
Beditz, Lindsay C., and Randy V. Bellomo
   1980   Excavations at Mound A, Shiloh National Military Park, Tennessee. *Bul-*
             letin of the Southeastern Archaeological Conference 23:20–22.
Bellomo, Randy V.
   1981   Field notebook on file at Southeastern Archeological Center, National
             Park Service, Tallahassee, Florida.
   1983   An Evaluation of Contemporary Digital Filtering Techniques Applied to
             Magnetometer Data from Archaeological Sites: Southeastern Examples.
             Unpublished Master's thesis, Department of Anthropology, Florida State
             University, Tallahassee.
Black, Glenn
   1967   *Angel Site: An Archaeological, Historical and Ethnological Study.* Indiana
             Historical Society, Indianapolis.

Blitz, John H.
1993   Big Pots for Big Shots: Feasting and Storage in a Mississippian Commu-
        nity. *American Antiquity* 58:80–96.
Blitz, John H., and Karl G. Lorenz
2003   The Early Mississippian Frontier in the Lower Chattahoochee-Apalachi-
        cola River Valley. *Southeastern Archaeology* 21:117–135.
Bohannon, Charles F.
1972   *Excavations at the Bear Creek Site, Tishomingo County, Mississippi.* Na-
        tional Park Service, Office of Archeology and Historic Preservation, Di-
        vision of Archeology and Anthropology, Washington, D.C.
Bond, Stanley C., Jr.
1981   Experimental Heat Treatment of Cedar Creek Cherts. *Journal of Ala-
        bama Archaeology* 27:1–31.
Boyd, C. Clifford, Jr.
1982   An Examination of the Variability in the Mississippian I and II Lithic
        Assemblages at the Martin Farm Site (40MR20), Tennessee. Unpub-
        lished Master's thesis, Department of Anthropology, University of Ten-
        nessee, Knoxville.
Brain, Jeffrey P.
1989   *Winterville: Late Prehistoric Culture Contact in the Lower Mississippi Val-
        ley.* Archaeological Report No. 23, Mississippi Department of Archives
        and History, Jackson.
Brewer, David M.
1987   An Archeological Overview and Assessment of Shiloh National Military
        Park. Report on file at Southeast Archeological Center, National Park
        Service, Tallahassee, Florida.
Bronk Ramsey, Christopher
2000   *OxCal Program v3.4.* University of Oxford Radiocarbon Accelerator
        Unit, Oxford.
Brown, James A., Richard A. Kerber, and Howard D. Winters
1990   Trade and the Evolution of Exchange Relations at the Beginning of the
        Mississippian Period. In *The Mississippian Emergence,* edited by Bruce D.
        Smith, pp. 251–280. Smithsonian Institution Press, Washington, D.C.
Butler, Brian M.
1991   Kincaid Revisited: The Mississippian Sequence in the Lower Ohio Val-
        ley. In *Cahokia and the Hinterlands: Middle Mississippian Cultures of the
        Midwest,* edited by Thomas E. Emerson and R. Barry Lewis, pp. 264–
        273. University of Illinois Press, Urbana.
Butler, Brian M., and Richard W. Jefferies
1986   Crab Orchard and Early Woodland Cultures in the Middle South. In
        Early Woodland Archeology, edited by Kenneth B. Farnsworth and Thomas
        E. Emerson, pp. 523–534. Kampsville Seminars in Archeology No. 2.
        Center for American Archeology, Kampsville, Illinois.

Cadle, Cornelius

   1902   A Remarkable Prehistoric Ceremonial Pipe. *Records of the Past* 1:218–220.
   1903   Letter to Maj. D. W. Reed dated August 28. Shiloh National Military
             Park archives Series 1, Box 38, Folder 628.

Cambron, James W., and David C. Hulse

   1975   *Handbook of Alabama Archaeology, Part I: Point Types.* The Archaeologi-
             cal Research Association of Alabama, Moundville.

Chambers, Moreau B. C.

   1933–   Excavations at Shiloh National Military Park, Pittsburg Landing, Tenn.
   1934   Unpublished field notes on file at the National Anthropological Ar-
             chives, Smithsonian Institution, Washington, D.C.
   1976   An Interview with Moreau Browne Congleton Chambers. Transcript on
             file at Mississippi Department of Archives and History, Jackson.
   n.d.   The Indian Mounds Shiloh National Military Park. Ms. on file, South-
             east Archeological Center, National Park Service, Tallahassee, Florida.

Chapman, Jefferson

   1995   *Tellico Archaeology: 12,000 Years of Native American History.* Rev. ed. Pub-
             lications in Anthropology No. 41, Tennessee Valley Authority, Knoxville.

Clay, R. Berle

   1997   The Mississippian Succession on the Lower Ohio. *Southeastern Archae-
             ology* 16:16–32.

Cobb, Charles R.

   2000   *From Quarry to Cornfield: The Political Economy of Mississippian Hoe Pro-
             duction.* University of Alabama Press, Tuscaloosa.

Cole, Fay-Cooper, and Thorn Deuel

   1937   *Rediscovering Illinois: Archaeological Explorations in and around Fulton
             County.* University of Chicago Press, Chicago.

Cotter, John L., and John M. Corbett

   1951   *Archeology of the Bynum Mounds, Mississippi.* Archeological Research Se-
             ries No. 1. National Park Service, U.S. Department of the Interior,
             Washington, D.C.

Dahlstrom, Ake, and Leif Brost

   1996   *The Amber Book.* Translated by Jonas Leijonhufvud. Geoscience Press,
             Tucson, Arizona.

DeBoer, Warren R.

   1993   Like a Rolling Stone: The Chunkey Game and Political Organization in
             Eastern North America. *Southeastern Archaeology* 12:83–92.

DeJarnette, David L., and Steve B. Wimberly

   1941   *The Bessemer Site.* Museum Paper 7, Geological Survey of Alabama, Tus-
             caloosa.

Dille, I.

   1867   Sketch of Ancient Earthworks in United States. *Smithsonian Institution
             Annual Report for 1934,* pp. 359–362.

Dye, David

2002 WPA Excavations at the Link Farm Site (40HS6), Humphreys County, Tennessee. Paper presented at the 59th Annual Meeting of the Southeastern Archaeological Conference, Biloxi, Mississippi.

Emerson, Thomas E., and Randall E. Hughes

2000 Figurines, Flint Clay Sourcing, the Ozark Highlands, and Cahokian Acquisition. *American Antiquity* 65:79–101.

Emerson, Thomas E., S. Wisseman, and D. Moore

2001 Cahokian Figurines in the Greater Southeast: The Use of PIMA Technology to Source Mississippian Art. Paper presented at the 58th Annual Meeting of the Southeastern Archaeological Conference, Chattanooga, Tennessee.

Emerson, Thomas E., Randall E. Hughes, Mary R. Hynes, and Sarah U. Wisseman

2003 The Sourcing and Interpretation of Cahokia-Style Figurines in the Trans-Mississippi South and Southeast. *American Antiquity* 68:287–313.

Ensor, H. Blaine

1980 An Evaluation and Synthesis of Changing Lithic Technologies in the Central Tombigbee Valley. *Southeastern Archaeological Conference Bulletin* 22:83–90.

1981 Classification and Synthesis of the Gainesville Lake Area Lithic Materials: Chronology, Technology and Use. In *Archaeological Investigations in the Gainesville Lake Area of the Tennessee-Tombigbee Waterway,* Vol. 3. Report of Investigations No. 13. Office of Archaeological Research, University of Alabama, University.

Feathers, James K.

1997 The Application of Luminescence Dating in American Archaeology. *Journal of Archaeological Method and Theory* 4:1–66

Fowler, Melvin L.

1997 *The Cahokia Atlas: A Historical Atlas of Cahokia Archaeology.* Rev. ed. Illinois Transportation Archaeological Research Program, Urbana.

Fuller, Richard S., and Noel R. Stowe

1982 A Proposed Typology for Late Shell-tempered Ceramics in the Mobile Bay/Mobile–Tensaw Delta Region. In *Archaeology in Southwestern Alabama: A Collection of Papers,* edited by Cailup Curren, pp. 45–102. Alabama-Tombigbee Regional Commission, Camden, Alabama.

Futato, Eugene M.

1975 The Champion Site. In *Archaeological Investigations in the Little Bear Creek Reservoir,* by C. B. Oakley and E. M. Futato. Research Series No. 1. Office of Archaeological Research, University of Alabama, University.

1977 *The Bellefonte Site, 1Ja300.* Research Series No. 2. Office of Archaeological Research, University of Alabama, University.

1980 An Overview of Wheeler Basin Prehistory. *Journal of Alabama Archaeology* 26:110–135.

1983   *Archaeological Investigations in the Cedar Creek and Upper Bear Creek Reservoirs.* Report of Investigations No. 29, Office of Archaeological Research, University of Alabama, University.

1987   *Archaeological Investigations at Shell Bluff and White Springs, Two Late Woodland Sites in the Tombigbee River Multi-Resource District.* Report of Investigations No. 20. Office of Archaeological Research, Alabama State Museum of Natural History, University of Alabama, University.

1988   Continuity and Change in the Middle Woodland Occupation of the Northwest Alabama Uplands. In *Middle Woodland Settlement and Ceremonialism in the Mid-South and Lower Mississippi Valley,* edited by Robert C. Mainfort, Jr., pp. 31–48. Archaeological Report 22. Mississippi Department of Archives and History, Jackson.

1998   Ceramic Complexes of the Tennessee River Drainage, Alabama. *Journal of Alabama Archaeology* 44:208–241.

Galloway, Patricia K.

1995   *Choctaw Genesis 1500–1700.* University of Nebraska Press, Lincoln.

2000   Archeology from the Archives: The Chambers Excavation at Lyon's Bluff, 1934–35. *Mississippi Archaeology* 35:23–90.

2002   Colonial Period Transformations in the Mississippi Valley: Disintegration, Alliance, Confederation, Playoff. In *The Transformation of the Southeastern Indians, 1540–1760,* edited by Robbie Ethridge and Charles Hudson, pp. 225–247. University Press of Mississippi, Jackson.

Garland, Elizabeth Baldwin

1992   *The Obion Site, An Early Mississippian Center in Western Tennessee.* Report of Investigations No. 7. Cobb Institute of Archaeology, Mississippi State University, Mississippi State.

Gibson, Arrell M.

1971   *The Chickasaws.* University of Nebraska Press, Lincoln.

Griffin, James B.

1952   Some Early and Middle Woodland Types in Illinois. In *Hopewellian Communities in Illinois,* edited by Thorne Deuel, pp. 95–128. Scientific Papers No. 5, Illinois State Museum, Springfield.

1993   Cahokia Interaction with Contemporary Southeastern and Eastern Societies. *Midcontinental Journal of Archaeology* 18:1–17.

Griffin, James B., and Richard G. Morgan (editors)

1941   *Contributions to the Archaeology of the Illinois River Valley.* Transactions of the American Philosophical Society (n.s.) 32(1):1–208.

Haag, William G.

1939   Pottery Type Descriptions. *Southeastern Archaeological Conference Newsletter* 1(1).

1942   A Description and Analysis of the Pickwick Pottery. In *An Archaeological Survey of Pickwick Basin in the Adjacent Portions of the States of Alabama,*

Mississippi, and Tennessee, by William S. Webb and David L. DeJarnette, pp. 509–526. Bulletin 129. Bureau of American Ethnology, Smithsonian Institution, Washington, D.C.

1986　Field Methods in Archaeology. In *American Archaeology Past and Future,* edited by David J. Meltzer, Don D. Fowler, and Jeremy Sabloff, pp. 63–76. Smithsonian Institution Press, Washington, D.C.

Haas, Mary R.

1978　*Language, Culture, and History: Essays by Mary R. Haas,* edited by Anwar S. Dil. Stanford University Press, Stanford.

Hally, David J.

1983　The Interpretive Potential of Pottery from Domestic Contexts. *Midcontinental Journal of Archaeology* 8:163–196.

Hays, Tony

1996　*On the Banks of the River: A History of Hardin County, Tennessee.* The Tennessee River Museum, Savannah, Tennessee.

2000　Developer Neglects Site, Blames State. Electronic document, http://www.archaeology.org/found.php?page=/0005/newsbriefs/tenn.html, accessed June 17, 2003.

Heimlich, Marion Dunlevy

1952　*Guntersville Basin Pottery.* Museum Paper 32, Geological Survey of Alabama, Tuscaloosa.

Hilgeman, Sherri L.

2000　*Pottery and Chronology at Angel.* University of Alabama Press, Tuscaloosa.

Holley, George R.

1989　*The Archaeology of the Cahokia Mounds ICT-II: Ceramics.* Illinois Cultural Resources Study No. 11, Illinois Historic Preservation Agency, Springfield.

Hudson, Charles

1976　*The Southeastern Indians.* University of Tennessee Press, Knoxville.

1997　*Knights of Spain, Warriors of the Sun: Hernando de Soto and the South's Ancient Chiefdoms.* University of Georgia Press, Athens.

Jackson, H. Edwin, and Susan L. Scott

1995a　The Faunal Record of the Southeastern Elite: The Implications of Economy, Social Relations, and Ideology. *Southeastern Archaeology* 14:103–119.

1995b　Mississippian Homestead and Village Subsistence Organization: Contrasts in Large-Mammal Remains from Two Sites in the Tombigbee River Valley. In *Mississippian Communities and Households,* edited by J. D. Rogers and B. D. Smith, pp. 181–200. University of Alabama Press, Tuscaloosa.

Jenkins, Ned J.

1981　*Gainesville Lake Area Ceramic Description and Chronology.* Report of Investigations No. 12, Office of Archaeological Research, University of Alabama, University.

2001 Terminal Woodland/Mississippian Development in West Central Alabama. Paper presented at the 58th Annual Meeting of the Southeastern Archaeological Conference, Chattanooga, Tennessee.

n.d. Terminal Woodland-Mississippian in Northern Alabama: the West Jefferson Phase. Unpublished manuscript prepared as a Master's thesis, Department of Anthropology, University of Alabama, Tuscaloosa.

Jenkins, Ned J., and Richard A. Krause

1986 *The Tombigbee Watershed in Southeastern Prehistory.* University of Alabama Press, Tuscaloosa.

Jenkins, Ned J., and Catherine C. Meyer

1998 Ceramics of the Tombigbee–Black Warrior River Valleys. *Journal of Alabama Archaeology* 44:131–187.

Jennings, Jesse D.

1941 Chickasaw and Earlier Indian Cultures of Northeast Mississippi. *The Journal of Mississippi History* 3:155–226.

Jewell, Willard B.

1931 *Geology and Mineral Resources of Hardin County, Tennessee.* Bulletin 37, Tennessee Division of Geology, Nashville.

Johnson, Jay K.

2000 The Chickasaws. In *Indians of the Greater Southeast: Historical Archaeology and Ethnohistory,* edited by Bonnie G. McEwan, pp. 85–121. University Press of Florida, Gainesville.

Johnson, Jay K., and James R. Atkinson

1987 New Data on the Thelma Mound Group in Northeast Mississippi. In *The Emergent Mississippian: Proceedings of the Sixth Mid-South Archaeological Conference,* edited by Richard A. Marshall, pp. 63–70. Occasional Paper No. 87-01, Cobb Institute of Archaeology, Mississippi State University, Mississippi State.

Judd, Neil M.

1966 Frank H. H. Roberts, Jr. *American Anthropologist* 68:1226–1232.

Justice, Noel D.

1987 *Stone Age Spear and Arrow Points of the Midcontinental and Eastern United States.* Indiana University Press, Bloomington.

Kelly, John E.

2001 The Historical and Distributional Significance of Wells Incised Plates. Paper presented at the 58th Annual Meeting of the Southeastern Archaeological Conference, Chattanooga, Tennessee.

King, Adam

2003 *Etowah: The Political History of a Chiefdom Capital.* University of Alabama Press, Tuscaloosa.

Kirkby, Anne, and Michael J. Kirkby

1976 Geomorphic Processes and the Surface Survey of Archaeological Sites in Semi-arid Areas. In *Geoarchaeology: Earth Science and the Past,* edited by David A. Davidson and Michael L. Shackley, pp. 229–253. Duckworth, London.

Knight, Vernon J., Jr.

1990 *Excavation of the Truncated Mound at the Walling Site: Middle Woodland Culture and Copena in the Tennessee Valley.* Report of Investigations No. 56, Division of Archaeology, Alabama State Museum of Natural History, University of Alabama, University.

1998 Moundville as a Diagrammatic Ceremonial Center. In *Archaeology of the Moundville Chiefdom,* edited by V. J. Knight, Jr., and V. P. Steponaitis, pp. 44–62. Smithsonian Institution Press, Washington, D.C.

Knight, Vernon James, Jr., and Vincas P. Steponaitis

1998 A New History of Moundville. In *Archaeology of the Moundville Chiefdom,* edited by V. J. Knight, Jr., and V. P. Steponaitis, pp. 1–25. Smithsonian Institution Press, Washington, D.C.

Knight, Vernon J., Jr., Lyle Konigsberg, and Susan Frankenberg

n.d. A Gibbs Sampler Approach to the Dating of Phases in the Moundville Sequence. Unpublished manuscript in possession of the author.

Lafferty, Robert

1981 The Phipps Bend Archaeological Project. Research Series No. 4. Office of Archaeological Research, University of Alabama, University.

Lafferty, Robert H., III, and James E. Price

1996 Southeast Missouri. In *Prehistory of the Central Mississippi Valley,* edited by Charles H. McNutt, pp. 1–45. University of Alabama Press, Tuscaloosa.

Lawrence, William L., and Robert C. Mainfort, Jr.

1993 Excavations at 40LK1, a Mississippian Substructural Mound in the Reelfoot Basin, Lake County, Tennessee. *Midcontinental Journal of Archaeology* 18:18–34.

1996 The Reelfoot Lake Basin, Kentucky and Tennessee. In *Prehistory of the Central Mississippi Valley,* edited by Charles H. McNutt, pp. 77–96. University of Alabama Press, Tuscaloosa.

Lewis, Thomas M. N.

1995 Architectural Industry. In *The Prehistory of the Chickamauga Basin in Tennessee,* edited by Thomas M. N. Lewis, Madeline D. Kneberg Lewis, and Lynne P. Sullivan, pp. 54–78. University of Tennessee Press, Knoxville.

Lorenz, Karl

1996 Small-scale Mississippian Community Organization in the Big Black River Valley of Mississippi. *Southeastern Archaeology* 15:145–171.

Lowthert, William, Carl Shields, and David Pollack
    1998   *Mississippian Adaptations along the Barren River in South Central Ken-
              tucky.* Research Report No. 1, Kentucky Archaeological Survey, Lex-
              ington.
Lumb, Lisa Cutts, and Charles H. McNutt
    1988   *Chucalissa: Excavations in Units 2 and 6, 1959–67.* Occasional Paper
              No. 15, Anthropological Research Center, Memphis State University,
              Memphis.
Lyon, Edwin A.
    1996   *A New Deal for Southeastern Archaeology.* University of Alabama Press,
              Tuscaloosa.
Mainfort, Robert C., Jr.
    1992   The Mississippian Period in the West Tennessee Interior. In *The Obion
              Site, an Early Mississippian Center in Western Tennessee,* by Elizabeth B.
              Garland, pp. 202–207. Report of Investigations No. 7. Cobb Institute of
              Archaeology, Mississippi State University, Mississippi State.
Mann, C. Baxter, Jr.
    1983   Classification of Ceramics from the Lubbub Creek Archaeological Lo-
              cality. In *Studies of Material Remains from the Lubbub Creek Archaeologi-
              cal Locality,* edited by Christopher S. Peebles, pp. 2–121. Report submitted
              to the Heritage Conservation and Recreation Service, U.S. Department
              of Interior, Atlanta.
Marcher, Melvin V., and Richard G. Stearns
    1962   Tuscaloosa Formation in Tennessee. *Geological Society of America Bulletin*
              73:1365–1386.
Markin, Julie G.
    1997   Elite Stoneworking and the Function of Mounds at Moundville. *Missis-
              sippi Archaeology* 32:117–135.
Marshall, Richard A.
    1977   Lyons Bluff (22OK1) Radiocarbon Dated. *Journal of Alabama Archae-
              ology* 23:53–57.
Mason, Ronald J., and Gregory Perino
    1961   Microblades at Cahokia. *American Antiquity* 26:553–557.
Maxham, Mintcy D.
    2000   Rural Communities in the Black Warrior Valley, Alabama: The Role of
              Commoners in the Creation of the Moundville Landscape. *American
              Antiquity* 65:337–354.
Meyer, Catherine C.
    1995   *Cultural Resources in the Pickwick Reservoir.* Report of Investigations
              No. 75, Division of Archaeology, Alabama Museum of Natural History,
              University of Alabama, Moundville.

Michals, Lauren M.

1998 The Oliver Site and Early Moundville I Phase Economic Organization. In *Archaeology of the Moundville Chiefdom,* edited by V. J. Knight, Jr., and V. P. Steponaitis, pp. 167–182. Smithsonian Institution Press, Washington, D.C.

Milner, George R.

1998 *The Cahokia Chiefdom: The Archaeology of a Mississippian Society.* Smithsonian Institution Press, Washington, D.C.

1999 Warfare in Prehistoric and Early Historic Eastern North America. *Journal of Archaeological Research* 7:105–151.

Mistovich, Tim

1988 Early Mississippian in the Black Warrior Valley: The Pace of Transition. *Southeastern Archaeology* 7:21–38.

Moore, Clarence B.

1905 Certain Aboriginal Remains of the Black Warrior River. *Journal of the Academy of Natural Sciences of Philadelphia* 13:124–244.

1915 Aboriginal Sites on Tennessee River. *Journal of the Academy of Natural Sciences of Philadelphia* 16:171–428.

Morse, Dan F., and Phyllis Morse

1983 *Archaeology of the Central Mississippi Valley.* Academic Press, New York.

1990 Emergent Mississippian in the Central Mississippi Valley. In *The Mississippian Emergence,* edited by Bruce D. Smith, pp. 153–173. Smithsonian Institution Press, Washington, D.C.

Munro, Pamela

1987 Introduction: Muskogean Studies at UCLA. In *Muskogean Linguistics,* edited by Pamela Munro, pp. 1–6. Occasional Papers in Linguistics 6, Department of Linguistics, University of California at Los Angeles, Los Angeles.

Nash, Charles

1968 *Residence Mounds: An Intermediate Middle-Mississippian Settlement Pattern.* Occasional Papers No. 2, Memphis State University Archaeological Research Center, Memphis, Tennessee.

National Anthropological Archives

2000 Frank Harold Hanna Roberts, Jr., 1897–1966, Papers. Electronic document. http://www.nmnh.si.edu/naa/guide/_r2.htm#jrg_c5

National Geophysical Data Center

2002 Compute Values of Earth's Magnetic Field, version 4.0. Electronic document. http://www.ngdc.noaa.gov/cgi-bin/seg/gmag/fldsnth1.pl

O'Brien, Michael J.

1977 *Intrasite Variability in a Middle Mississippian Community.* Ph.D. dissertation, Department of Anthropology, University of Texas, Austin.

Parmalee, Paul W., and Arthur E. Bogan

    1998   *The Freshwater Mussels of Tennessee.* University of Tennessee Press, Knoxville.

Pauketat, Timothy R.

    1993   *Temples of the Cahokia Lords: Preston Holder's 1955–1956 Excavations of Kunnemann Mound.* Memoir No. 26. Museum of Anthropology, University of Michigan, Ann Arbor.

Payne, Claudine

    1994   *Mississippian Capitals: An Archaeological Investigation of Precolumbian Political Structure.* Ph.D. dissertation, Department of Anthropology, University of Florida, Gainesville. University Microfilms International, Ann Arbor, Michigan.

Peacock, Evan

    1986   A Comparison of Late Woodland, Mississippian, and Protohistoric Triangular Points from the Central Tombigbee Drainage. *Journal of Alabama Archaeology* 32:108–129.

Perino, Gregory

    1960   The Micro-drill Industry at Cahokia. *Central States Archaeological Journal* 7:116–120.

    1971   The Mississippian Component at the Schild Site (No. 4), Greene County, Illinois. In *Mississippian Site Archaeology in Illinois I: Site Reports from the St. Louis and Chicago Areas,* edited by James A. Brown, pp. 1–148. Illinois Archaeological Survey Bulletin no. 8. University of Illinois, Urbana.

Phillips, Philip

    1970   *Archaeological Survey in the Lower Yazoo Basin, Mississippi, 1949–1955, Part One.* Papers of the Peabody Museum of Archaeology and Ethnology, vol. 60. Harvard University, Cambridge.

Pope, Melody

    1989   Microtools from the Black Warrior Valley: Technology, Use, and Context. Unpublished Master's thesis, Department of Anthropology, State University of New York at Binghamton.

Prentice, Guy

    2000   *Ancient Indian Architecture of the Lower Mississippi Delta Region: A Study of Earthworks.* 2d ed. Southeast Archeological Center, National Park Service, Tallahassee, Florida.

Rafferty, Janet

    1986   Summary and Conclusions. In *Test Excavations at Two Woodland Sites, Lowndes County, Mississippi,* by Janet Rafferty and M. E. Starr, pp. 135–139. Report of Investigations No. 3, Cobb Institute of Archaeology, Mississippi State University, Mississippi State.

    1995   *Owl Creek Mounds: Test Excavations at a Vacant Mississippian Mound*

Center. Report of Investigations No. 7, Cobb Institute of Archaeology, Mississippi State University, Mississippi State.

Rathbun, R.

1914 Letter to Superintendent DeLong Rice dated 29 August. Shiloh National Military Park archives Series 1, Box 15, Folder 204.

Reed, David W.

1914 Prehistoric Mounds at Shiloh. *Illinois Central Magazine* 3(2):20–22.

Roberts, Frank H. H., Jr.

1933– Shiloh Battlefield Project. Unpublished field notes on file at the National
1934 Anthropological Archives, Smithsonian Institution, Washington, D.C.

1935 Indian Mounds on Shiloh Battlefield. *Explorations and Fieldwork of the Smithsonian Institution in 1934.* Smithsonian Institution, Publication 3300, pp. 65–68. Smithsonian Institution, Washington, D.C.

Ross, Andrew

1998 *Amber.* Harvard University Press, Cambridge.

Scarry, C. Margaret

1995 *Excavations on the Northwest Riverbank at Moundville: Investigations of a Moundville I Residential Area.* Report of Investigations No. 72, Office of Archaeological Services, University of Alabama Museums, Tuscaloosa.

Scarry, C. Margaret, and John F. Scarry

1995 Artifact Analyses. In *Excavations on the Northwest Riverbank at Moundville: Investigations of a Moundville I Residential Area,* pp. 17–90. Report of Investigations No. 72, Office of Archaeological Services, University of Alabama Museums, Tuscaloosa.

Scarry, C. Margaret, and Vincas P. Steponaitis

1997 Between Farmstead and Center: The Natural and Social Landscapes of Moundville. In *People, Plants, and Landscapes: Studies in Paleoethnobotany,* edited by Kristen J. Gremillion, pp. 142–156. University of Alabama Press, Tuscaloosa.

Scarry, John F.

1984 *Fort Walton Development: Mississippian Chiefdoms in the Lower Southeast.* Ph.D. dissertation, Department of Anthropology, Case Western Reserve University, Cleveland, Ohio. University Microfilms, Ann Arbor, Michigan.

Schiffer, Michael B.

1987 *Formation Processes of the Archaeological Record.* University of New Mexico Press, Albuquerque.

Schroeder, Sissel

2003 Leadership in a Contested Land. Paper presented at the 20th Annual Visiting Scholar Conference, Center for Archaeological Investigations, Southern Illinois University Carbondale.

Schroedl, Gerald F., Clifford Boyd, Jr., and R. P. Steven Davis, Jr.

    1990   Explaining Mississippian Origins in East Tennessee. In *The Mississippian Emergence,* edited by Bruce D. Smith, pp. 175–196. Smithsonian Institution Press, Washington, D.C.

Schroedl, Gerald F., R. P. Stephen Davis, Jr., and C. Clifford Boyd, Jr.

    1985   *Archaeological Contexts and Assemblages at Martin Farm.* Report of Investigations No. 39. Department of Anthropology, University of Tennessee, Knoxville.

Schumm, S. A.

    1966   The Development and Evolution of Hillslopes. *Journal of Geological Education* 14:98–104.

Sierzchula, Michael C.

    1980   Replication and Use Studies of the Zebree Microlith Industry. Master's thesis, Department of Anthropology, University of Arkansas, Fayetteville.

Smith, Bruce D.

    1984   Mississippian Expansion: Tracing the Historical Development of an Explanatory Model. *Southeastern Archaeology* 3:13–22.

Smith, Gerald

    1969   *Ceramic Handle Styles and Cultural Variation in the Northern Sector of the Middle Mississippi Alluvial Valley.* Occasional Papers No. 3, Memphis State University Archaeological Research Center, Memphis.

    1977   Archaeological Investigations of the Indian Mounds Area, Shiloh National Military Park. Report on file at the Southeast Archeological Center, National Park Service, Tallahassee, Florida.

    1996   The Mississippi River Drainage in Western Tennessee. In *Prehistory of the Central Mississippi Valley,* edited by Charles H. McNutt, pp. 97–118. University of Alabama Press, Tuscaloosa.

Smith, Kevin E.

    1992   *The Middle Cumberland Region: Mississippian Archaeology in North Central Tennessee.* Ph.D. dissertation, Department of Anthropology, Vanderbilt University, Nashville, Tennessee. University Microfilms International, Ann Arbor, Michigan.

Smith, Kevin, and Mary Beth Trubbitt

    1998   The Gordontown Ceramic Assemblage from a Regional Perspective. In *Gordontown: Salvage Archaeology at a Mississippian Town in Davidson County, Tennessee,* edited by Michael C. Moore and Emanuel Breitburg, pp. 129–131. Research Series No. 11, Division of Archaeology, Tennessee Department of Environment and Conservation, Nashville.

Smith, Marvin T.

    2000   *Coosa: The Rise and Fall of a Southeastern Mississippian Chiefdom.* University Press of Florida, Gainesville.

Smith, Timothy B.

2004   *This Great Battlefield of Shiloh: History, Memory, and the Establishment of a Civil War National Military Park.* University of Tennessee Press, Knoxville.

Southside Baptist Church

2001   A Short History of the Royal Ambassador Program. Electronic document. http://royalambassadors.home.att.net/RAHistory.html

Speck, Frank G.

1907   Notes on Chickasaw Ethnology and Folk-lore. *Journal of American Folk-Lore* 20:50–58.

Stelle, J. Parish

1871   An Account of Aboriginal Ruins at Savannah, Tennessee. In *Annual Report of the Board of Regents of the Smithsonian Institution, Showing Operations, Expenditures, and Condition of the Institution for the Year 1870,* pp. 408–415. Government Printing Office, Washington, D.C.

Steponaitis, Vincas P.

1980   Some Preliminary Chronological and Technological Notes on Moundville Pottery. *Southeastern Archaeological Conference Bulletin* 22:46–51.

1981   *Ceramics, Chronology, and Community Patterns: An Archaeological Study at Moundville.* Academic Press, New York.

1992   Excavations at 1Tu50, an Early Mississippian Center near Moundville. *Southeastern Archaeology* 11:1–13.

Stirling, Matthew

1935   Smithsonian Archaeological Projects Conducted under the Federal Emergency Relief Administration, 1933–34. *Smithsonian Institution Annual Report for 1934,* pp. 371–400. Smithsonian Institution, Washington, D.C.

Stowe, Noel R., and Richard S. Fuller

1993   The Bottle Creek Mounds: History of Archaeological Research Prior to 1990. In *Bottle Creek Research: Working Papers on the Bottle Creek Site (1Ba2), Baldwin County, Alabama,* edited by Ian W. Brown and Richard S. Fuller, pp. 10–29. *Journal of Alabama Archaeology* 39(1–2).

Sullivan, Lynne P.

1995a   Foreword. In *The Prehistory of the Chickamauga Basin in Tennessee,* by Thomas M. N. Lewis and Madeline D. Kneberg Lewis, compiled and edited by Lynne P. Sullivan, pp. xv–xxi. University of Tennessee Press, Knoxville.

1995b   Mississippian Household and Community Organization in Eastern Tennessee. In *Mississippian Communities and Households,* edited by J. Daniel Rogers and Bruce D. Smith, pp. 99–123. University of Alabama Press, Tuscaloosa.

Swanton, John R.

1946   *The Indians of the Southeastern United States.* Bulletin 43. Bureau of American Ethnology, Smithsonian Institution, Washington, D.C.

Sword, Wiley

    1988   *Shiloh: Bloody April.* Press of Morningside Bookshop, Dayton, Ohio.

Tanner, Helen Hornbeck

    1989   The Land and Water Communication Systems of the Southeastern Indians. In *Powhatan's Mantle: Indians in the Colonial Southeast,* edited by Peter H. Wood, Gregory A. Waselkov, and M. Thomas Hatley, pp. 6–20. University of Nebraska Press, Lincoln.

Turgeon, D. D., A. E. Bogan, E. V. Coan, W. K. Emerson, W. G. Lyons, W. L.

Pratt, C. F. E. Roper, A. Scheltema, F. G. Thompson, and J. D. Williams

    1988   *Common and Scientific Names of Aquatic Invertebrates from the United States and Canada: Mollusks.* American Fisheries Society, Special Publication 16. Bethesda, Maryland.

United States Department of Agriculture (USDA)

    1998   *Keys to Soil Taxonomy.* 8th ed. USDA, Natural Resources Conservation Service. Washington, D.C.

Vogel, Joseph O.

    1975   Trends in Cahokia Ceramics: Preliminary Study of the Collections from Tracts 15A and 15B. In *Perspectives in Cahokia Archaeology.* Illinois Archaeological Survey Bulletin No. 10, Urbana.

Walling, Richard, Robert C. Mainfort, Jr., and James R. Atkinson

    1991   Radiocarbon Dates for the Bynum, Pharr, and Miller Sites, Northeast Mississippi. *Southeastern Archaeology* 10:54–62.

Walthall, John A.

    1980   *Prehistoric Indians of the Southeast: Archaeology of Alabama and the Middle South.* University of Alabama Press, Tuscaloosa.

    1981   *Galena and Aboriginal Trade in Eastern North America.* Scientific Papers Vol. 17. Illinois State Museum, Springfield.

Webb, William S.

    1939   *An Archaeological Survey of Wheeler Basin on the Tennessee River in Northern Alabama.* Bulletin 122. Bureau of American Ethnology, Smithsonian Institution, Washington, D.C.

Webb, William S., and David L. DeJarnette

    1942   *An Archaeological Survey of Pickwick Basin in the Adjacent Portions of the States of Alabama, Mississippi, and Tennessee.* Bulletin 129. Bureau of American Ethnology, Smithsonian Institution, Washington, D.C.

Welch, Paul D.

    1990   Mississippian Emergence in West Central Alabama. In *The Mississippian Emergence,* edited by Bruce D. Smith, pp. 197–225. Smithsonian Institution Press, Washington, D.C.

    1991   *Moundville's Economy.* University of Alabama Press, Tuscaloosa.

    1994   The Occupational History of the Bessemer Site. *Southeastern Archaeology* 13:1–26.

    1996   Mississippian Occupations at Shiloh and Savannah, Tennessee. Paper presented at the 53rd Annual Meeting of the Southeastern Archaeological Conference, Birmingham, Alabama.

1998a   Middle Woodland and Mississippian Occupations of the Savannah Site in Tennessee. *Southeastern Archaeology* 17:79–92.

1998b   Preliminary Report on Excavations at the Shiloh Indian Mounds Site (40HR208), Shiloh National Military Park, Tennessee, in July, 1998. Report submitted to the Southeastern Archeological Center, National Park Service, Tallahassee, Florida.

1998c   Outlying Sites within the Moundville Chiefdom. In *Archaeology of the Moundville Chiefdom,* edited by V. J. Knight, Jr., and V. P. Steponaitis, pp. 133–166. Smithsonian Institution Press, Washington, D.C.

1999   Mississippian House Mounds at Shiloh, Tennessee. Paper presented at the 56th Annual Meeting of the Southeastern Archaeological Conference, Pensacola, Florida.

2000   Shiloh: A Major Mississippian Mound Center on the Tennessee River. Paper presented at the 58th Annual Meeting of the Southeastern Archaeological Conference, Macon, Georgia.

2001   Archeology at Shiloh Indian Mounds, 1899–1999. Report on file at the Southeastern Archeological Center, National Park Service, Tallahassee, Florida.

2003   40HR16 Swallow Bluff Island Mounds: Preliminary Report of 2003 Fieldwork. Ms. on file, Anthropology Department, Southern Illinois University, Carbondale.

2004   Fieldwork at Swallow Bluff Island Mounds, Tennessee (40Hr16) in 2003. *Tennessee Archaeology* 1:36–48. Electronic document, http://histpres.mtsu.edu/tennarch/V1I1 1Welch.pdf, accessed January 17, 2005.

Welch, Paul D., and C. Margaret Scarry
1995   Status-Related Variation in Foodways in the Moundville Chiefdom. *American Antiquity* 60:397–419.

Welch, Paul D., David G. Anderson, and John E. Cornelison
2003   A Century of Archaeology at Shiloh Indian Mounds. Paper presented at the 68th Annual Meeting of the Society for American Archaeology, Milwaukee, Wisconsin.

Wesler, Kit W.
2001   *Excavations at Wickliffe Mounds.* University of Alabama Press, Tuscaloosa.

Williams, Stephen, and Jeffrey P. Brain
1983   *Excavations at the Lake George Site, Yazoo County, Mississippi, 1958–1960.* Papers of the Peabody Museum of Archaeology and Ethnology, vol. 74. Harvard University, Cambridge.

Wilmsen, Edwin, and Frank H. H. Roberts, Jr.
1978   *Lindenmeier, 1934–1974: Concluding Report on Investigations.* Contributions to Anthropology No. 24. Smithsonian Institution, Washington, D.C.

Wilson, Gregory
   2001   Crafting Control and the Control of Crafts: Rethinking the Moundville
           Greenstone Industry. *Southeastern Archaeology* 20:118–128.

Yerkes, Richard W.
   1983   Microwear, Microdrills, and Mississippian Craft Specialization. *American Antiquity* 48:499–518.
   1987   *Prehistoric Life on the Mississippi Floodplain.* University of Chicago Press, Chicago.

Index